BY RICHARD MARSCHALL

ABBEVILLE PRESS · PUBLISHERS · NEW YORK

A Roundtable Press Book
Directors: Susan E. Meyer, Marsha Melnick
Editor: Virginia Croft
Assistant Editor: Marguerite Ross

Published by Abbeville Press
Project Editor: Walton Rawls
Designer: Renée Khatami
Copy Chief: Robin James
Production Supervisor: Hope Koturo

Library of Congress Cataloging-in-Publication Data
Marschall, Richard.
America's great comic-strip artists / by Richard Marschall.
p. cm.
Includes index.
ISBN 0-89659-917-5 : $55.00
1. Cartoonists—United States—Biography.   2. Comic books, strips, etc.—United States.   I. Title.
NC1426.M28   1989
741.5′0973—dc20   89-35461
                                                             CIP

The author wishes to thank and acknowledge those who have lent artwork for use as illustrations in this volume: Gordon Campbell, pages 19, 29 (top), 34 (bottom), 130, 136; Rob Stolzer, page 282; Bill Blackbeard, pages 155, 158, 159, 161, 194, 202-203; and Jim Ivey, page 136. All other illustrations are from the collection of Richard Marschall. The author acknowledges the assistance of comics scholars Ron Goulart, Alan Kaplan, Jim Lowe, and Steve Thompson, whose suggestions and corrections were willingly offered and gratefully received; they are blameless, however, for opinions and viewpoints of the author.

The author gratefully acknowledges a grant-in-aid from the Swann Foundation for Caricature and Cartoon that assisted in the research for Chapter 2 of this book.

Pierre Couperie of France and Donald Phelps of the United States are friends of the comic strip and friends of mine. American popular culture is richer for the former fact, and I am grateful for the latter. Scholars and gentlemen who have seen the comics in special ways, they have taught the rest of us what we have been looking at and why it is worthwhile to continue digging, discovering, criticizing, and appreciating this marvelous art form. This is their book.

CONTENTS

The comic strip, like jazz, is a uniquely American art form. In less than a century, the comic strip—with its own language, structure, and integrities—produced a great many artists who worked masterfully within a complex set of rules.

Accorded little recognition in its birthplace, the comic strip is widely celebrated around the world, where American cartoonists of the past are culturally lionized and their works anthologized. American critics finally

are beginning to acknowledge what the rest of the world has long known, that this art form encompasses a body of astonishing masterpieces created by a number of true graphic geniuses. By chiefly focusing on sixteen of the most gifted masters of the comic strip, this book not only celebrates the achievements of these great artists but tells the story of the art form as it has evolved from the time of the earliest creators to the present day. The comic strip is also a dynamic, formative means of communication, but it is composed of certain irreducible elements: a succession of panels (in contrast to the single-panel cartoon); a story that is told (not a vignette illustrated); a written language enclosed in dialogue "balloons" (except in pantomime strips) and placed within the image frame, serving somehow a visual as well as narrative function; presentation through mass media; and a distinctive new vocabulary.

The comics' vocabulary transcends the written words of balloons and captions; it extends—expands—to unique and meaningful signs and symbols: motion lines, sweat beads, stars of pain, sound-effect indications, all hovering physically within the comic-strip universe. They are not crutches for the cartoonist but splendid means to tell stories in a way different from, say, the novelist.

Most art through the ages has been designed to tell a story. Cave paintings, for example, can be thought of as long, drawn-out picture stories. They used no words, of course, but they did depict action, motion, characters, and some kind of story. Egyptian art likewise depicted stories and the passage of time. Roman friezes and, during the Middle Ages, tapestries, triptychs, stained-glass windows, mosaics, and illuminated manuscripts all did things the comics eventually were to do—utilized signs and symbols, incorporated text on occasion, and basically told stories.

It was the invention of the printing press and the rise of literacy that disrupted the almost primal intellectual imperative to relate stories in ways that combined visual and narrative elements. The printed word subsequently became the major vehicle of communication, education, and persuasion, and artwork was increasingly relegated to decoration. Illustration thrived, but otherwise art had to become art for art's sake.

Closely related to the development of the comic strip were the works of three forefathers of continuity graphics. William Hogarth, in late eighteenth-century England, drew series of satirical cartoon prints that told stories within the frame of each image that were part of a larger story when the series was viewed in sequence (usually morality tales with enough scatological detail to satisfy all purchasers of the prints). These well-known series included *The Harlot's Progress, The Rake's Progress,* and *Marriage à la Mode.*

In the 1830s and 1840s the Swiss logician and mathematician Rodolphe Töppfer, a friend of Goethe, wrote *An Essay on Physiognomy,* which contains his observations on the role of pen lines in depicting character and on the conceptual implications of drawn symbols; the modern theory of semiotics owes its inception in large part to Töppfer's work. As an amateur cartoonist, Töppfer told picture-stories—prototypical comic strips—about hapless heroes like Crepin and Cryptogramme.

The German cartoonist and poet Wilhelm Busch more closely united picture and word with narrative sequence in his many *bilderbogen* (picture-stories), beginning in 1865 with *Max und Moritz,* a collection still in print in many countries around the world. Subtitled *A Story in Seven Tricks,* the book can be seen as an early panel-by-panel type of comic strip; the protagonists later became models for the American classic *The Katzenjammer Kids.*

In nineteenth-century England, the serialization of illustrated popular fiction in the newspapers established another of the comics' characteristics. Weekly installments of stories by writers like Charles Dickens and Wilkie Collins were printed with copious illustrations by popular cartoonists of the day. As printing technology (in addition to growing literacy, affluence, and leisure time) fueled the popular press, fundamental developments in graphic figuration sped the evolution toward the comic strip. The photography and stop-action motion studies of Eadweard Muybridge did not just settle arguments about whether a horse's hooves were ever *all* off the ground when galloping; they enabled talented artists and cartoonists to dissect the logic of movement and anatomy in a new way. Cartoonists were soon dispersing form and motion in their drawings over several successive panels, in order to show it better (or distort it according to

This full-page cartoon was published on the front page of the *New York Journal*'s "American Humorist" section for March 13, 1898. In it the Yellow Kid—America's first popular newspaper-cartoon character, whose popularity was beginning to wane—is kidded by the Katzenjammer Kids, recent creations of Rudolph Dirks. There are other transitions present here: this was one of Dirks's last single-panel cartoons before definitively establishing the sequential-panel format for storytelling. The page also reveals the immigrant nature of early comics' themes, and no doubt the source of much of its readership as well. From the windows in the building on the right peer Mama and Papa Katzenjammer; the kids' father was soon to disappear from the feature.

YELLOW KID? ACH, NO! IT'S ONLY THE KATZENJAMMER KID—
(And His "Brudder.")

narrative, if not textual, demand). As film was evolving from the snapshot to the motion picture, so the cartoon was evolving toward the strip, and the same dynamic was at work: to tell stories rather than to depict incidents; to achieve a sophisticated narration; to employ new visual techniques; to not merely expand on artwork or traditional fiction, but to borrow elements from both to create a new language.

Cartooning developed a separate lifeline in America, the largely graphic side, which had its origins with Benjamin Franklin. He drew a brilliant propaganda cartoon, *Join or Die*, depicting a severed snake, each segment representing a different colony, to illustrate his warning to fellow revolutionaries: "If we do not hang together we shall surely all hang separately." Another early American cartoonist was Paul Revere, whose *Boston Massacre* print was a drawing full of incendiary lies but masterful for its persuasion.

For a generation or more after the Revolution, most American cartooning was political and fiercely partisan in nature. With the advent of wood engraving and lithography and the establishment of comic almanac magazines—the assertion, again, of technology and commerce—humorous illustration became a discipline in American art. The cartoon prints of Currier and Ives and the brilliant, influential cartoons of Thomas Nast, who single-handedly routed the corrupt Democratic party in New York City, served to popularize cartoons throughout America.

The 1870s saw the birth of humor-and-cartoon weeklies, the most popular being *Puck, Judge,* and *Life.* They mixed political themes among social cartoons, and soon their single-panel drawings yielded to more and more "series." At first, the multipanel sequences were pantomime stories in cartoon form, and usually they featured slapstick action. A.B. Frost was an early master of the series form but he is remembered chiefly as a great illustrator; others who refined the format are forgotten, like F.M. Howarth, who featured full text and dialogue beneath his panels instead of balloons within. But by the 1890s the multipanel mode was in full vogue and moved from the humor magazines to their new competitors, the comic (humor) supplements in Sunday metropolitan newspapers.

In major cities, but especially in New York, newspapers were fighting mighty battles for readership. The circulation wars were waged with many weapons, including sensationalism, scandal, sex, and exposé; women's features, children's pages, and quality fiction; color artwork and, ultimately, the comic strip.

Considering the motives and methods of press barons like Joseph Pulitzer and William Randolph Hearst, one might doubt that anything of merit could emanate from their journalistic peregrinations. Yet they must be seen as modern Medicis, for they were patrons of the new art of the comic strip as it was developing in their newspapers, granting cartoonists enormous freedom to experiment. Combining technology and art, the publishers invested heavily in the refinement and deployment of color printing presses. A novelty at the time, color was meant to attract circulation, but it also gave cartoonists a wonderful showcase, one they were then obliged to stock every week. Finally, the publishers married commerce to art as the comic strip itself (as much as the section it was printed in) became a weapon in circulation wars. When interesting characters could be counted on to appear weekly in the comics, readers were likely to remain faithful; cartoonists, therefore, became stars to be promoted; strips became properties

to be developed. The cartoonists at the turn of the century lived in an astonishing environment. There was a feeling of intense artistic excitement as artists had a format of technical brilliance—the color of those early sections was superior to today's—the support of generous publishers, and a receptive public. The comic strip, having taken so long to evolve, finally coalesced and established its formal conventions in the decade between 1895 and 1905.

The comics were—and still are in their vitality—many things to many people. Although often promoted toward children, the "funnies" were usually drawn for adults. They were often the first literature read by immigrants but in the beginning often dealt with stereotypes. Eventually strips evolved from featuring stereotype to archetype, from harried suburban "little man" to dashing hero, and soon the comic strip became the new democratic art, enthusiastically seized upon by all segments of society, all ages, all classes. Virtually every newspaper in the country—with *The New York Times* and the new *Christian Science Monitor* lonely exceptions—had to have its own comics.

The story of comics' evolution and life since their inception in the 1890s is the subject of this book, told through the lives and work of sixteen great cartoonists. The period before 1910 was a time of experimentation in form and theme. The following decade saw a standardization of formats, largely due to syndication (the means of distribution to newspapers), and the 1920s was a time of standardization of themes, with the advent of categories like suburban-life strips and working-woman strips. The 1930s brought a renaissance—the comics' second birth—with the dominance of continuity episodes (as distinct from simple gags) and a variety of realistic styles; adventure entered the story as illustration flavored the art. In the 1950s, perhaps reacting to television, stories were shortened or eliminated, humor strips returned to gag-a-day modes, and new brands of satire and sarcasm entered the field.

There have been many new comic strips but few trends since the 1950s, a situation that falls somewhere between sad and frightening. Commerce, once such a benign partner, today smothers the newspaper comic strip in America. Licensing and merchandising considerations now often precede the creation of a strip, rather than the reverse. Printing quality has declined, and coloring is not as brilliant as it once was. Formats have shrunk, and Sunday comics are now crowded several to a page instead of each filling a whole sheet. New features seen imitative; the gag-a-day mode has degenerated into stale punch lines; and newspapers themselves no longer promote—or, evidently, appreciate—comic strips as they once did.

One must not conclude that the art form only had creative possibilities for a finite period of time; it is the creative community that has stultified. Bill Watterson (*Calvin and Hobbes*) is an exception to the rule and proves daily that there yet can be life in newspaper comics, but perhaps the future lies in areas where Europeans have trod: quality formats, longer lengths, books of 96 pages instead of strips 4 inches long.

Just as there have been sharply defined chronological periods in comics history, there have also been larger thematic categories or major eras.

The age of the founding fathers was marked by genuine experimentation—

even more by absolute freedom growing from absence of precedent. Frederick Opper was a veteran cartoonist, known throughout America for his political and social drawings, but otherwise the pioneer cartoonists who entered the strip field were as fresh as the medium itself. Men like Jimmy Swinnerton in San Francisco and Charles Saalburg in Chicago experimented with, respectively, animal cartoons in black and white and kid cartoons in color, while in New York, R.F. Outcault (*The Yellow Kid* and *Buster Brown*) and Opper (*Happy Hooligan* et al.) established the language and structure of comic-strip expression.

The period between 1905 and 1915 was a time of fantasy in the comics—a thematic preoccupation strangely, and sadly, absent today—and its foremost exponent was Winsor McCay, whose *Little Nemo* and other creations were elegant explorations of daydreams and nightmares. George Herriman created dozens of clever strips before settling in with *Krazy Kat,* the surreal masterpiece generally

A panel from Winsor McCay's *Little Nemo in Slumberland* for March 11, 1906. McCay's stunning artwork was enhanced by superlative color-printing technology in its home paper, the *New York Herald.* This was the first comic strip to rely on sophisticated coloring techniques. McCay was inspired by art nouveau sensibilities, and the color of Slumberland was as integral as the beauties, demons and imps whom Nemo met there each week.

acknowledged to be the greatest comic strip of all time. Cliff Sterrett invested *Polly and Her Pals* with no less whimsy—graphic or narrative—yet he has been less celebrated.

As continuity entered the comics, around the mid-1920s, some humor strips straddled the line between laughs and thrills and often retained an element of fantasy as well. E.C. Segar's *Thimble Theatre,* starring Popeye, compensated for its somewhat pedestrian artwork with a gallery of memorable characters and some of the wildest scenarios in strip history. Al Capp is likewise to be remembered for his plot lines and dialogues, as well as for the social commentary he injected in *Li'l Abner,* and Walt Kelly did the same in *Pogo,* a strip that combined more strains and disciplines of comic-strip expression than any other single title. The 1920s to the 1950s was the period of the classic continuity strips, when, among

A comic-strip artist creates a universe, and the greatest cartoonists invest theirs with a consistent vision and a population of resonant characters with distinctive voices. A supreme example is Walt Kelly's *Pogo*; the wordplay, charm, and literate nonsense were fringe benefits. *(Facing page)*

others, Frank King's *Gasoline Alley* (humor, sentiment, and fantasy), Billy DeBeck's *Barney Google* (farce and melodrama), Harry Tuthill's *The Bungle Family* (sardonic surrealism), and Frank Willard's *Moon Mullins* (burlesque and slapstick) displayed the plasticity of the form.

The same period was also the golden age of the adventure-continuity comic, when nonhumorous elements dominated the now-inaccurately termed comics. Roy Crane infused his picaresque *Wash Tubbs* (later *Captain Easy*) with good-natured élan but later got grimmer and more realistic in wars real and cold with *Buz Sawyer*. Illustrative realism entered the comics a surprising three decades after the art form's birth through the work of Harold Foster, who, first in *Tarzan* and then in his own epic *Prince Valiant*, emulated artists like Edwin Austin Abbey and Howard Pyle in historical detail and graphic majesty. Milton Caniff, whose work in *Terry and the Pirates* can be seen as the high-water mark of the story strip, mastered the elements of plot, art, and characterization—what else is there?—leaving a legacy that showed the creative heights comics could achieve. Caniff's contemporary Alex Raymond relied more on his illustrative skills in *Secret Agent X-9*, *Flash Gordon*, and *Jungle Jim* until his storytelling powers asserted themselves solidly in *Rip Kirby*.

Caniff has been referred to as a comic-strip impressionist, using his brushwork and chiaroscuro technique to great effect. By similar analysis we may see Harold Gray (*Little Orphan Annie*) and Chester Gould (*Dick Tracy*) as the expressionists of the comics. Soul mates and cell mates (they both worked for the conservative *Chicago Tribune*), each artist asserted a fiercely personal worldview in his strip—not just through story lines, but through complex characterizations, repeated motifs, sophisticated construction, and even the very artwork of their daily sagas; their brilliant achievements are multifaceted. During the golden age of the story strip, other cartoonists like Burne Hogarth (who drew *Tarzan* after Foster), George Storm (*Bobby Thatcher*), and Jerry Siegel and Joe Shuster (*Superman*) also contributed memorable work.

Although story strips still exist, the field clearly has returned to the domain of humor. The strong rebirth is exemplified by the modest Charles Schulz and

Classic comic strips grow and evolve organically. Al Capp's *Li'l Abner* began as a screwball comedy of the 1930s—the impoverished hillbilly repeatedly found in affluent urban settings. (These strips are from *Abner*'s first year.) Capp's comic preoccupations grew beyond such devices as the strip evolved from a burlesque of society to a commentary on human nature.

There was little that was orthodox about Chester Gould's compositions or anatomical renderings; but his sense of comic-strip design was powerful and his characters' personalities were memorable.

his quiet colossus *Peanuts*. Besides creating a vital comic strip, Schulz defined a new type of construction and fashioned a style that is paid silent homage through the construction and style in contemporary strips such as *Doonesbury* that seem so different from *Peanuts*. In the otherwise dismal—clone-prone and bland—second era of the humor strip since World War II, some very bright moments have been provided by Crockett Johnson's *Barnaby*, Jack Kent's *King Aroo*, Mort Walker's *Beetle Bailey*, Johnny Hart's *B.C.*, Mell Lazarus's *Miss Peach*, Dik Browne's *Hagar*, and Bill Watterson's *Calvin and Hobbes*.

The artists in this book, *in corpus*, are truly representative of the history of the art form. Their selection may seem arbitrary to some comics enthusiasts except for one common factor—all are enshrined in the Hall of Fame by the Museum of Cartoon Art in Rye Brook, New York. They are the best of the best. Others mentioned here but not represented are arguably, but perhaps marginally, less qualified as "greats." Decisions also had to be made that would keep the book a manageable length and allot enough pages to illuminate each selected cartoonist's work; to give short shrift would have defeated the purpose of this book. Nostalgia is certainly one of the warmest fringe benefits of the comic-strip experience, but it is to be hoped that pure nostalgia will not be the animating force behind regrets over omissions.

The comics routinely have been dismissed, yet they have been durable and vital for nearly a century. They have been denigrated, yet they are read by millions—perhaps even a billion people—every day.

However, readership alone is not reason to assert the validity of the comic strip. Its formal aspects are respectable enough. Many critics have judged comics by their worst examples—and there are many—but if paintings, poetry, and architecture of any given era and culture were similarly judged, they might also be held in contempt. When great works are celebrated, the forms themselves are not dismissed. In this book we shall finally judge the comic strip by its greatest artists and their finest works.

Of all the founding fathers of the comic strip, Richard Felton Outcault usually is the one credited with being the most influential. At the time of his death, newspapers across America hailed him as creator not only of memorable characters, including the Yellow Kid and Buster Brown, but of the comic strip itself.

Myths, however, can be stronger than truth in comics history, just as in other forms of popular culture like jazz and the movies. Outcault was not the first cartoonist to draw newspaper comic strips, and the *Yellow Kid*, the feature popularly credited with commencing the art form, was not even a strip. Other "firsts" traditionally ascribed to the *Yellow Kid* are first titled character to appear every week and first cartoon series in color. The feature supposedly had its debut in 1896, a year that—because of faulty history—has assumed an almost holy status in comics chronologies. None of these widely accepted "facts" is true.

R. F. OUTCAULT

MY 'POP SEE

1863-1928

The *Yellow Kid* was *not* a comic strip. Except for a few multipanel episodes near its end, it was always a large, single image genre cartoon. But the cartoon's massive popularity made the colored funny section a necessity in every major Sunday newspaper in America, and those supplements proved to be pulp-paper versions of petri dishes for the evolving art form that became the comic strip. And no less significantly, Outcault became an integral part of the ferment he inspired via the immortal *Buster Brown,* which he created a few years later. It was a bona fide comic strip, popular with the public and influential among other cartoonists. Even after subtracting the false claims of historians, then, Outcault is indeed worthy of consideration. Without his work, comic strips might have taken a different direction in different outlets, and their inception might even have been delayed.

Richard Felton Outcault was born in Lancaster, Ohio, on January 14, 1863, during the fury of the Civil War. He was descended from Germans who arrived in America in the 1720s and spelled the surname Altgelt. R.F. displayed an early interest in art and was encouraged by his father, a cabinetmaker of modest means, to take lessons with a local nun. At fourteen he left home and enrolled in McMicken University's School of Design in Cincinnati. After three years of study, he found employment as an artist painting pastoral scenes on safes for the Hall Safe and Lock Company.

In 1888 the Centennial Exposition of the Ohio Valley and Middle Atlantic States was held in Cincinnati, and the grandest exhibit of the fair was a massive electric-light display organized on a $40,000 budget by William J. Hammer of the Edison Laboratories. As part of the publicity Hammer arranged to have an account of the Edison exhibit published in *Electrical World* magazine. For the article he needed sophisticated illustrations, and Outcault—who had been visiting the exposition and making sketches on his own—was engaged for the princely sum of $400. Hammer was so pleased that he further commissioned Outcault to depict inventions and diagrams for a series of lectures he was to deliver at Philadelphia's Franklin Institute on the subject of Edison's life and work. Ultimately Outcault was hired as a full-time employee and moved to Edison's West Orange, New Jersey, headquarters.

Thomas Alva Edison was planning another grand exhibit of his work, but this time at the Paris World's Fair of 1889—for which Eiffel was constructing his tower—and Hammer was once again in charge. Outcault was named official artist for the entire traveling exhibit, and he then formed a lasting friendship with Edison. One night Outcault was startled to hear somebody in a shadowy corner of the laboratory singing operatic arias, and he whacked the singer from behind with a ruler. To Outcault's embarrassment, the singer was Edison, who was testing the range of a new phonograph. Soon after, Edison playfully retaliated when the artist was catnapping during the painting of a mural, with the same ruler on the same portion of the anatomy. Outcault later remembered he felt like framing the seat of those pants except that they were his sole pair of trousers at the time.

Edison's exhibit at the Paris World's Fair was a notable sensation, covering nine thousand square feet and consisting of nineteen separate compartments where visitors could listen to the new phonographs (Edison's latest success) or, in some compartments, have their performance on a grand piano recorded on the spot. Outcault busily sketched all aspects of the exhibit, as well as its prominent visitors; in return, Edison and Hammer paid for Outcault to study art in the Latin Quarter.

Back in New York in 1890, Outcault illustrated another major Edison show and then joined the art staff of *Electrical World,* which was edited by Hammer's friend T. Comerford Martin. During the early 1890s Outcault combined his talent with an irrepressible sense of humor, freelancing cartoons—or jokes, as he called them—to weekly humor magazines. In a few years, when he was more

In its seminal period the comic strip was struggling for its definitive forms. R. F. Outcault's *Yellow Kid* was almost always a single panel, but here is an early example (1896) making use of multiple panels (but no framed borders), balloons (but also "speech" on the Kid's nightshirt), and a sequential narrative. Outcault had once worked for Edison, and here he ribs the great inventor while plugging the new color comic section of the *New York Journal*.

accomplished and more famous, he was able to sell his cartoons to major markets like *Judge* and *Life*, but at the beginning he was only able to crack small-circulation magazines like *Capital Chips* of Albany; *Harlem Life* (rural Harlem Heights was where Outcault and his bride settled when they moved to New York); *Truth; Oakes' Dyary; Godey's Ladies' Book;* and *Harper's Bazaar.*

The Harper Brothers' women's magazine provided fair exposure, but none of Outcault's sales promised to spread his reputation as a cartoonist. A new outlet, however, was hungry for cartoons by virtually anyone and, surprisingly, was seen by more readers than almost any other publication in America: the *Sunday World.* Joseph Pulitzer had fashioned the *World*, daily and Sunday, into the biggest-circulation newspaper in the nation and, incidentally, the official organ of the Democratic party. As part of Pulitzer's ongoing, eternal, obsessive circulation-building promotions, the *Sunday World* was offering a colored section replete with reproductions of fine art, fashion drawings, society illustrations, news pictures, and cartoons. Cartoons were reprinted from overseas, copied from *Puck* and *Life*, and bought from freelancers. The *World's* own staff artists contributed as many as they could, but there was a golden opportunity for journeymen cartoonists like R.F. Outcault.

His signature began appearing with regularity through 1894 and 1895, usually beneath drawings of tenement urchins and ragged gamins. Many cartoonists of the day had specialties, and Outcault's, it developed, was to be immigrant ragamuffins.

Such thematic preoccupation was not unusual. In the humorous weeklies, cartoonists like Michael Angelo Woolf fashioned careers on such subjects. In the literary monthlies, writers like Stephen Crane and William Dean Howells were using such settings and such people in their fiction, now known as Naturalism. Jacob Riis took his camera to the neighborhoods Outcault depicted for his memorable book *How the Other Half Lives.* Soon artists who were to concentrate on the less attractive sides of urban life were said to be of the Ashcan School. And papers like the *World* frequently focused on stories of the slums. Like others,

Outcault saw humor in these environments, but he also saw pathos and depicted both strains. His cartoons provoked chuckles, but they also purposefully pricked the conscience.

Outcault's cartoons proved popular, and his work occupied more space in the *World's* feature section each week throughout 1895—more in number, more in details, larger in space. Finally, on May 5, 1895, Outcault adapted the opening words of the song "Maggie Murphy's Home" from a contemporary Broadway musical, *O'Reilly and the Four Hundred* ("Down in Hogan's Alley…"), and titled a cartoon showing a motley collection of kids, dogs, and goats in a back-tenement lot.

There was nothing particularly remarkable about this cartoon, at least compared to other Outcault slum drawings, except perhaps that it was more involved—a genre drawing in the tradition of Hogarth, swarming with figures, bursting with personality, suggestive in its implied stories and activities in every corner. One detail, however, is notable in retrospect: a little fellow off to the side, jug-eared, barefooted, wearing a soiled nightshirt with handprints over its front. He was *different*. Other children around him had bare feet, but he looked different. Others wore clothes, but he, for some reason, was in a gown. He was bald and the others were not. He stood out but was not central in any fashion to the cartoon's action.

In succeeding weeks and months—and as Outcault's work grew in prominence and color—the *Hogan's Alley* cartoons became fixtures in the *World's* funny pages. This was evolution of the purest sort; Outcault's work gradually caught the fancy of readers. That kid evolved too.

He popped up with amiable obtrusiveness a little more prominently in each cartoon. He was, of course, to become in visage and name the Yellow Kid, but during his evolution his nightshirt changed from blue to green to pink to white to red with black dots. And then yellow. Why yellow—or, rather, why did yellow become the Kid's *mode de rigueur*? That fact is lost to history, if there ever was a specific reason at all, but one myth must be dispelled; it was not because yellow printing inks were drying improperly and a large blank area was needed on which to test a new formula. Comics histories have nurtured this pleasant and convenient canard for years, but in fact newspapers—the *World* certainly included—had been printing beautiful color work since 1893, with yellows bright, attractive, and well behaved. (Another popular impression can also be dispelled here; the Kid, despite his generally Asian features, and despite the implication of his Yellow monicker, was not Chinese but rather Irish. Mickey Dugan was his name.)

By early 1896—not quite overnight, but soon enough to have surprised Outcault and Pulitzer both— *Hogan's Alley* became a sensation with readers. As Stephen Becker noted, the cartoon series evoked "that first, gentle wave of mass hysteria which accompanies the birth of popular art forms." It seemed that everyone in New York was talking about those funny kids in *Hogan's Alley*, especially the Yellow Kid, and the *World's* circulation zoomed. Pulitzer responded by promoting the Yellow Kid widely, in newspaper ads, on billboards, on big posters astride his delivery wagons.

It is hard to overstate the impact the Yellow Kid had on New York and whatever parts of America that received the New York *World* (which, with the

The Yellow Kid grew from being a bit player in *Hogan's Alley* to playing host to the action, a sometimes-silent Greek chorus. The Kid's name was Mickey Dugan, and this 1896 page shows his family's eviction—a typically serio-comic genre scene in Casey's Flats on Hogan's Alley.

Readers saw much humor in *Hogan's Alley* cartoons that depicted slum kids mimicking the activities of adults and society folk—debutante balls, yachting events, country jaunts, and days at the races. From the *New York World* of May 24, 1896.

MOVING DAY IN HOGAN'S ALLEY.

THE RACING SEASON OPENS IN HOGAN'S ALLEY.

New York *Tribune*, was the closest thing to a national newspaper of the day). Not only did the Yellow Kid, in larger, more colorful, more involved cartoons, seem to dominate the whole paper, but soon there were Yellow Kid cigarettes on the market, as well as crackers, buttons, fans, a *Yellow Kid* magazine, and eventually a Broadway musical. And not only did the *World* have to have a visit from Outcault's Yellow Kid in the every Sunday editon, but the very existence, and security, of the color comic section was being assured. And it had to be filled with other cartoons.

Hogan's Alley drawings were not strips; the multipanel form would come soon, but from other hands. Nor did *Hogan's Alley* rely on speech balloons for communication with its readers; there were captions and labels, and even dialogue appeared on the Kid's nightshirt in an almost surreal fashion, but other cartoonists were to institutionalize the speech balloon. In fact, *Hogan's Alley* actually was similar in several remarkable ways to a feature that has been completely unnoticed for almost a century. In the Chicago *Inter-Ocean* of 1893, cartoonist and editor Charles W. Saalburg created a cast of gamins called the *Ting-Ling Kids*. Their title prefigured the Yellow Kid, the Katzenjammer Kids, and other early comic kids. They were in fact Asian; they appeared every week; they were identifiable characters; their adventures ran in color—all innovations traditionally assigned to Outcault. The Ting-Lings were popular, too, running into 1897 and even achieving success in England as well. Perhaps coincidentally, Saalburg by 1895 was a cartoonist on the staff of the New York *World*.

Nevertheless, it was *Hogan's Alley* starring the Yellow Kid that truly turned the newspaper world upside down. Every paper had to have its own color comic section, and every publisher longed to have his own counterpart of the Yellow

Kid. One publisher actually wanted the Kid himself for himself, and he would have him, at any cost.

That publisher was William Randolph Hearst—an upstart, at least in the eyes of the mogul Pulitzer. Hearst (who had served on the staff of Harvard's humor magazine, the *Lampoon*, and was expelled for playing practical jokes) had used several million dollars of his father's fortune to turn the struggling San Francisco *Examiner* into the largest newspaper in the West, and he did so by emulating Pulitzer's formula of sensation, promotion, scandal, and an unceasing devotion to diversity, talent, entertainment, and genuine fun in his newspaper. In 1895 Hearst moved East, bought the flagging *Journal* from Pulitzer's brother Albert, and within months turned it into a fire-breathing, circulation-threatening rival to the *World*. What could complete Hearst's conquest?

"Eight pages of polychromous effulgence that make the rainbow look like a lead pipe!" Hearst would have his own color comic section, and he would have Outcault and the Yellow Kid. And he did. By offering the cartoonist an outrageous increase in salary, he secured Outcault's services. Of course Pulitzer countered, but so did Hearst again. Soon journalism had its own inky version of the Oklahoma land rush. Hearst at one point hired an entire floor of the World Building—the staffs of Pulitzer's feature sections of the *Sunday World*. There is a report that the popular cartoonist T.E. Powers stood at a Park Row saloon one afternoon doing nothing but drinking and receiving reports of which publisher was raising his salary to what levels. Such raiding, coupled with lurid headlines and wild promotions, was ignited by Outcault's Yellow Kid, and the practices were tagged, in his honor, "yellow journalism."

After the *World* lost Outcault, it offered readers a consolation prize—*Hogan's Alley* drawn by another staff cartoonist. George Luks inherited the slum saga, and he invested the weekly genre drawings with regular characters, in-jokes, and enough action to involve readers for twenty minutes. It is interesting to speculate whether his assignment on *Hogan's Alley* influenced his subsequent focus as a fine artist, but George Luks later became one of the Eight, a member of the Ashcan School.

Luks's valiant attempt at imitation notwithstanding, Joseph Pulitzer sued to stop Outcault from drawing the *Yellow Kid* for Hearst's *Journal*. The result of the notorious court case was that Outcault could draw his *character* for whomever he wished, while publisher Pulitzer could continue the *feature* with whatever artist he chose to employ. So New York had two Yellow Kids—one in *Hogan's Alley* in the *World* and one in the *Yellow Kid* in the *Journal*. (Since the legal issues revolved around likenesses and distinguishing characteristics, Luks's character for a few weeks wore bloomers instead of the gown and was once even green instead of yellow!)

Outcault's slums were less manic than Luks's, and he settled into a masterful formula for his cartoons. There was always a central theme, and it usually concerned the slum children simulating a high-society event. Hence there were mock weddings, excursions, parades, races, and dog shows. In the beginning there were touches of melancholy—evictions of the Dugan family, for instance—but later there were more outrageous scenes, including, under Hearst, a ballyhooed trip around the world by the urchins. The trip presented a great opportunity for newspaper promotions, and color-lithograph posters covered New York, especially

THE WORLD: SUNDAY, AUGUST 9, 1896.—COLORED SUPPLEMENT. 3

The True Story of Mr. Blue Beard.

Many years ago there lived a nobleman who possessed some wealth, but not enough to be the high-flyer his ancestors had been, nor yet enough to renew the plumbing and make other repairs in his ancestral castles.

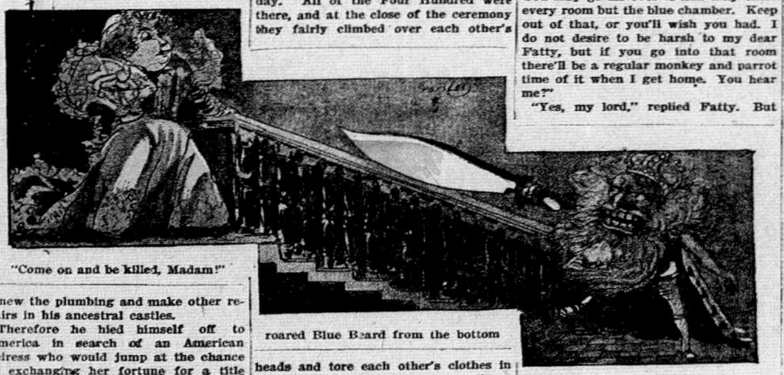

"Come on and be killed, Madam!" roared Blue Beard from the bottom of the stairs a minute later.

Therefore he hied himself off to America in search of an American heiress who would jump at the chance of exchanging her fortune for a title and a fixed residence in dear old England. He had heard that our grand free country had in it a number of feeble-minded females of this kind, and when he arrived on our shores he found that the report was quite true, and that he could have his pick and choice of a large number of American heiresses, regardless of the fact that he was a wizened, shrunken, evil-looking old wretch, with so little moral character left that it would have taken the big telescope at the Lick observatory to have discovered it. He was a choice specimen of the type of individuals we call "a tough." He had, moreover, an indigo blue beard, but his title would have made him eligible to a certain type of the American heiress had he been ringed, streaked and striped with a pea-green beard.

Blue Beard, after being lionized to even his own disgust at Newport, Bar Harbor and Lenox, and after rejecting the offers of many heiresses, decided upon one of two sisters as the future Mrs. Blue Beard. Her name was Fatima, but as she was a young lady of the most generous physical proportions she was playfully called Fatty by her intimates. Her sister's name was Anne. They were shrewd young women in some respects, and they wished to be dead sure that Blue Beard's castle was not a fake. Expressing this wish to him he invited them to go over to England and see it for themselves. The young ladies accepted the invitation and were soon in England, where they satisfied themselves that the castle and the nobleman's social standing were all he had represented, whereupon Fatty threw herself into his arms, saying:

"My noble, generous lord! I am yours, for I am sure, quite sure, that I love you now!"

"My own darling!" he said, embracing as much of her as he could reach around, "I have you not only on your own account, but on your bank account."

"It is all yours," she murmured.

Fatty and Anne then returned to New York, and the wedding, which came off in Grace Church, is talked about to this day. All of the Four Hundred were there, and at the close of the ceremony they fairly climbed over each other's heads and tore each other's clothes in their frantic endeavors to possess themselves of the flowers Blue Beard had imported for the occasion from his English conservatories. The strife for these souvenirs of nobility was so hot and eager that the famous Mrs. Van Million, who was noted for her regal manners, came out of the church with her magnificent Worth gown in rags and her $100 Virot bonnet torn from her head, while her beautiful wavy false front dangled over one ear.

The haughty Mrs. K. De Forest De Ducats so far forgot herself as to accuse the superb Mrs. Royal St. Hauteur of being "no lady" because that individual snatched a choice rose that Blue Beard's own royal foot had trod upon from Mrs. De Ducat's hand after she had crawled under ten pews of the church to get possession of this souvenir of royalty. The police had to come in and use their clubs to restore order, and it was extremely mortifying to the proud family of Fatty to have her carefully planned and enormously expensive English wedding partake so largely of the elements of an Irish wake.

Fatty's gown was a Worth creation of ivory-white satin, with a train so long and so profuse in real old point lace that it filled many a woman with such envy that she would willingly have torn it to rags rather than to have had Fatty possess it. She wore an enormous diamond sunburst and a diamnd necklace and tiara, gifts of the generous Blue Beard, the bills for which were sent to Fatty's father. This was all very lovely for Fatty, and it put Blue Beard into such a good humor that he was kind and polite to his wife for nearly a week after the wedding.

They sailed for England amid the loudly uttered good wishes of many who at heart wished that the Cunarder Blue Beard and his wife were on would go to the bottom of the ocean rather than that Fatty should reap the rewards of what she had paid the money for.

Two days after their arrival at Blue Beard's castle he said to Fatty:

"My dear Fat, I must go away to see a man and may be gone a day or two. Here are the keys of the castle. You may go all over it and may enter every room but the blue chamber. Keep out of that, or you'll wish you had. I do not desire to be harsh to my dear Fatty, but if you go into that room there'll be a regular monkey and parrot time of it when I get home. You hear me?"

"Yes, my lord," replied Fatty. But the moment Blue Beard was gone Fatty ran to her sister, who was visiting her, and said:

"What do you think, Anne? My lord says I am not to enter the blue chamber while he is away."

"I guess I'd show him that I'd enter any room I pleased in this house after all the money you've got to spend on it to put it into decent shape," said Anne, with much asperity.

"I'd just like to know what's in that room," said Fatty.

"Why don't you go and see?"

"He might not like it."

"Pooh! Now see here, Fatty; if you give in to your husband in the beginning you'll have it to do all of the time. I'd just let him know at the outset that I came from a country in which a wife is not only the equal, but a good deal the superior of her husband. I'd like to see the man who could boss me!"

"I dare say that you would," said Fatima, a little tartly, "but I believe that you are right, so come on and we'll see what's in that room, and if Blue Beard don't like it he can lump it."

So the two sisters went to the blue chamber and Fatty opened the door and stepped in.

"My soul and body!" she exclaimed, throwing up both hands and dropping the key, whereupon it fell with a dull thud to the floor, and Fatima came near following suit, for there, ranged along the wall, were the thirteen dead wives of Blue Beard, while above each hung a life-size Rembrandt of herself.

"The old wretch, to go and make a cemetery of his own house!" said Anne. "He's a regular Holmes! If I were you, he'd hear from me the moment he got home, and there'd be some house-cleaning done here and those ladies should be carted off to the crematory."

"It's where they belong," said Fatima. "I call it anything but pleasant to have them around here. But what is that? Oh, Anne, it is Blue Beard returning already!" She picked up the key and found that there was a drop of blood on it she could not wash off. While she was rubbing away at it Blue Beard came in and, striking an attitude, said:

"Aha, madam! What do I see? My orders have been disobeyed. Your life shall pay the penalty of this wilful disobedience!"

"Now, don't get rattled," said Fatima, calmly seeking to engage her lord in a dispute while Anne went down to the telephone and rang up No. 642, which was the police station.

"Madam!" roared Blue Beard, "your time is short!"

"Spare me long enough to crimp my bangs," said Fatima with true American spirit and independence, feeling buoyantly confident that America had beaten England once and could do it again.

Blue Beard was dazed by this splendid exhibition of nerve. He could not but admire Fatima's courage, and he said:

"Well, you're a good one. Time to crimp of your hair? Well, I like that! I'll give you ten minutes while I go down to the grindstone and sharpen my sword."

"Thanks!" said Fatima, tittering in her sleeve. Then she joined Anne, and said:

"Did you ring up the police station?"

"Yes, and the patrol wagon is now on its way to the house."

"Good enough," said the plucky Fatima; "it'll just about paralyze my precious husband when he sees it."

Come on and be killed, Madam!" roared Blue Beard from the bottom of the stairs a few minutes later.

"Coming, dear," replied Fatima, airily, for she had caught sight of four of the "finest" coming towards her house. When Blue Beard saw them enter the door he hissed out:

"Betrayed! But I'll never be taken alive!" Nor was he. When they dragged him from his hiding place a few minutes later it was found that he had swallowed an enormous dose of Rough on Rats, and in three minutes Fatima was a widow.

"And the social season at its height," said Fatima, sadly. "But black is wonderfully becoming to me," she added more cheerfully.

Fatima's first care was to have her thirteen predecessors cremated along with the husband who had been so much to them in life, and when her year of mourning was done she became one of the most dashing widows England had ever known.

MAX MERRYMAN.

"Sezi" and "Sezee."

She was a "saleslady" of the type that chews gum and wears fourteen rings on one hand, the aggregate value of the lot being about a dollar and seventy-five cents. She had had a "falling-out" with her "best fellow" and was giving an account of the tragic event to another "saleslady," whose own wad of tutti-frutti was gracefully poised between her half-parted lips.

"Yes, Mag," said the bejewelled saleslady, "I've give him the G. B. for good and all."

"La, Mame, you ain't!"

"Ain't I, though? Well, I guess. I let him know that I don't play second fiddle to no fellow an' that he couldn't take Jennie Simpson to the ice-cream saloon one night and take me to walk round in the park next night an' never get me so much as a soda. I guess I paralyzed him!"

"What did he say?"

"Well, I'll tell you the whole story, Mag. I didn't let out on 'im till we'd got clean back to our house and then sezi to him, sezi:

"'You think you're blamed smart, don't you, Jim Hixon,' sezi, an' he sez, sezee:

"'What do you mean, Mame?' sezee, an' sezi to him, sezi:

"'Oh, you're mighty innocent, now, ain't you?' sezi, an' he sez, sezee:

"'Pon honor, Mame, I don't know what you're drivin' at,' an' I up an' sez, sezi:

"'You don't know anything about a certain feller takin' a certain freckle-nosed, tallow-complexioned, pop-eyed, lop-eared girl to the ice-cream saloon last night, now, do you?' sezi, right out, flat-footed, like that, an' he looked as if he'd drop, an' he sez, sezee:

"'So you're onto that, are you, Mame,' an' I sez, sezi:

"'Yes, I am, my youthful friend, an' I'm onto the rest of your curves,' sezi, 'an' I'll thank you to address me as Miss Hobbs hereafter,' sezi, 'an' I don't want you to even speak to me on the street,' sezi, 'for you're no more to me than the dirt an' grime under my feet,' sezi, 'an' if you think, Jim Hixon, that I'll play second fiddle to Jen Simpson you're most beautifully left,' sezi. 'I'm accustomed to receiving attentions from gentlemen, an' I'm sorry I ever lowered myself by condescending to even look at such a squint-eyed, bow-legged, pimple-faced, drab-haired chump as you are,' sezi."

"Oh, Mame, you didn't?"

"Didn't I though? I tell you my dander was up an' I let 'im have it right in the neck."

"'The next time a lady condescends to look at you,' sezi, 'an' give you her comp'ny, I hope you'll treat her as a lady expects to be treated,' sezi, an' he sez, sezee:

"'Shucks, Mame!' sezee; 'you know I don't care two wrappings of my finger for Jen,' sezee, an' I sez, sezi:

"'That's more'n I care for you, Jim Hixon, an' now you git,' sezi.

"La, Mame, what did he do?"

"He got."

"He did?"

"You kin just bet he did."

"An' ain't you goin' to make it up with 'im?"

"Me? What you take me for, Mag Higgins? When I go to craw fishin' you'll know it, for—there's the floor-walker watchin' us, the old bloke."

The "All Right" Friend.

I'm not well posted in the tricks
Of policy or politics;
The East and West can fight it out—
I don't know what it's all about.
But I am waiting till the time
Allows me to commit a crime.
I wish to single out the man,
And slaughter him, that's if I can—
The man who on election night
Insists on saying "He's all right!"

LA TOUCHE HANCOCK.

FRANKNESS.

She—To what am I indebted for the pleasure of this call?

He—To the fact that the other girl I called on was not at home.

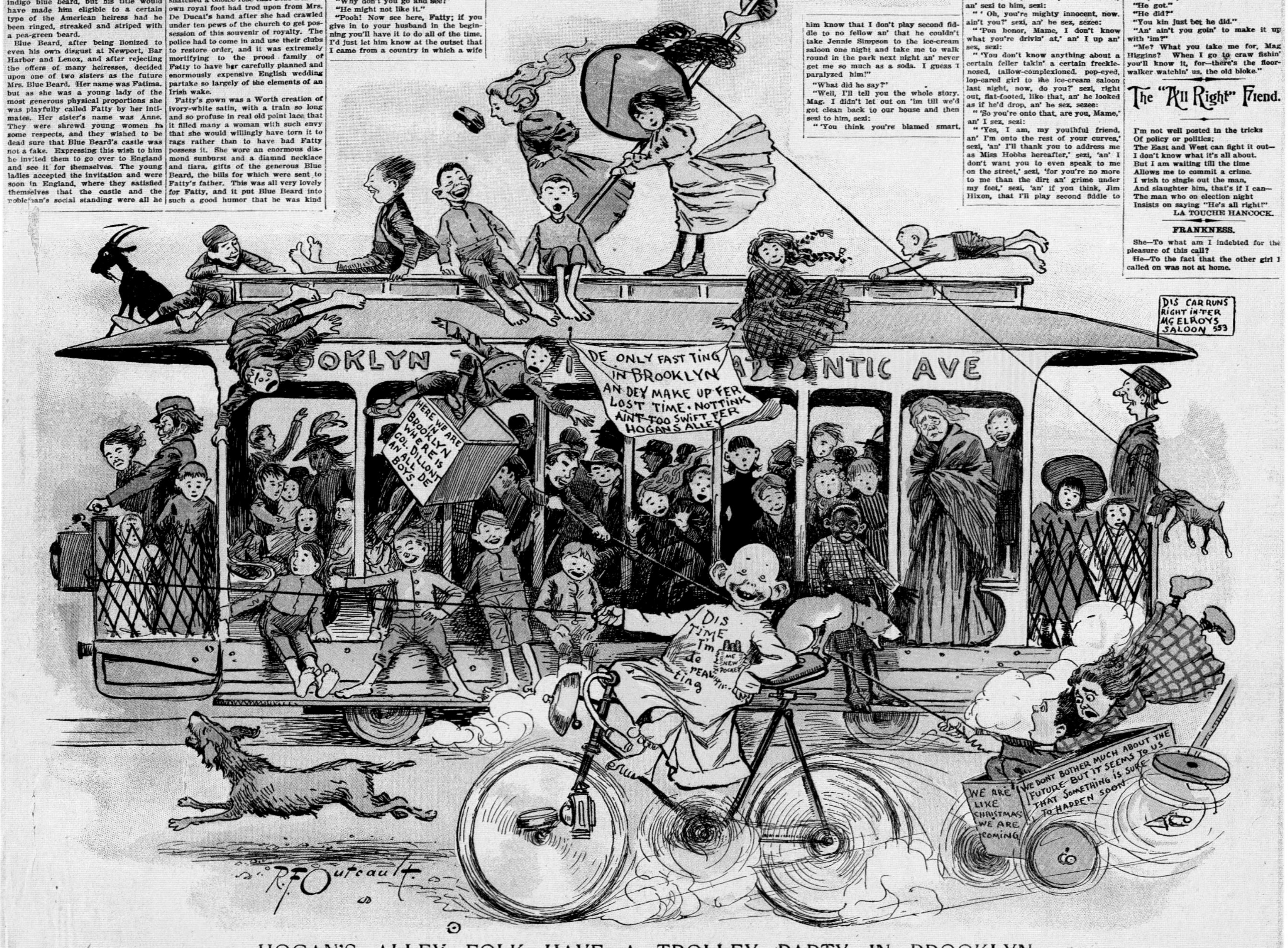

HOGAN'S ALLEY FOLK HAVE A TROLLEY PARTY IN BROOKLYN.

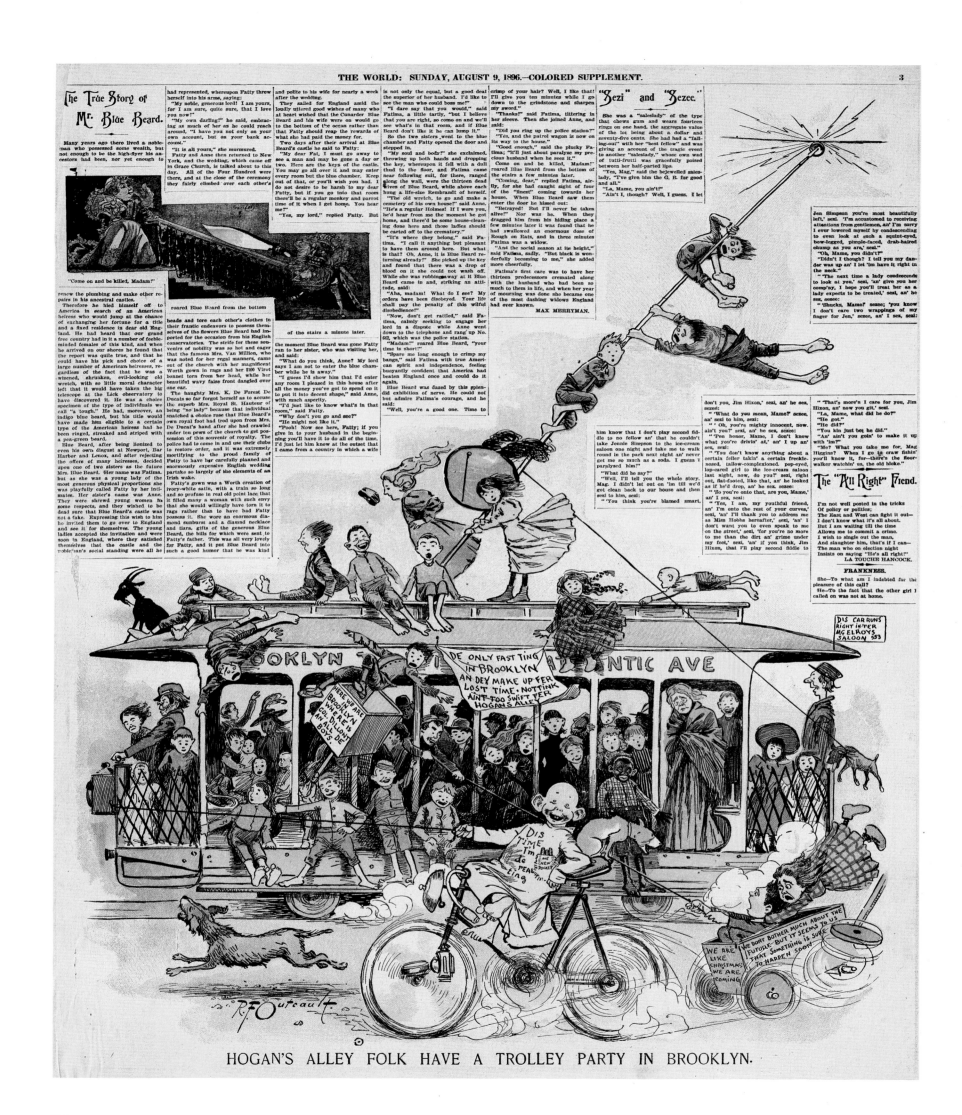

in neighborhoods where immigrant residents could see their homelands respectfully delineated. But the premise of the cartoon series was becoming diluted; perhaps Outcault was tiring of the back lots.

More likely, both Outcault and Hearst were reacting to a backlash against the Yellow Kid's popularity. Educators and clerics objected to the vulgar cartoons in the color supplements and to Outcault's Kid in particular. The preoccupation with tenement life was unseemly enough, but the comic details horrified some readers—details like eyes being gouged, dogs being kicked, and invariably, somewhere in each cartoon, a kid falling from a fire escape. Such light touches soon became the slapstick staples of many comic strips and early comedy films, but in the *Yellow Kid* they became one more reason for public libraries to refuse subscriptions to Hearst papers. And they became a handicap that comic strips had to contend with for a generation.

Ironically, Outcault's artwork mirrored little of the raucous themes of the cartoon, and perhaps the juxtaposition of a refined line and anarchic mayhem

T he Yellow Kid's name and image were festooned on all manner of products. Indeed it was the character's commercial popularity, perhaps more than the cartoons themselves, that was responsible for the establishment of comic sections as necessary components of Sunday newspapers.

C ould this have been the inspiration for Outcault's *Yellow Kid*? Charles Saalburg drew the *Ting-Ling Kids* in Chicago as early as 1893, employing a regular cast of characters in color genre drawings every week; they even vaguely resembled the kid who became Mickey Dugan. And in 1895 Saalburg had moved to New York, where he was Outcault's art director on the *New York World*. *(Right)*

T he "comic" of the Sunday comic sections in newspapers like the *World* referred more to the tone of the whole section—cartoons, poems, articles, jokes—than to what evolved into the "comic" strip. Accordingly, as in this example (August 9, 1896), the cartoons were often integrated with other matter. *(Facing page)*

Copyright, 1894, by C. W. Saalburg. THE TING LINGS GO A FISHING.

accounted for part of the *Yellow Kid's* appeal. Outcault always tended toward realism in his drawings, exaggerating little and attempting to emulate the illustrator's techniques of crosshatchings and delineating the finest details. In fact, the Yellow Kid was always and exclusively the one figure in each cartoon that deviated from a realistic depiction. As his popularity widened, his role in the cartoons became standard—the Kid established eye contact with the reader, inviting the reader into the scene or commenting on it. Thus this wise-guy update of the Greek chorus pioneered a special form of communication between cartoon characters and readers.

By 1898, however, the Kid's welcome had worn out, perhaps because of protests from respectable readers or Outcault's restlessness or, most likely, a combination of both. Outcault returned to Pulitzer's *World* (there are no hard feelings when marketable talents are concerned) and created a short-lived feature, *Kelly's Kindergarten.* It was *Hogan's Alley* without the Yellow Kid and inspiration for another Broadway musical, but basically it passed with little flurry. Outcault kept busy during the late 1890s freelancing to *Life* and *Judge* (he specialized in cartoons about the rural black community of Possumville) and joined the staff of the *New York Herald*, as respectable a newspaper as was published in New York at the time.

Perhaps Outcault joined the *Herald* to escape the low-life associations of the *World* and the *Journal*; certainly his cartoons were more genteel. For the *Herald* he drew realistic captioned cartoons of rural blacks; he created a popular series of genre drawings in the form of illustrated letters called *Pore Li'l Mose* (the little black boy and his animal friends once visited Edison in his laboratory!); and he finally experimented with strips on a regular basis. Outcault drew Sunday multipanel episodes of comic events from real life and a strip about a bizarre boy in clown costume, *Nixie*, as well as one about a junior bellhop, *Buddy Tucker.*

All of this work—even *Mose*, which was collected in one of the first comic books—helped Outcault refine his realistic drawing style and kept his work before the public, but it hardly rivaled his earlier success with the Yellow Kid. In 1902, however, he introduced a new strip, and a new character, to the genteel readers of the *Herald*.

Buster Brown was the mischievous son of prosperous parents. The Browns lived in an elegant home with maids and servants; they summered in the country and traveled abroad. Buster wore Little Lord Fauntleroy outfits, and his dog,

The Yellow Kid was the first of many comic characters to dance across Broadway stages. Others to come included Buster Brown, Foxy Grandpa, Little Nemo, Li'l Abner, the *Peanuts* cast, and Little Orphan Annie.

After Outcault moved to the *Journal*, the *World* continued the *Hogan's Alley* cartoons, although the Kid wore various costumes, including a white gown. Cartoonist George B. Luks later became a respected member of the Eight, which ironically—considering Luks's training in Hogan's Alley—was dubbed the Ashcan School of painting. *(Page 30)*

In one of the last appearances of the *Yellow Kid*, from the *New York Journal* of January 23, 1898, his yellow had changed to orange, and he was appearing in strips—although still not with formal conventions like panel borders and speech balloons. *(Page 31, above)*

Outcault's major feature after the *Yellow Kid* was *Pore Li'l Mose*. The cartoonist remained with his urban settings, but he was groping toward a broader storytelling mode via "letters" to Mammy, assorted vignettes, and awkwardly placed speech balloons. *(Page 31, below)*

When he licensed his own characters, R. F. Outcault often drew the images himself and eventually arranged the licenses through his own advertising agency, which was based in Chicago and managed by his son.

William Randolph Hearst ballyhooed his own comic section—eight pages of color, compared to four color pages in an eight-page section in Pulitzer's *World*—with the newly acquired Outcault. The first *Yellow Kid* cartoons appeared as parts of tenement stories by Edward W. Townsend, later a U.S. congressman.

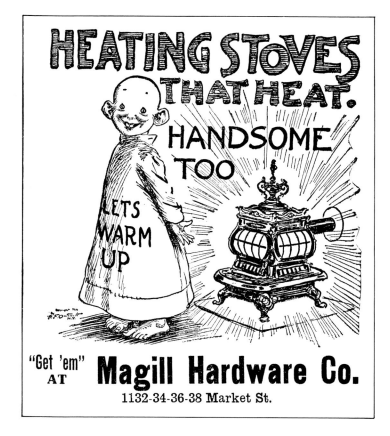

THE OPEN-AIR SCHOOL IN HOGAN'S ALLEY.

THE YELLOW KID EXPERIMENTS WITH THE WONDERFUL HAIR TONIC.

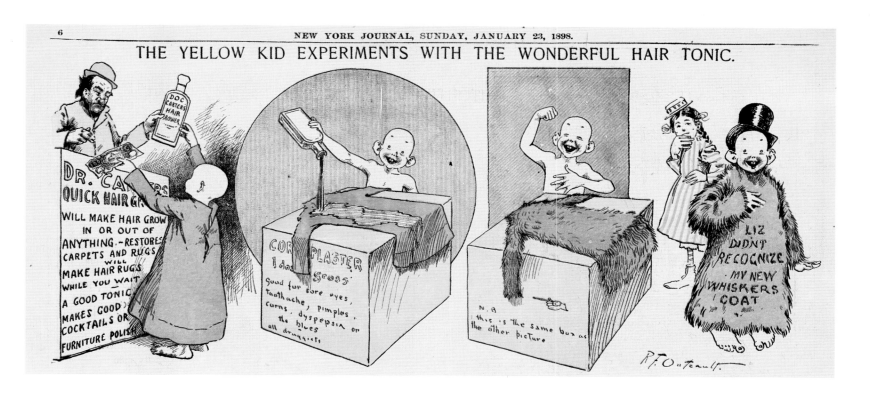

SUNDAY, SEPTEMBER 8, 1901.   3

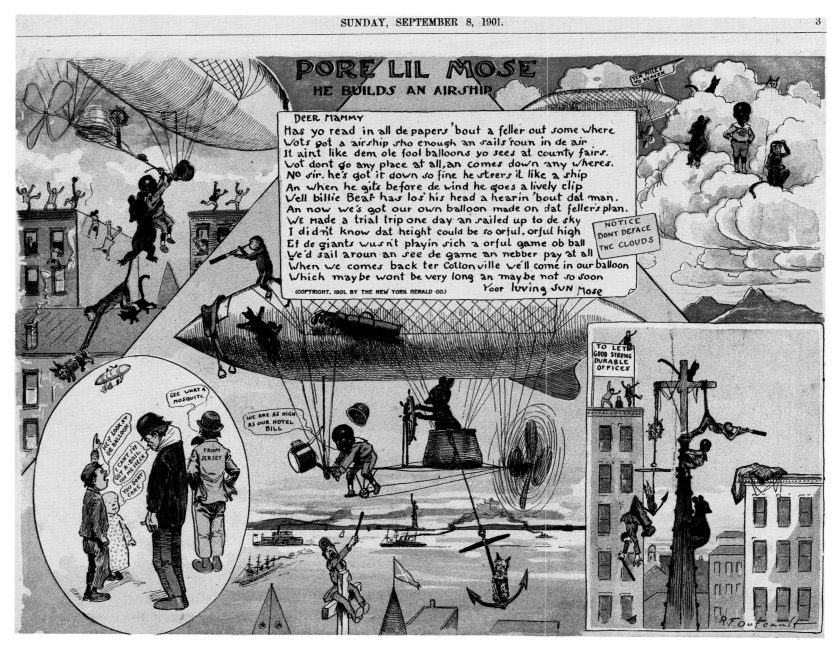

Tige, was not a one-eyed mutt of the slums but a pedigreed bulldog. Could anything be more different in tone and style from *Hogan's Alley*?

In fact, Mickey Dugan and Buster Brown were brothers under the skin. Buster was more than mischievous; he was a congenital prankster. His aggressive, crazed expression during the first few weeks of newspaper life was soon modified to an angelic countenance, but it set the tone for Buster's *modus*. In fact, the comedic mayhem in *Buster Brown* was more central than in *Hogan's Alley* (where it was a side effect). Buster wrecked his parents' ballroom, terrorized the help, sabotaged dinners, frightened elderly relatives, and reveled in every moment of scheming and execution. So did the public, which took Buster Brown to heart as enthusiastically as they had the Yellow Kid.

There were several factors that must have prevented the storms of protest that Buster Brown's rampant naughtiness might have incurred. For one thing, simply, the setting was more polite; the horrid slums were replaced by society folk in gowns and tuxedos. For another, there was *always* retribution; Buster got spanked or punished or thwarted at the conclusion of every Sunday episode. Finally, in a palatable bit of overkill that might have served as a concession to moralists, every page ended with a "Resolution." These resolutions were in Buster's hand and formed little homilies—virtually sermons—on lessons learned, observations about disobedience, and, eventually, reflections on life, philosophy, and religion. This aspect surely mirrored Outcault's own personal interests. His studio was filled with books by Emerson, Thoreau, and Henry George.

The resolutions neutralized potential complaints, and readers could simply sit back and enjoy Outcault's wonderful new world of high-society playfulness. Buster was sometimes an angel with a dirty face and sometimes a devil with a tin halo, and readers loved the formula. Tige was the character who established eye contact with the readers and forever attempted to be Buster's prudent adviser. In the process he became the first major talking animal of the comics, ancestor of Mickey Mouse, Felix the Cat, and Snoopy.

The formula that assured *Buster Brown's* success might well have been due to some calculation by Outcault, but it probably was due more to his genius for structuring comic situations and developing memorable characters. The atmosphere of the strip reflected a change in Outcault's own surroundings; "We were going up the social scale ourselves," Outcault's daughter, Mary Jane, remembered.

Mary Jane was the model for Buster's girlfriend, Mary Jane, but his young son, Richard II was not the model for Buster, despite the undying contentions of publicists and fans. Mrs. Outcault was the model for Mrs. Brown (Outcault resisted the temptation to depict himself as the Brown paterfamilias), and outfits worn by Outcault's wife and daughter would often appear in the comic strip a week later. When *Buster Brown* achieved national success, Outcault embarked on speaking tours; invariably his real-life family would accompany him, and invariably little Mary Jane Outcault would appear in costume as the fashionable girlfriend of Buster Brown.

The success of *Buster Brown* once again catapulted Richard Felton Outcault to the forefront of a profession he had helped create but which was now crowded with many other impressive talents. The popularity of his Sunday strip resulted in the publication of more than a dozen reprint volumes and two hardcover storybooks. The popularity of his character resulted in the merchandising and

When *Buster Brown* made its appearance—these early examples are from his first weeks in the *New York Herald*—he was manifestly manic. Outcault was learning to construct strips and use balloons, although he clung to labels in the form of Buster's trademark "resolutions" throughout his career.

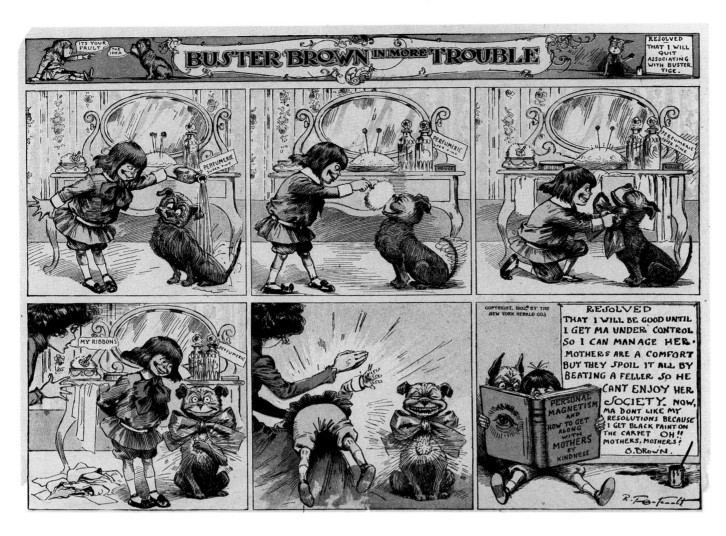

Some of the first "comic books" were reprints of newspaper strips, and, predictably, Outcault was a pioneer in this form of licensing. At left is the cover of an early volume featuring Buster's girlfriend, who was modeled after Outcault's own daughter, Mary Jane.

By the time *Buster Brown* moved to the *New York Journal* in 1906, Outcault had begun asserting more control over his creation and was generating an active licensing program; note the "Buster Brown Co." tag line at the bottom of the clothing ad at left. The activities were so fierce that the cartoonist crowed a little while having fun with Buster's omnipresence in this December 17, 1905, page for the *Herald* (right), one of Outcault's last for that paper.

licensing of scores of products named for Buster Brown: bread, chocolates, children's clothing, candy, postcards, hosiery, coffee, apples, cups, rubber stamps, games, shirt collars, razors, and soap, as well as shoes and textile products still produced today by two separate Buster Brown companies. Once again Outcault saw one of his characters become the inspiration for a Broadway musical and long-running stock touring show, and Buster Brown also starred in early animated

THE NEW YORK HERALD.

NEW YORK, SUNDAY, DECEMBER 17, 1905.—CHRISTMAS EDITION.—BY THE NEW YORK HERALD COMPANY. PRICE FIVE CENTS.

cartoons. For a second time Outcault was able to transcend mere slapstick on paper as his comic strip ignited a response among readers across America.

Ironically, after 1906 the name that R.F. Outcault was to license so widely was denied to him for use on his own comic strip. The situation was the result of another complicated, landmark lawsuit. Once again it was because the cartoonist switched papers, and once again his new employer was William Randolph Hearst. Hearst and assistant E.F. Flynn had met with Outcault in, of all places, Stratford-upon-Avon while the cartoonist was traveling with his family abroad (during the vacation, Buster visited foreign capitals in pages sent back to New York). The immediate result was a five-year exclusive contract with Hearst and the *Denver Post;* the longer-term result was a copyright suit that sent fur flying when the *Herald* engaged anonymous artists to continue *Buster* in its pages. The decision was similar to the Yellow Kid's: Outcault could draw Buster's adventures for

S everal times through the years Outcault resurrected the Yellow Kid as a visitor in *Buster Brown*.

B uster Brown's adventures were decidedly—and by design—less urban than those of the Yellow Kid. And when Buster even ventured onto the mean streets, he was punished. The page at left is reproduced from Outcault's original art, which shows the cartoonist's marks for the color engraver.

  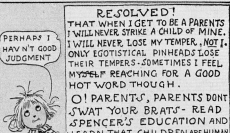 

whomever he pleased but could not use the title, which belonged to the *Herald,* and the *Herald* could freely continue *Buster Brown* with a cartoonist of its choosing.

The cartoonists of the *Herald's* choosing were uniformly terrible, and its version of *Buster Brown* died quietly in a few years (it was overshadowed, besides, by *Little Nemo* in the *Herald's* pages). And for years Outcault had to cope with drawing *Buster Brown* without being able to call it such. He resorted to simple episodic titles ("Getting an Education"; "It Was All Tige's Fault") or sometimes visual tricks ("Mary Jane and…" with a portrait of Buster). Ultimately it was a negligible thorn in Outcault's side. *Buster Brown* retained its popularity through the early 1920s, when Outcault retired from active cartooning.

The cartoonist was by then assured of his role in comic-strip history and of the immortality of his characters. Outcault also had other pursuits. The wealthy suburbanite (he had settled in what was then the affluent countryside of Flushing, Long Island) inaugurated several enterprises, including the Outcault Lecture Bureau and the Buster Brown Amusement Company. Around 1906 he was invited to invest in a Chicago firm that became the Outcault Advertising Agency. A man named Crewdson established the enterprise (and was later convicted of siphoning profits to invest in Washington State apple orchards); James F. Pershing, brother of General Pershing and soon father-in-law to Outcault's daughter, was treasurer, and Outcault's own son, R.F. II, eventually ran the operation after his graduation from business school. Although the elder Outcault had a hand in the agency's direction and Buster Brown images promoted his own and others' products, he remained in Flushing through the years, primarily devoted to the strip.

When Outcault died in 1928, newspaper articles hailed him as Father of the Comic Strip; those notices that called him Father of the Funnies were closer to the truth. The comic section, not the comic strip, was his legacy and is his monument. For years prototypical versions of comic strips—usually black and white, usually pantomimic—had been appearing in places as diverse as the back sections of literary monthlies and the penny prints. Because of the Yellow Kid, the comic strip had a place to experiment, innovate, expand, and mature.

At the turn of the century many comic-strip characters appeared on postcards—some printed by the prestigious Raphael Tuck & Sons, "Art Publishers by Appointment to Their Majesties the King and Queen" of England—and besides Buster there were the Katzenjammer Kids, Happy Hooligan, Foxy Grandpa, Little Jimmy, and Little Nemo.

Right at the birth of the art form, Outcault institutionalized several thematic conventions. His range was broad: slums, high society, ethnic subjects. He was a pioneer at injecting politics into his cartoons; years before *Doonesbury,* Outcault freely dealt references to McKinley, Bryan, Roosevelt, and local politicos. (On the other hand, as strips evolved from panel cartoons, it remained for some to *emancipate* the form from political preoccupations.) For all the refinement of his line, Outcault happily trafficked in slapstick.

There is one more aspect to Outcault's contributions that has been little commented upon—that is, his appeal to both adult and child readers. Virtually all of his comic series were devoted to children as characters, yet the tone and references within the drawings were often aimed at older readers and more sophisticated sensibilities. Whether it was the pathos in *Hogan's Alley* or the high-society milieu in *Buster Brown,* whether the political comments were tucked away in labels in the *Yellow Kid* or in Tige's sarcastic asides, there was material enough to attract older readers while the children laughed at the mayhem and pranks.

In this way Richard Felton Outcault established more than the raw popularity of the newspaper cartoon and color comic section; he ensured that its appeal would be universal. The downside of his virtuosity is that, even years later, the comic strip is denigrated in some quarters for its juvenile appeal and unappreciated for its more sophisticated levels. However, while the debate goes on, so do the comics, thanks in large part to the father of two remarkable comic offspring, the Yellow Kid and Buster Brown.

2

The newspaper comic strip was a genuine phenomenon when it emerged around 1895, but it was also the product of a long evolution. Somehow it seems fitting that, just as its showcase, the colored supplement, was a brand-new medium, so the one cartoonist who fused many of its essential elements was a newcomer on the scene.

Rudolph Dirks was that cartoonist, and he made his contributions through the *Katzenjammer Kids,* a strip that became a major contribution itself. Dirks took the new convention of a regular cast—tried tentatively by James Swinnerton as well as Charles Saalburg and more resolutely by R.F. Outcault—and became the first cartoonist who specialized in just a single feature from the start. (Other cartoonists freelanced before settling into a series or continued to draw other artwork.) Dirks also made routine use of sequential panels to tell a story, which others only had experimented with. A.B.

RUDOLPH DIRKS

AHOY, LOAFER! VOT'S DER BIG IDEA?

1877-1968

Frost and F.M. Howarth, among others in the magazines, made use of paneled "comic series," as they were called, but Dirks made the practice standard in his work.

Many historians have ascribed the pioneering of dialogue balloons in comic strips to Dirks, but actually he used them as redundant or superficial appendages to his drawings, almost afterthoughts at first; it was Frederick Opper who would later establish the dialogue balloon in sequential panels. Nevertheless, Dirks played a pivotal role in the development of the comic strip. Because of him, the comics told tales, not just jokes. They made sense instead of merely making points. Where once cartoons—even crowded, elaborate ones like the *Yellow Kid*—stood as vignettes, the newspaper comic strip began telling stories, developing characters, sustaining continuities, and, eventually, stretching beyond humor to other literary forms and beyond newspapers to media like graphic novels.

Incidentally, in creating the *Katzenjammer Kids*—what they were and what they portended—Dirks served to reinforce the comics' young but hardly fragile role as promotional tool for the newspapers in which they appeared. More than the colored supplement itself, the regularly appearing strip with an established cast encouraged readers to follow favorite features each edition—and buy the papers in which they starred.

Rudolph Dirks was born in 1877 in Heinde, a town in the Schleswig-Holstein region of Germany. The son of a woodcarver, he moved with his family to Chicago when he was seven; ten years later he was freelancing cartoons, and three years after that, in 1897, he was drawing cartoons in New York for William Randolph Hearst's *Journal*.

Dirks's inspiration flowed more directly from the great German story-cartoonist Wilhelm Busch than from Americans like Frost and Howarth. Busch's *Max und Moritz, a Story in Seven Tricks* had been a classic since its first publication in Germany in 1865. It was a *bilderbogen*—a picture-story book of cartoons and verse that resembled a prototypical comic strip. Max and Moritz were two devilish brothers whose pranks (and eventual demise) were published around the world, including America. It is known that Hearst, when he was a young boy touring the Continent with his mother, acquired a copy of *Max und Moritz*. Legends would imply that Busch's little book became a sort of Rosebud, hidden away in Hearst's memories until the advent of his colored newspaper supplement.

Although Dirks was drawing in the most cosmopolitan city in the United States, at a time when a distinctively American art form was evolving, ironically he was asked by his editors to look back, not forward. His assignment actually came from comics editor Rudolph Block, who, as a humor writer, adopted the pseudonym Bruno Lessing. On December 12, 1897, three boys appeared in the *American Humorist* section of the *Journal* (the next week and forever after, their number was two) in a succession of panels that depicted a backyard tempest between the boys, a gardener, and a hose.

From the start the elements were in place—Busch's conventions, young male pranksters (mischievous pairs formed a long literary tradition), a generational confrontation—and the premises, style, and substance of the strip have changed little from 1897 to today. The Katzenjammers were German, to be sure; even before dialogue revealed the fact, the titles were in pidgin German dialect. The characters' costumes and the homely household decorations confirmed their nationality, and the very name erased all doubt. *Katzenjammer,* literally "the howling of cats," is German slang for a hangover.

There was no coyness about the Katzies' origin, either inspirationally or ethnically; in fact, the prime motivator was probably commercial. A German-born cartoonist drawing a feature about Germans reminiscent of a German children's book classic was obviously meant not to lampoon but to attract German readers. Immigrants still composed a large percentage of urban sub-

In the beginning there was *Max und Moritz*, the 1865 picture story by the German cartoonist Wilhelm Busch.

Although Dirks facilely established the conventions of storytelling and panel progression early in the *Katzenjammer Kids*, he eschewed the use of dialogue balloons. This 1898 example, from the *New York Journal*'s "American Humorist" section, displays Dirks's preoccupation with gadgets, appliances, and machines, and how they could be turned to mischievous ends.

duction to the language, and publishers aimed, by simplified dialogue, clearly delineated drawings, and sympathetic character types, to cater to these readers.

In the beginning there was a Grandfather and a Papa Katzenjammer. Both were to disappear in short order. The father was a mere ornament who would either observe pranks played upon Mama or be the butt of some disasters himself without ever being moved to anger ("Such a family!" was his frequent, and most emotional, response). There was Mama Katzenjammer, dumpling-like, forever baking pies and forever oblivious to the mayhem being plotted and perpetrated around her. Other characters followed, notably Der Captain, a corpulent sea dog who appeared in 1902 as a target for the boys (and not, as the public has assumed, the boys' father), and Der Inspector, who first was cast as a bloodhound of a truant officer but later mellowed—or surrendered—into a docile role as the Captain's card-playing partner.

And then, of course, there were Hans and Fritz.

Could such boys be the agents of chaos? They were not bullies; neither were they mean spirited. They were hardly prigs, and their outfits—wide collar and floppy bow tie for dark-haired Hans and lace collar for blond Fritz—were more camouflage than tip-off. Hans and Fritz were not the embodiments of evil, but they certainly were the manifestations of mischief.

The brothers were usually partners, although occasionally Dirks would have them turn tricks on each other. Hardly ever were they seen to conspire; rather, they intuitively sensed opportunities for pandemonium. Sometimes, in delicious sequences, Dirks would show the pair exchanging glances, their eyes growing wild with anticipation, their smiles reflecting joy unrestrained; in such episodes Hans and Fritz would even proudly compare notes while cheeks were still wet after the inevitable spanking. Readers must have felt lucky to witness such craftsmanship and pride—and felt relieved to be spectators, not victims.

Dirks's strip was an instant hit and appeared with increasing frequency through early 1898, just as the Yellow Kid was fading from the *American Humorist* pages of Hearst's newspaper; the *Katzenjammer Kids* became the most prominent

The Katzenjammer Kids Explore a Ship.

of the section's titles. Dirks's success was due to more factors than luck and circumstance. He was a gifted cartoonist who had the perfect instincts for the comic-strip form. He was one of the first cartoonists to "spot" blacks, eliminating details and using large areas of black to aid his compositions. His arrangement of characters and props and his masterful sense of balloon placement led the reader's eyes through his strips. His comic sense of anatomy was sure, and he imbued his figures with believable movements, reactions, and attitudes.

It is remarkable how Dirks, especially given his lack of experience as a cartoonist, defined a vocabulary of comics language—after having already contributed so much to its structure by the sequential panels he constructed in order to tell his stories. Seemingly by instinct, he either invented or standardized the use of many visual shorthand symbols. Motion lines, stars of pain, footprints

the use of many visual shorthand symbols. Motion lines, stars of pain, footprints indicating changed positions, dotted lines along the sharp focus of attention, sweat beads: today these are clichés of comic-strip expression, and Dirks must be acknowledged as their architect.

If ever the comics were faced with a gestalt equation, it is with the *Katzenjammer Kids.* For all the other factors so evident in Dirks's success, it must be recognized that there is a virtually indescribable attractiveness to the simple formula based on the mischievous pair. Not only has the *Katzenjammer Kids* been the most durable of all American comic strips (it is still running today), but it has spawned nearly a dozen imitations, countless licensing permutations, and a host of counterfeit versions—even in other nations and cultures.

The most notable spin-off, although not the first chronologically, was by Dirks himself. Every comics history recounts how the cartoonist wanted to take a lengthy cruise around 1912 and Hearst asked him to draw a year's worth of pages a year in advance. Such was not the scenario. In fact, Dirks had taken long vacations earlier, and other artists, including Frederick Opper, had filled in on the *Katzies* (Dirks, it seems, was the first artist to employ ghosts). The cause of Dirks's rupture with Hearst in 1912 was the autocratic attitude of Hearst's comic editor, Rudolph Block. (Through the years other leading cartoonists, including Opper, Outcault, and Frank Willard, also expressed disgust with Block, and it seems amazing that Hearst retained him.) The Hearst–Pulitzer rivalry had not died with the *Yellow Kid,* and in 1912 the rising star George McManus (later to draw *Bringing Up Father*) deserted Pulitzer for Hearst. The *World's* persistent publisher merely played tit-for-tat by enticing Rudolph Dirks across the street.

Echoing the court battles over the *Yellow Kid* and *Buster Brown* and foreshadowing a similar dispute over rights to *Mutt and Jeff,* the fight for Hans and Fritz lasted well over a year. The invective between cartoonists, editors, and publishers spilled over onto the front pages. The landmark case's Solomon-like decision granted Dirks the physical likenesses and names of his characters, and Hearst the title of the strip.

In late 1914, the kids began appearing on the front page of the Pulitzer chain's funny sections and were syndicated to other papers as well. At first the episodes carried descriptive, rather than running, titles but soon the strip was dubbed *Hans and Fritz* (in the twenties it became *The Captain and the Kids*). The credit was always given as "by the famed originator of the Katzenjammer Kids, R. Dirks."

Back at the Hearst papers, an artist named Harold H. Knerr inherited the *Katzenjammers,* and his work was polished, fresh, and lively. He continued the strip with such ease that one might have thought he had been drawing it for a decade already. As a matter of fact, Knerr *had* been virtually auditioning for the previous ten years, in a strip he drew for the *Philadelphia Inquirer* and its nationwide syndicate. Called the *Fineheimer Twins,* it featured a blond boy and a dark-haired boy; familiar outfits; a Mama and an overweight, retired sea dog; German accents; and much more. The resemblance was hardly accidental, but curiously there seemed to be no effort by Dirks or Hearst to enjoin the sincere form of flattery Knerr or his successors perpetrated. Possibly in a bit of puckishness

but more probably to keep within the letter of the judicial decision, Knerr rechristened his kids. Hans became Fritz and Fritz became Hans. It is likely that not one reader in a hundred knew the two kids by their names anyway, since they were seldom addressed individually in the strip.

That the *Fineheimer Twins* was not the only imitation to flourish is another testament to the astounding durability of theme and premise, and the visceral response of readers everywhere through the years. Dirks himself duplicated the setup in two short-lived strips during a hiatus from Hearst in 1900: *The Pinochle Twins* for the *Philadelphia Inquirer,* and *Alfred's Little Cousin and Alfred* for the *New York World.* Also in the *World* was C.W. Kahles's brittle imitation, *Tim and Tom, the Terrible Twins,* although this pair shared black hair. In the twenties they became *Tim and Tom, The Kelly Kids* and lost their German accents, but the costumes and hair color once again approximated the Katzenjammers'. An artist named Karls drew *Dem Boys* for the World Color Printing Company, and about the only difference between his kids and Dirks's—besides a scabrous drawing style—was their names, Max and Chulius. So popular were the premise and theme that, for several years during the teens, five separate versions were appearing simultaneously: *Katzenjammer Kids* by Knerr; *The Katzies,* Hearst's reprints of earlier Dirks pages; *Hans and Fritz* by Dirks himself; *Dem Boys* by Karls; and the *Fineheimer Twins* by Jack Gallagher.

The theme and premise—and imagery—were just as popular and durable abroad. As early as the turn of the century, Dirks's characters were well known in France, where mechanical toys of the Katzenjammers were pictured on the front page of the *Printemps* catalog. Soon France had its own *Pim, Pam, Poum,* which has amused more than two generations and still exists in a comic book, starring the entire cast of Katzenjammers in identical settings but drawn by a succession of French artists with no acknowledgement to the American original (or to its German inspiration, for that matter; Dirks occasionally paid silent homage to Busch by reworking some of Busch's classic sequences). In Great

Britain *The Terrible Twins* and *The Twinkleton Twins* were mirror images of the Dirks designs, as were the characters in one-shot series by Tom Browne and Tom Wilkinson. Since 1912 Norway has issued reprints of their version, *Knoll og Tott,* and as far back as 1899 the Portuguese magazine *Carantonha* (*Big Ugly Face*) featured copies of kids, redrawn from the American by engraver Pires Marinho. Italy, Denmark, Sweden, and even Israel have had their versions, and in many European countries the actual vintage work of Dirks and Knerr has been anthologized through the years.

Not even the intense anti-German propaganda in the United States through two wars could dampen the popular enthusiasm for the Kids. Only during World War I (when government-sponsored hostility to ethnic Germans was actually more virulent than later) were adjustments made. In the *Katzenjammers* page, Knerr had the Captain apply for a legal name change—implying, by the way, that the Captain was the Kids' father—because the family was Dutch but too often taken for "dod-gasted Choimans." The page was also retitled *The Shenanigan Kids* during the war, and the boys were rechristened Mike and Aleck. Dirks, in his strip, also implied the family was Dutch, not German, and simply dropped any trace of accents. After the war there was a "Return to Normalcy" on the comic pages, as in all of Harding's America. During World War II no such silly realignments occurred.

It is astonishing that the worldwide appeal and longevity of Dirks's characters have not been duplicated by any other popular comic strip. Busch's original *Max und Moritz* is still in print in Germany and around the world—but not imitations of it (save the Katzies, which only began thirty years after Busch's work.) Mickey Mouse and Snoopy are virtual icons around the world—but in their original images, not countless counterfeits and imitations. Dirks's creation continues both ways—almost a century of the *Katzies* (with reprints, licensed products, animated cartoons, and such) as well as a host of carbon-copy imitators. What is it about those kids?

Clearly Rudolph Dirks touched some primal chord, not only in devoting his feature to a traditional mischievous pair, but in choosing the manner, type, and style of the unfolding antagonisms he chronicled in each episode. To some readers Hans and Fritz have consciously or subconsciously represented the manifestations of pure anarchy. They live to destroy and reduce, and no characters in the comics or all of fiction take more undiluted delight in such mayhem. "Mit dose kids, society is nix!" is an epithet ascribed to the Inspector, and while not every reader has wished to duplicate the kids' iconoclastic vengeance, many have been happy voyeurs.

For readers with a more authoritarian strain, there was the comfortable assurance that justice would always reign in the Katzenjammers' world. Almost every prank succeeded, but just as often a spanking would follow. The only thing more certain than retribution was the inevitability of more mayhem next week; it was as if apprehension and punishment were only challenges rather than deterrents to Hans and Fritz.

A certain matriarchal flavor must be recognized in Dirks's epic. In the first few years of *Katzenjammer Kids,* Mama was the recipient of ink in the perfume bottle and buckets of water over the door and sometimes crueler fates. But eventually—especially after the Captain's appearance as a pliable, inviting target—

The restless Dirks drew two other strips during a break from the *Katzenjammers*, possibly during a contract dispute or possibly just as moonlighting forays—*The Pinochle Twins* for the *Philadelphia Inquirer* and *Alfred's Little Cousin and Alfred* for the *New York World*. Drawn just a few weeks apart in 1900, both were built around mischievous pairs like the Katzies.

1 THE TWINS ARE KIDNAPPED BY A BOLD BAD MAN

2 WHO TAKES THEM TO HIS CAVE FOR RANSOM AND TELLS THEM WHAT A WICKED MAN HE IS AND—

3 HOW MANY LITTLE BOYS HE HAS KILLED BECAUSE THEY RAN AWAY FROM HIM BUT THE KIDS DON'T BELIEVE A WORD OF IT

4 WHICH MAKES THE BAD MAN ANGRY

5 BUT HE SOON FINDS HE IS NO MATCH FOR THE TWINS

6 AND IS GLAD TO MAKE HIS ESCAPE AND THE TWINS ARE NOW OUT FOR A NEW ADVENTURE

THE PINOCHLE TWINS IN AN ADVENTURE WITH A BRIGAND

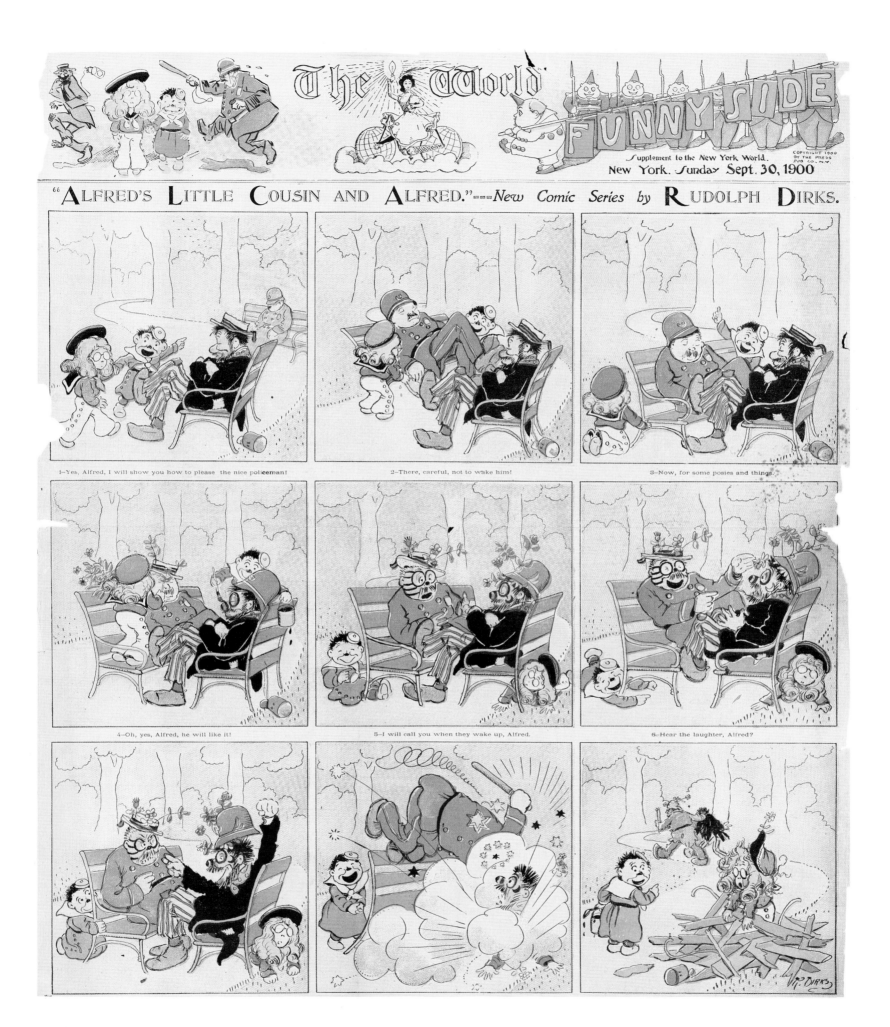

Mama was recast in the role of the protectress. Hans and Fritz could rely on her everlasting forbearance, as well as her eternal faith in their innocence; she was always willing to believe the best about her "anchels" and the worst of the Captain and the Inspector.

The constant battles evolved into a fascinating schizophrenic duality of types, and the variation on the theme must have attracted some readers. The Captain and the Inspector never ceased being the butt of the Kids' pranks, as Mama had, but their roles changed: they became grown-up kids themselves, avoiding chores, sneaking away to play cards, stealing pies. The Inspector was transformed, in a manner of speaking, into the truant he originally was dedicated to pursuing. And the Kids, while never losing the irreducible playfulness of their characters, provided a new dimension by frequently becoming agents of Mama's hounding justice.

For all the German flavor, there is a particularly American characteristic that both Dirks and Knerr grafted onto the Katzies' persona: a glorification of the mechanical. A sort of comic Industrial Revolution visited the Katzenjammer household, as pranks involved machines and devices and inventions. Many gadgets turned upon themselves and their intended functions. Hans and Fritz became little mad scientists as they seized upon, for instance, appliances that were supposed to help in the modern household and transformed them into instruments of mayhem. Knerr, incidentally, was an avid balloonist and delighted in setting some of his weekly riots in airships and hot-air devices.

Finally there is the aspect of Hans and Fritz as incorruptible happy savages in an adult world. Obviously Dirks made the Rousseauvian ideal humorous by using it as a comic strip—but we can be reasonably certain that he was not philosophically oriented. Nevertheless, his lifelong output stands as a statement and invites speculation. With hardly an exception the Kids' antagonists were adults, and except for some early gags centered in the schoolroom, Dirks seldom even pictured other children. Is it possible that the generational warfare he dwelt upon appealed to both the children in his audience and the children present in the psyches of his adult readers? Self-evidently Hans and Fritz were *not* incorruptible. They were wild and free and immune to nobility, innoculated with the comics' version of original sin. Following Mark Twain, most of the boys in fiction were rather insipid, from the Little Lord Fauntleroy in the pages of *St. Nicholas* magazine to the Little Lord Fauntleroy played by Freddie Bartholomew in the movie. Scruffy hell-raisers—in other words, real boys—lived mostly in the funny pages, and the Katzenjammer Kids were their foremost exponents.

The idea of Hans and Fritz as pure types in a representative world was further enhanced by the physical setting in which both Dirks and Knerr placed the cast. After several world cruises launched on paper by each cartoonist, the Katzenjammers eventually settled in generic tropical lands that were variously identified as Panama, the South Sea Islands, and German East Africa. These settings were festooned with anomalies that in the comics surrealistically reinforced rather than undermined the usual goings-on. The tropical background seemed to be a virtual Garden of Eden (again highlighting the Kids' comically intrusive personalities), except that modern conveniences were present wherever needed. Pirates occasionally invaded the serenity, but of course their deviltry was effortlessly outpaced by that of Hans and Fritz. And the local population consisted of dark-hued natives in grass skirts, but they were invariably more sophisticated than any of the Katzenjammer adults and spouted not pidgin English, as readers might have expected, but cultivated Oxford English.

There is reason to believe that Rudolph Dirks himself would have endorsed these speculations, for the Katzenjammer impact grew beyond the confines of his own drawing board. As to any motivations or intellectualized theories, however, he might have said "Piffle!" which was, according to his son John, his favorite debunking expletive. He was just doing a comic strip, and although he was proud of his work and achievements, he fell prey to creative *wanderlust*.

We can marvel at a career that sustained weekly bursts of comedic confrontations from 1897 to Dirks's death in 1968, but it was a career punctuated by sabbaticals; very possibly, Dirks needed time off to preserve his sanity and thus preserve his strip's insanity. During the Spanish-American War he enlisted and left the strip to his brother Gus (a talented cartoonist who committed suicide in 1903). In 1900 Dirks briefly left Hearst. In 1912 the mutiny-cum-vacation freed him from "those damn kids" for almost two years. He frequently traveled to the Southwest and places like Iceland in the company of fellow cartoonists Jimmy Swinnerton, George Herriman, and Dan Smith, and occasionally he left the Katzenjammer Kids in the hands of ghosts, including Gus Mager and Oscar Hitt. Between 1932 and 1937 Dirks quit his strip entirely and left it in the hands of Bernard Dibble (whose name seemed more appropriate as the title, not the creator, of a comic strip). And beginning in the 1940s Dirks's son John assisted on *The Captain and the Kids,* assuming virtually all the duties in 1958. He added some touches—science fiction and continued stories—that pleasingly combined the early flavor with contemporary trends.

In these detours Rudy Dirks was not merely resting from the grind of comic-strip production; he pursued a number of other artistic interests. He was a frequent contributor of cartoons to *Life* magazine at the turn of the century, and drew in radically different styles from the one he used for the *Katzenjammer* page. He was a painter of accomplishment and respect, a confrere of many Ashcan School painters. In 1913 he exhibited in the landmark Armory Show in New York and two years later won a bronze medal at the Panama-Pacific Exposition. He established an artists' colony that survives today in Ogunquit, Maine; among the artists he drew around him were Walt Kuhn and Yasuo Kuniyoshi, and the cartoonists included Cliff Sterrett (*Polly and Her Pals*), Gus Mager, and caricaturist Peggy Bacon.

In 1979 United Feature Syndicate decided to end *The Captain and the Kids.* In a gesture symbolic of the changed nature of the comic industry, the strip was unceremoniously dropped—this feature so vitally important to the art form and once fought over tooth and nail by titans. The fate of the original version was in the hands of the Hearst syndicate, King Features, which bestowed its venerable treasure on a long line of largely uncaring guns for hire who progressively made the *Katzenjammer Kids* a virtual parody of itself. After Knerr's death in the early 1950s the roster included Doc Winner, Joe Musial, Mike Senich, Angelo deCesare, and Hy Eisman; the only artist undeserving of either criticism or embarrassment is deCesare, who thoughtfully attempted to recapture the authentic flavor of the glory days.

Of all the work discussed in this volume, the *Katzenjammer Kids* is probably

The Katzenjammer Kids—*sans* their title but with everything else reasonably intact—moved with Dirks from Hearst to Pulitzer. In addition to all of his technical contributions, Dirks displayed a flawless sense of comic action and composition. "Vot a life" indeed. *(Overleaf)*

Meanwhile, back at the Hearst farm, Harold H. Knerr was drawing the "original" version of the *Katzenjammer Kids*, unchanged except for Hans becoming Fritz and Fritz becoming Hans (except during World War I, when the strip became the *Shenanigan Kids* and the names became Mike and Aleck). Knerr's work, which many critics considered more structured than Dirks's, paralleled *The Captain and the Kids*, the title into which Dirks settled. The two cartoonists reportedly never met. *(Page 55)*

Hans und Fritz—Forty Vinks   By R. Dirks — *Originator of the Katzenjammer Kids*

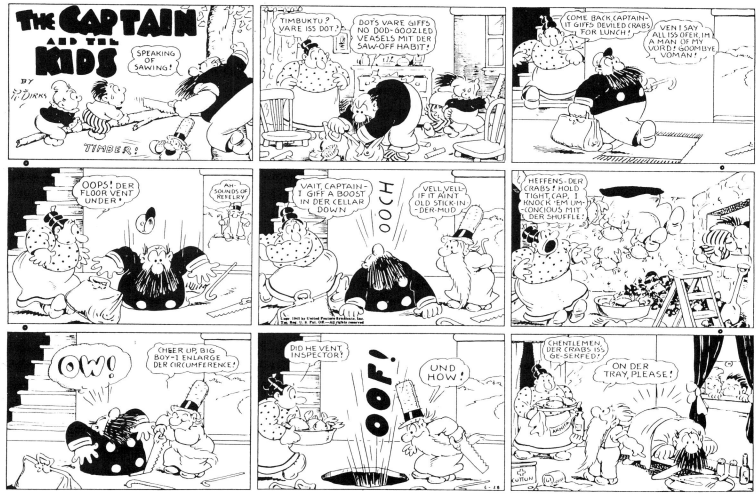

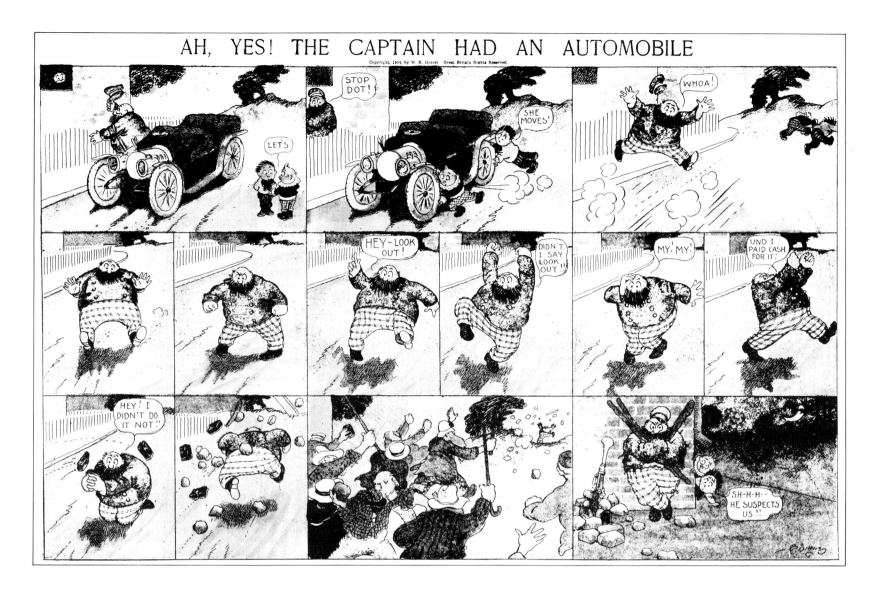

A stunning, and early, *Katzies* page shows that Dirks had already become a master of the strip form and was proving himself an innovator besides. This entire tale is told without divulging any of the carnage to the reader. Everything is seen—and heard through the Captain's voice—in his reactions and those of the offended parties. Dirks set himself a challenge in this page and succeeded masterfully in a comic strip tour de force.

T wo of the eternal themes of the eternal strip—Mama becoming unsuspecting protectress of the Kids, and the Captain and the Inspector becoming naughty truants themselves. These Sunday pages date from 1938 and 1942, a period when Dirks was still going strong after forty years of drawing the Kids. *(Facing page)*

the only strip that is as important as its creator—and Rudy Dirks was a genius of prodigious talent. Although it was the first real comic, it immediately captured the essence of comic-strip fundamentals. Later cartoonists, particularly the adventure-strip creators, embellished the art form in ways undreamed of by such as Dirks, but their contributions were just that—embellishments. Dirks truly laid the cornerstone.

The remarkable reception, longevity, and universal appeal of the *Katzies*, completely without parallel in comics history or that of other popular arts, also mark the strip as perhaps the most representative and archetypal of any yet produced. Without a doubt later generations were to take the comics to wondrous levels of nuance and characterization. Dirks took the young art form's basic formula—peace, scheming, mayhem, exposure, punishment—and made it appeal to all ages and types of readers, expressed through a new vocabulary appropriate to comic strips alone. Hans and Fritz's endless explosions and chases may have seemed trivial, yet they endure. After almost a century, the *Katzenjammer Kids* can be read as a virtual "dod-gasted" blueprint of what a comic strip is.

3

The simple signature F. Opper belonged to the most prolific of all cartoonists. Frederick Burr Opper cartooned professionally for more than half a century, one of the longest careers in the comics. He was called the "Mark Twain of cartooning," not so much for his fame or omnipresence as for his humanity and breadth. He created a staggering number of strips, characters, and series. Although a founding father of the comic strip, Opper was also a prolific magazine cartoonist—producing thousands of gags and social cartoons—

and at the same time ential political car- almost incidentally, lustrator for major and illustrated his stories for children. ing strip creations Maud the Mule, and but his considerable art form of the comic ated with specific

FREDERICK B. OPPER

1857-1937

a powerful and influ- toonist. In addition, Opper was a book il- authors, and he wrote own poems and own His longest endur- are Happy Hooligan, Alphonse and Gaston, contributions to the strip are not associ- features. First, his

very presence was vital to the survival of the fledgling comic-strip form in ways that are difficult to comprehend in retrospect; he appeared at a moment of crisis. Newspaper publishers had not relied upon big-name cartoonists to build their comic sections. Outcault and Dirks are virtual prototypes of the unknown artists who found success in this virgin field of endeavor. Publishers filled their color supplements with work by minor freelance cartoonists from the magazines *Puck, Judge,* and *Life* and even old journeymen artists from Currier and Ives.

The early success of the comic sections, however, was constantly nagged by protests; complaints—from clergymen, educators, librarians—were plentiful against the vulgarity, violence, and anarchic influence in these pages. Such protests very likely contributed to R.F. Outcault's decision to abandon the Yellow Kid to create the more palatable prankster Buster Brown. William Randolph Hearst—as ever displaying a fine instinct beyond mere business acumen— recognized the necessity for respectability in his Sunday funnies.

Opper, as the dean of American cartoonists, provided that respectability in 1899. Not only the most revered, he was perhaps the most dignified of all illustrator/cartoonists, and he agreed to work for the sensationalistic Hearst— and in the raucous color comic section besides. Surely Opper would be adding more stature to the supplements, and the new form, than any slapstick series could add to his laurels. Except that he excelled in a fashion that probably surprised even Hearst. Opper silenced both the friends who undoubtedly advised him against such a career move and a great many critics of the vulgar funny papers. Not only did he deign to grace the garish pages, but he was to shine with a comic brilliance that gave the comics legitimacy. His reputation alone transformed readers' perceptions of slapstick strips of cartoon drawings.

The second major contribution Opper made to the comics' development— apart from his inventive features themselves—was technical. He completed the innovations begun by a host of cartooning predecessors, particularly Outcault and Dirks. Artists like A.B. Frost and F.M. Howarth in the magazines and Dirks in the funnies had standardized the use of panels to advance a story line. James Swinnerton, Charles Saalburg, and Outcault had experimented with the use of continuing, identifiable characters. It remained for Opper to sum up their experiments and to codify the utilization of one last ingredient: the speech balloon.

Opper's adaptability is all the more remarkable given the fact that he had been drawing cartoons without multipanel displays and speech balloons for a full quarter century. Many cartoonists might have been able to cast away one crutch, that of traditional expression, but unable to sacrifice the other, that of habit. But Frederick Opper switched from single-panel cartoons with printed captions to sequential-panel strips with balloon-encased dialogue with the apparent ease of changing his work address. And the mode he adopted was largely without precedent; in fact, he blazed many of the paths he was to tread.

Speech balloons had been used occasionally throughout cartoon history— rather awkwardly in Colonial-era prints and Currier and Ives lithographs, for instance, and even in illuminated religious manuscripts of the Middle Ages. Opper combined the trend toward sequential art in cartooning with the necessity of telling stories in an allotted space in color newspaper supplements. Others— even Dirks, who mostly relied on the pantomime technique—did not seem to realize that the wordless series was wearing thin in the weekly funnies.

Opper's balloons were more than superfluous accompaniment to visual action. With his strips, readers were just as dependent upon words as pictures; the comic strip had finally become a synthesis of artwork and text.

If Frederick Opper ever intellectualized about what he was doing in those days of creative ferment at the turn of the century, it has been lost to the ages. Nevertheless the art form he synthesized was not just the result of fortuitousness. He was a cartoonist always sure of himself, and his gift for innovation was as

Frederick Opper's immortal Happy Hooligan.

certain as his purposefulness. Because of the scope of his talent, he is, with Dirks, the artist most responsible for the conventions, clichés, and techniques of the comics, as well as the very direction in which they were to develop.

Frederick Burr Opper was born in Madison, Ohio, on January 2, 1857. His father was of Austrian immigrant stock, and his mother was descended from Aaron Burr. Opper attended local schools until the age of fourteen, then went to work in a Madison store, where he remembered drawing more than clerking. Afterward, at the *Madison Gazette,* he set type and served as a printer's devil. A year later, convinced that he could draw professionally, Opper moved to New York City. Realistic enough not to expect overnight success, he planned to work as a compositor and draw cartoons as a sideline. He was crushed to learn—after burning all manner of bridges behind him—that compositors in New York City were obliged to serve three-year apprenticeships. He eventually secured a position painting window cards and still cartooned as a freelancer.

He began selling humorous ideas and rough sketches and, ultimately, finished cartoons to magazines like *Wild Oats, Phunny Phellow,* and *Budget of Fun.* Two of New York's leading cartoonists of the day, Frank Beard and Edward Jump, encouraged the young Opper in his artistic progress. *Budget of Fun* was one of the many humor and cartoon magazines launched by Frank Leslie, and in 1878 Opper was offered a position on *Frank Leslie's Illustrated Newspaper,* a rival to *Harper's Weekly,* and was assigned news sketches, topical art, and cartoon subjects.

One of Opper's predecessors at *Leslie's* was Joseph Keppler, who had left in 1876 to found *Puck* magazine. *Puck* was the first successful weekly humor magazine in America, after scores of efforts by many publishers. Keppler eclipsed Thomas Nast as America's premier cartoonist, and in February of 1880 Frederick Opper was invited to join his staff.

Puck at the time was adding to its fame with virtually every issue; clever cartoons, pointed political jabs, quotable verse—America had never seen such a magazine. People might have to pay for Currier and Ives color prints, but *Puck* was offering three brilliantly colored lithographed cartoons in every issue. Growing prosperity permitted the luxury of a cartoon journal; growing literacy allowed a sophistication in *Puck*'s humor that could surpass the local color and dialect humor of the reigning establishment. A heavy dose of politics in its pages ensured *Puck* of being up-to-date and controversial.

Actually, it was *Puck*'s emphasis on politics that probably led to Opper's invitation and his instant prominence in its pages. Keppler concentrated on political cartoons, as did *Puck*'s other major cartoonist, J.A. Wales. Most of the black-and-white cartoon space inside the magazine was reserved for purely humorous subjects—social commentary, the lighter side of daily news, ethnic cartoons, and such. *Puck* was in sore need of an artist to handle those "chores," and Opper filled the bill with a mirthful vengeance. He drew as many as ten cartoons a week—some of them multipanel affairs, either prototypical strips or variegated comments on a theme—and provided gags for other cartoonists. He also occasionally drew lithographed political cartoons as well.

Opper's early drawing style had a naive quality that in his case represented lack of sophistication rather than lack of talent. The scratchy drawings nevertheless shine with spontaneity and are bursting with hilarity. In the early 1880s popular

F rederick Burr Opper was a master at depicting character and personality. An interesting reference is his subtitle for this Sunday page, "A Kinetoscopic Study," indicating an early cross-pollination of the related strip and cinema forms. *(Overleaf)*

H ooligan *en famille.* Several things are at work here besides the comic mayhem. The nation's most distinguished humorous illustrator is gracing a new phenomenon, the comic strip, which is under heavy attack for crudity, and he is doing it with as much broad humor as he can muster. At the same time Opper is establishing a device—the well-meaning Hooligan is trounced in the end—used for thirty years of *Happy Hooligan* as well as for other tramps who followed in his footsteps. Gloomy Gus, by the way, for a while rivaled Hooligan himself in popularity among readers, and his name has gone into the language. *(Page 63)*

ONLY A COMIC VALENTINE
A Kinetoscopic Study of Human Nature.

COMIC SUPPLEMENT
OF
The Examiner.
SAN FRANCISCO.

NOVEMBER 16th 1902.
COPYRIGHT 1902 BY W·R·HEARST   ALL BRITAIN RIGHTS RESERVED.

The Hard Luck of Happy Hooligan.

He Is Not Out of Jail Three Minutes Before He Is Locked Up Again.

(Copyright, 1902, by W. R. Hearst. Great Britain Rights Reserved.)

humor was visual and visceral, but as the decade progressed, both America's taste in humor and *Puck*'s style grew more sophisticated, and so did Opper's work. In a remarkable evolution, his drawing style by 1887 became that of a realistic illustrator, and his style of humor turned from slapstick to social commentary.

Opper was a pioneer of the social cartoon. In a few years he was eclipsed by Charles Dana Gibson, whose themes took a slightly different direction; the Gibson Girl belonged to high society while Opper's subjects were suburbanite and middle class. With a sympathetic eye, Opper examined the minutiae of everyday life—raising children, meeting bills, keeping servants, catching trains, growing gardens—and he explored the fancies of late Victorian America, such as cigarette smoking, parlor games, and bicycle riding. He continued to draw political and ethnic cartoons, but in the social cartoon he displayed a brilliant talent for observation and left America with a portrait of a time and a people that no other form of historical record could provide. The usual name for Opper's focus was the Suburban Resident, and one of his recurring characters was the figure Howson Lott, whose name was a weak pun. Opper's habitats were the outlying, sparsely settled areas around New York, which in those days meant Brooklyn and Harlem.

As *Puck* grew less political and more literary, Opper's fame and influence increased. He had imitators—Grant Hamilton on the back pages of *Judge,* for example—and *Puck* began publishing anthologies of his cartoons. When Keppler died in 1893, Opper became the magazine's chief cartoonist, a young veteran who was certainly first in the affection of its readers.

In 1897 Frederick Opper accepted an invitation to freelance cartoons for the *New York Herald*'s Sunday color sections. The new work meant extra income for the cartoonist, but hardly disrupted his routine. Unlike Pulitzer's raucous *World* or Hearst's garish *Journal,* the *Herald* was as respectable and literary as *Puck* (a fact that ultimately led to the decline of both journals in the face of the sensationalist press), as Opper merely drew *Puck*-style commentaries. But in 1899, barely three or four years after the success of Outcault's *Yellow Kid,* the forty-two-year-old dean of cartoonists descended from the heights of journalism to dive head first into waters that must have seemed both inviting and murky— the comic supplement.

Opper not only returned to slapstick, but evinced aspects of his humor that

Two early Opper drawings show his evolution as a cartoonist. The first, from *Puck*, is a political cartoon from 1880 on the factionalism between Stalwarts and Half-Breeds in the Republican Party. The second drawing is an 1887 illustration from the humorous novel *Samantha in Saratoga* by Marietta Holley. Opper's style had grown more sophisticated and understated in a short period of time.

We rapped, but nobody answered.

The Suburban Resident was a regular butt of Opper's social cartoons in *Puck*—this example is from 1889—and kept his character Howson Lott around through his career, even in Sunday pages for Hearst around 1910. Eventually Opper became a suburban resident himself, first in Bath Beach, Brooklyn, and later in New Rochelle, New York.

SUBURBAN RESIDENT (to FRIEND from the city). — Don't be startled, my boy; it's only our Tramp-Alarm

The Suburban Resident making a pleasant evening call on a neighbor.

One of the Suburban Resident's Strange Habits — The Bundle Habit.

Another of the Suburban Resident's Strange Habits — The Riding-in-the-Baggage-Car-Habit.

One of the pleasures of being a Suburban Resident — He has so many opportunities of contributing his mite for sweet Charity's sake.

Who are these unhappy people looking at this wretched performance. Hush, reader. These are Suburban Residents, and this is the village "Opera House."

his most devoted fans had never seen: sarcasm, in-jokes, vaudeville-type asides, and lowbrow themes, all of which represented neither conceptual slumming nor a patronizing attitude, but rather the liberating effect of the comic strip on American modes of humor. It was comic-strip humor, largely identified with the Hearst press, and Opper contributed importantly to its acceptance.

Happy Hooligan was Opper's first comic-strip success with Hearst. It starred a character type now familiar; Hooligan was the essence of the well-intentioned little guy whose good deeds went awry, went unnoticed, and, in fact, invariably went kaflooey. Disaster, rather than success, was Fate's inevitable

COMIC SUPPLEMENT OF HEARST'S BOSTON SUNDAY AMERICAN JANUARY 15th 1905. COPYRIGHT 1905 BY THE AMERICAN-JOURNAL-EXAMINER ALL BRITAIN RIGHTS RESERVED.

IT WAS AT THE ROYAL CHARITY BAZAAR

Among the Fashionable Throng Were Happy Hooligan, Montmorency and Gloomy Gus

From the days of uninhibited fun in the funnies, this *Happy Hooligan* page for January 15, 1905, was drawn by America's dean of cartoonists, Frederick Burr Opper. Happy and his brothers, Gloomy Gus and the feckless poseur Montmorency, are in England during a protracted round-the-world tour, discovering that whatever the locale the denouement would always be the same. Behind the bologna-fingers and absurd expressions, Opper displayed a sure sense of anatomy, composition, and animation. *(Facing page)*

One of the comics' first major features with a standard running title, *And Her Name was Maud!* by Opper, this is representative of many comics from the first decade built upon a single theme—played endlessly. The only thing more predictable than Maud's kicks were reader's laughs at the ridiculous scenarios and Si Slocum's frustrations with his bad-penny mule.

perversion, and the tramp Hooligan would end each episode in handcuffs or with an elderly lady's umbrella broken over his head or with a bulldog's jaws firmly attached to the seat of his ragged trousers.

Although Happy Hooligan superficially resembled hundreds of tramp characters Opper drew for *Puck,* he represented a departure. In a bow to the comic section's established atmosphere of exaggeration and trivialization, Hooligan was drawn with a large head and a nonsensical tin can as a hat; his appearance may have seemed a parody of what the funny papers did to standard cartoon icons. In amiable defiance of the comics' young tradition, however, Hooligan became the first major character to be the victim, not the instigator, of comic-sadistic turns.

On this single premise, Happy Hooligan amused readers between 1900 and 1932; Frederick Opper was as adept at varying a theme as was Mozart. Hooligan acquired two brothers, Gloomy Gus and the aristocratic *poseur* Montmorency, and his misadventures, rather than dividing, actually tripled. The brothers traveled the world in the early years of the strip—in some of the first continuities in the comics—only to prove that it was humanity in general, not American cops and shopowners and streetcar conductors, that seemed somehow to conspire against the Hooligans. Happy, for a time, was proprietor of the butterfly net in a lunatic asylum, and eventually he courted the fair Suzanne, with as much luck as in his less romantic endeavors.

In this period most comic strips did not have running titles but separate episodic descriptions over each week's page. Nevertheless, a frequently employed title over Opper's second memorable feature during his comic-strip days was almost poetic and somehow encapsulated the screwball nature of the feature: *And Her Name Was Maud!* Maud was a mule, but not just any mule. She was endowed by her creator with certain inalienable rights—stubbornness, orneriness, fierce independence—that seemed to be the very distillation of mulish attributes. Maud was mute (this was generally the age before talking animals in strips),

AND HER NAME WAS MAUD!

but she did have thoughts, shown not in thought balloons but in wondrous, comical facial expressions. Added to her character traits was loyalty; Maud's owner, the hayseed farmer Si Slocum, simply could not lose, sell, or even, in moments of crazed frustration, incapacitate her. Maud resolved the impasse as someone—usually Si himself—became the recipient of her explosive kicks. In

One of Opper's happiest creations was *Alphonse and Gaston*, which became another entry in the American language. Here are the original Alphonse and Gaston routines, replete with absurd exaggeration, action, slapstick, and comic characterization. Opper's portrayals also succeeded in cementing an image of stereotypical Frenchmen in American minds.

succeeding panels her expression would turn from innocence to mischief to wild-eyed setup behind the hapless victim, who was then seen in long shot, sailing across the landscape. Dare to attempt a trade of Maud to an unsuspecting farmer? Hee-haw!

Opper's third success in the funnies was one that possibly lived the longest, at least in its influence in American manners and phrases. In *Alphonse and Gaston*, it was not just the characters but the very practice of *politesse* that was exaggerated, stretched, and lampooned. Alphonse and Gaston (and eventually their friend Leon) became the stereotypical Frenchmen—and it was a stereotype that Opper in this strip helped define. In idiotic extensions of formal courtesy, such dialogue as "After you, my dear Alphonse!" "No, no—I insist; after you, dear Gaston!" might precede the terrible onrush of a freight train from whose tracks the pair were inviting each other to depart. Numbing disasters scarcely shook the Frenchmen from their rule-book etiquette, but occasionally there would be the lament to return to the happy days in—not Paris—but East Paterson, New Jersey, or some such geographical *non sequitur*.

These three strips by Opper were hits with readers of the Hearst chain of newspapers and eventually with all of America through syndication and anthologies. On some Sundays Opper drew three separate strips featuring his new characters, and frequently they passed through each others' strips. He also collaborated on occasion with his fellow cartoonists, and Happy Hooligan was prone to guest-star in the *Katzenjammers, Foxy Grandpa, Little Jimmy,* and *Lulu and Leander.*

It was a time of few restrictions, and Opper's creativity and playfulness constantly outpaced that of his younger colleagues. He created dozens of other features, including *Hans from Hamburg; Our Antedeluvian Ancestors; Willie; On the Farm;* and a resurrected *Howson Lott.* In his latter incarnation, Lott was no longer the beleagurered suburbanite but an exurbanite convert to the "charms" of rural life. Each week his city guests would suffer comic anguish at the vicissitudes of the country as they encountered swarms of mosquitoes, farm animals in the bedroom, or nitwit handymen.

Opper continued, and actually accelerated, his career as a political cartoonist after joining Hearst's comic-strip ranks. Probably his most enduring and effective series was his first: *Willie and His Papa.* Conceived during the 1900 presidential campaign, Willie was President McKinley, and Papa was a bloated malefactor labeled the Trusts. Industrial monopolies, or trusts, were enjoying their most unrestrained period of activity at the time, and William Randolph Hearst was America's chief critic of their existence. Opper's icon of the overstuffed plutocrat became as recognizable and serviceable as Uncle Sam, and so did his conceptualization of the Common People as a bespectacled and victimized wimp. Two generations of cartoonists were to adopt Opper's characters as symbols.

Papa cared for Willie in a coercive, avuncular relationship, and McKinley's real éminence grise, Mark Hanna, was pictured as a nursemaid. When the hero of San Juan Hill, Theodore Roosevelt, was nominated for vice president, Opper pictured him as a ridiculous infant with wooden sword and hobby horse. It is reported that Teddy himself was good-natured about Opper's daily barbs, but that his wife Edith found them hilarious and kept them in a scrapbook that she delighted in showing to guests. Couching his barbs in humor was forever an Opper trait. Hearst's other political cartoonist was Homer Davenport, whose own

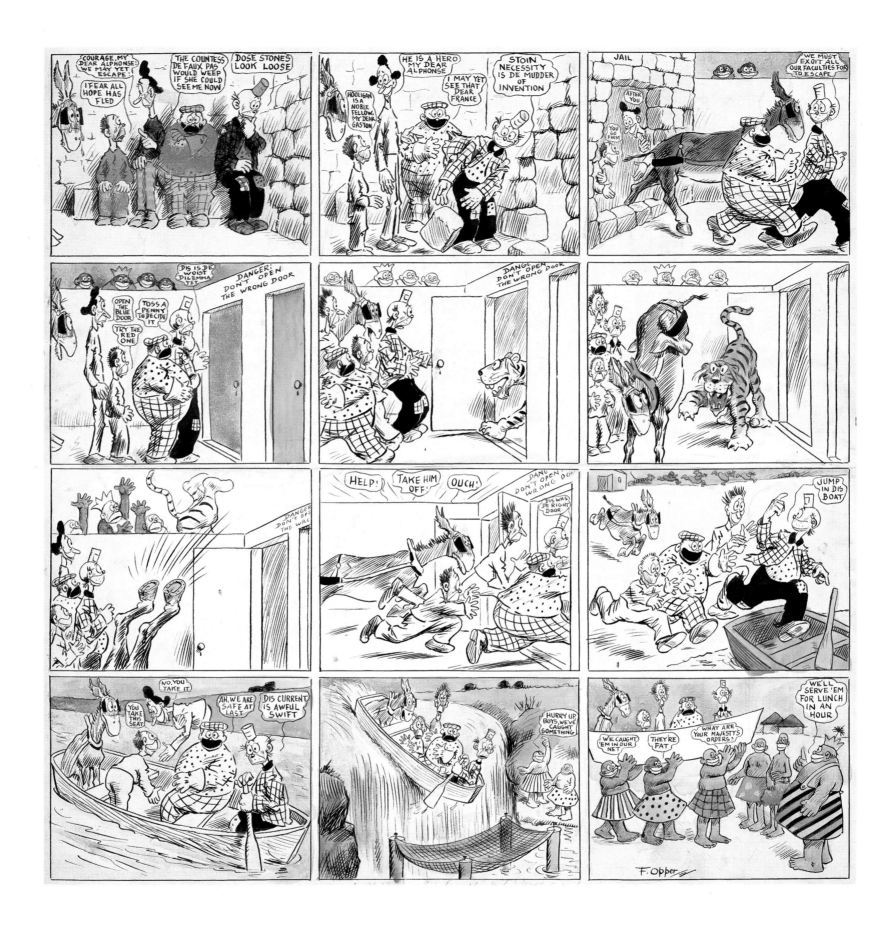

Many of the early strip cartoonists, including Opper, would "jam" on each other's strips. And sometimes Opper would mix his own characters from several strips, as in this 1907 page with Happy Hooligan, Maud the Mule, Alphonse and Gaston, and even their friend Leon. The original art reproduced here is partially colored because elements were tinted as a guide to engravers and, once established, did not have to be colored in succeeding panels. *(Facing page)*

Two exceptional political cartoons by Opper. The first, from a series on the 1900 presidential campaign, was widely noted for its venom and its humor (Theodore Roosevelt's wife found the cartoons hilarious and kept a scrapbook) and was published in a reprint book. The second, drawn twenty years later, also calls on visual humor but employs even simpler symbols and is rather more direct than the earlier cartoon. In addition to his strip work, Opper drew political cartoons for Hearst into the 1930s.

Trusts were loathsome, ravenous monoliths and whose Mark Hanna was an avaricious monster with the skulls of workingmen on his watch fob. It is interesting to speculate upon which cartooning style affected and persuaded more readers.

During his comic-strip days, Opper continued a pursuit he began shortly after joining *Puck,* that of book illustration. In 1884 he illustrated articles by the humorist Bill Nye, and a decade later he illustrated Nye's most popular book, the best-selling *Comic History of the United States.* The signature of F. Opper also graced the works of Marietta Holley ("Josiah Allen's Wife"), Finley Peter Dunne ("Mr. Dooley"), George V. Hobart ("Dinkelspiel"), H.C. Bunner, Mark Twain, and Eugene Field. He also contributed children's verse and illustrations to *St. Nicholas* magazine and wrote several of his own picture books, including a version of *Aesop's Fables.*

Opper's later work in cartooning included notable editorial series—commentary on foreign relations and Prohibition during the 1920s; a series on human nature, this time titled *Wouldn't It Jar You?;* and a feature called *The Freeneasy Film Company.* Happy Hooligan eventually married Suzanne (and they had a son who wore a miniature tin-can hat in the nursery!), but the hapless hero was to solo again for a while; he survived some mock adventures in the 1920s and even some science-fiction escapades. He teamed with the half-pint Mr. Dubb in futile battles with the wealthy Mr. Dough, and their episodes could be read as pure gags or as Bunyan-like portrayals of life's trials.

Opper's wit and versatility remained sharp to the end of his career, but his eyes did not. Even though during his lifetime cartoonists began using ghost artists, and almost everyone in the profession had an assistant, Opper continued to draw every line himself until 1932, when poor eyesight forced him to retire. His drawings had grown simpler, with thicker lines, and did not have the illustrator's finesse that marked his earlier work.

"WHAT AILS YOU, WILLIE?"
"LOOK AT THAT CAMPAIGN BANNER THAT TEDDY HAS PAINTED!"

Perhaps, in his last cartooning years, Frederick Opper produced those crudely rendered masterpieces as much by instinct and memory as by sight. The composition and pacing were still brilliant—almost textbook examples of character and balloon placement and storytelling. Just as Beethoven could compose when deaf, and the blind Bach, in his own twilight, dictated instead of autographed his supreme musical composition of Baroque theory, *The Art of the Fugue,* Frederick Opper, through painful squinting in the months before he lay down his pen, proved that he could be at once the most consciously innovative cartoonist of his time and yet the most instinctive. He died on August 27, 1937, in New Rochelle, New York, finally a Suburban Resident himself.

Opper can be assessed by the formal contributions he made to the development of the comic strip, and he can be appreciated through the many titles and series he drew. Further, he can be revered for the coruscating quality of his wit; his work from any period of his long career seems less stale to modern tastes than almost any work by his contemporaries. What is more difficult to measure is Frederick Opper's impact.

He obviously—the testimonials are numerous—inspired young artists to become cartoonists, and he later influenced the work of many of them. Not only did he adapt to several trends in American humor, but he largely helped define them. His slapstick and his tramp hero may very possibly have been responsible for the figures who evolved into W.C. Fields's Tramp Juggler (the comedian's first persona) and Charlie Chaplin's Tramp; at the least Happy Hooligan created a climate receptive to such characters. In the comic strips, Rube Goldberg's Boob McNutt and Al Capp's Li'l Abner were direct descendants of Hooligan, and in literature, Hooligan prefigured the Little Man of the twentieth century as chronicled by Robert Benchley, James Thurber, and Ring Lardner. In his style of humor, Opper inaugurated the schools of irony, commentary, human-nature themes, and ubiquitous catch-lines whose students were to include TAD Dorgan, Milt Gross, and H.T. Webster. And even if Opper had never drawn a single comic strip, his political cartooning would have assured him a place in the hall of fame.

Not to be overlooked in discussions of Opper's many attributes is his drawing style. He was a cartoonist when he worked at the drawing board, but first he was an artist. He knew anatomy, and even as bodies flew, fell, flopped, and flattened, they were real. Opper drew hands just right and could depict the human form—even clad in patches and tin-can hat—correctly. The strip artist, like no other artist, must be conscious of the placement of every figure, prop,

In his later years, when eyesight was failing (this daily *Hooligan* strip is from the mid-1920s), Frederick Opper displayed almost instinctive powers of comic-strip creation. This simple sequence betrays masterful technique: the woman subtly grows more optimistic and Hooligan progressively grows shocked. The reaction of each in the last panel is classic—and delicious—comic-strip cliché.

Even Opper's minor strips are masterpieces. *King Jake* ran briefly in 1908, careening brilliantly between nonsense and surrealism. Opper was not afraid to crowd his comic strips with figures and not capable of drawing any incorrectly, even in wildest contortions. He was a cartoonist who invariably had fun going about his work.

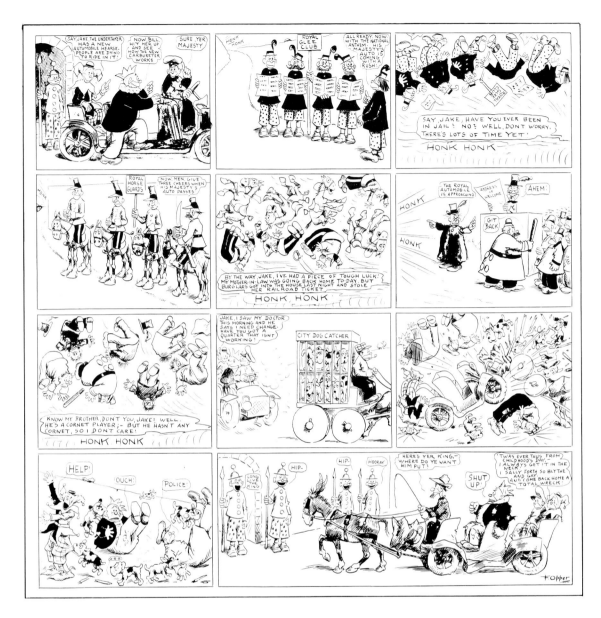

and even text in each panel, because the reader's eye must be subliminally led through the frames and strip. Opper used his space and wasted none. His compositions were flawless.

Rube Goldberg once stated that Frederick Opper had a glass eye, "and you could tell which one it was because it was the kindly one." Although a memorable anecdote, it is the only first-person comment by anyone who knew Opper that he was anything but generous with his affections, talent, and advice (or even that he had a glass eye). It is possible, since Goldberg's *Boob McNutt* was practically a clone of *Happy Hooligan*—down to Boob's personality, predicaments, tiny hat, and dippy pursuit of a True Love—that Goldberg might have been conscious of a withering glance or was simply self-conscious. Certainly Opper himself never had cause to borrow from anyone. He built on the past, he melded opportunities at hand, and he possessed an embarrassment of riches in both talent and achievement.

Frederick Barr Opper
Feb 3 1932

It was a remarkable piece of luck that the comic strip was blessed from its inception with an array of talent that secured its foundations. Although there were pedestrian journeymen filling the early color supplements, there was also a breed of cartoonists whose instincts fully complemented their abilities and whose creativity did not stop at playfulness but advanced to a mature, pioneering attitude. We can but wonder where the comic strip would have strayed if cartoonists like Opper and Dirks and other seminal proponents had

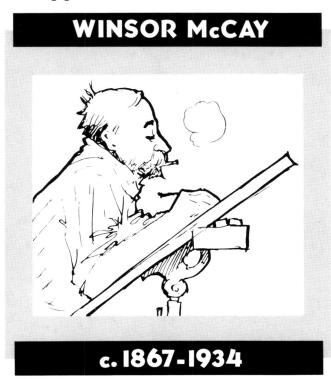

WINSOR McCAY

c. 1867-1934

not been present from the early days to define, chart, explore—and inspire others. No discussion of the comic strip is complete without lingering on Winsor McCay and his astonishing contributions. Indeed, the history of American graphic art is poorer for the neglect he has traditionally received. It can be said of McCay as of few others (his contemporary Lyonel Feininger being one exception) that he stretched and thereby virtually defined the outer perimeters of formal comic-strip expression, and that, in the years since, other cartoonists have occasionally met but none has surpassed the imaginative and structural excellence of his work.

McCay's accomplishments are all the more remarkable when considered in their chronological context: most were achieved a scant decade after the birth of the art form. The individual masterpieces of this fecund genius are numerous, and many professional cartoonists would be proud to claim the crumbs off his table. He created detailed Sunday pages, intricate editorial cartoons, and frame-by-frame animated cartoons (all simultaneously!).

Aside from being remembered for his actual work, however, Winsor McCay must be honored also for his furtherance of an early school of comic art, one that is strangely absent today: fantasy. Fantasy was a creative concern of many cartoonists in the comics' first days. Perhaps the themes mirrored the uninhibited nature of the entire art form at the time, whereas today's cramped formats seem to inspire stultification. McCay was but one—albeit the most prominent—of a school of fantasy artists in the comics. And within that category he developed his own specialty, a theme he explored his entire career: the world of dreams.

Just at the time when practitioners of the modern alchemy known as psychology were investigating dreams and manufacturing theories about them (Freud's *Interpretation of Dreams* was published in 1900), Winsor McCay was doing his own investigating, but he manufactured graphic images, not abstract theories. His fascination, if not obsession, with dreams was as compelling as that of Freud, Jung, or Adler (and there is no evidence that McCay read or subscribed to any of their theories), but his concentration was manifested through early magazine illustrations, daily comic strips, large Sunday pages, and detailed editorial cartoons that were really metaphorical and metaphysical essays in line.

Zenas Winsor McCay was born, according to his gravestone, in 1869, but in autobiographical articles he stated his birth year as 1871. Reliable evidence, however, points to 1867 as the actual year of his birth (it seems possible that he altered the facts to appear closer in age to his wife, whom he married when she was fourteen and he twenty-four). Likewise there is mystery concerning the place of his birth, which seems to have been in his mother's native Canada, but McCay claimed it was Spring Lake, Michigan, where he was raised—fires in his boyhood town obliterated definitive documentation.

McCay's very personality was paradoxical. He was in many ways reticent, reserved, and conservative; yet he enjoyed a career as a vaudeville performer. A man who clearly wore his psyche on his sleeve was chary of exposing it in less public, more personal, ways. His work glows with an almost psychedelic radiance, yet by all accounts the diminutive McCay was a modest, middle-class bourgeois fellow who reported to his drawing table every morning, rolled up his sleeves, composed his wondrous work in silent, businesslike fashion, rolled down his sleeves, and returned to his home in the suburbs. Not a Freudian, and certainly not a Conceptualist, Nominalist, or Surrealist, Winsor McCay was an imaginative cartoonist who was fortunate to work in a form of expression, the comic strip, that encouraged his speculations and unorthodox figuration. His fantastic visions were reveries, not hallucinations.

One thing was certain about McCay: he loved to draw, and he drew compulsively from his earliest days. His parents indulged their son's proclivities but sent young Winsor to business school in Ypsilanti, Michigan. The early chapters of nearly every great cartoonist's biography contain tales of literally irrepressible urges to draw, of menial jobs in newspaper art departments and the like, and McCay's story is no different. He played hookey from business school, traveling to Detroit, where he was intrigued by the Wonderland sideshow. He liked sketching the bizarre attractions and even profited from the sale of drawings for twenty-five cents each.

Eventually McCay was noticed by a venerable art teacher at the Michigan

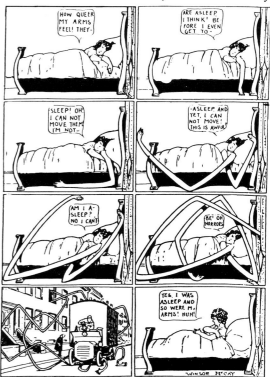

DAY DREAMS   By Winsor McCay

Daydreams—and nightmares—were the province of Winsor McCay.

State Normal School, John Goodison. According to McCay, the professor "was a great drawing teacher, but retired at an advanced age, feeling that all his teaching had gone for naught. Then a new idea of teaching perspective came to him and with the enthusiasm of renewed youth he gathered about him six youngsters who seemed to have talent for drawing, the idea being to 'try it on the dogs.' I was one of the 'dogs.' " Goodison, it seems, was fanatical not only about the principles of perspective, but also about their fundamental importance to all other forms of composition. McCay absorbed and cherished Goodison's theories and also learned much about color, as his professor had once been a stained-glass craftsman.

McCay's first formal employment in his chosen field was in 1889 as an artist with the National Printing and Engraving Company of Chicago. He likely worked as a sign painter at the same time, and he shared lodgings with Jules Guerin, later a noted illustrator specializing in architectural and travel subjects. In 1891 it was again a sideshow that attracted McCay and caused him to move to Cincinnati. He accepted employment from the Vine Street Dime Museum, where he executed backdrops, posters, portraits, and whatever else was necessary to add to the establishment's garish, otherworldly atmosphere.

In 1898 McCay joined the staff of the Cincinnati *Commercial Tribune* and began freelancing cartoons to the respected national cartoon weekly *Life*. For the *Tribune* he did illustrations and strips (some of which prefigured his later work featuring dreams of "rarebit fiends"), and for *Life* he established a specialty of anti-imperialist, futuristic, and fantasy cartoons. For *Life,* too, McCay experimented with multipaneled strips.

Also foreshadowed at this time were McCay's later fascination with grand architectural scale and his interest in theatrics. Although he was clearly opposed to the Spanish-American War during its brief duration, McCay immersed himself in celebrations after America's victory. He designed papier-mâché fleets for street parades in Cincinnati and elaborate temporary arches through which the festivities passed, and he dressed up as Spanish Admiral Cervera on a river-borne float.

In 1900 McCay moved to the *Cincinnati Enquirer,* where he created his first Sunday color comic feature, *Tales of the Jungle Imps* ("by Felix Fiddle"), which was a fantasy page of poems and cartoons that centered on wild animals and their origins. Sales of freelance cartoons to *Life* (according to the magazine three decades later) financed McCay's move to New York in 1903. He joined the *Telegram* and the *Herald,* owned by James Gordon Bennett, newspapers whose appeal was high-toned and respectable. They engaged in little of the sensationalism of the Hearst and Pulitzer papers, but Bennett did not eschew competitiveness, and his weapon was the most advanced color presswork among all American newspapers. McCay was promised a splendid showcase for his graphic talents in the *Herald*.

His work for Bennett generally was in two categories, black and white and color; the *Telegram* had no Sunday supplement. McCay was prolific enough for two cartoonists, and perhaps Bennett wished to foster the illusion that he had hired two artists when he asked McCay to sign his *Telegram* work "Silas," a name McCay later claimed he appropriated from a local trash hauler in the Herald Square neighborhood. Overnight the cartoonist was producing copious and impressive work: story illustrations and editorial art; decorations for titles and portraits; futuristic drawings for a science-fiction series, *The Spectrophone,* by John Kendrick Bangs; short-lived comic creations like *Mr. Goodenough, A Pilgrim's Progress by Mr. Bunion,* and *Poor Jake;* and two impressive Sunday comic strips.

One color strip was *Little Sammy Sneeze,* a weekly half page featuring a little boy whose curse was massive sneeze attacks that upset the order of each episode's setting. Sammy had no personality beyond his disruptive function, a singular pattern of character development that typified most of McCay's fictional characters in the years to follow. His other color strip in the *Herald*'s pages was *Hungry Henrietta;* the heroine, a little girl, was also vapid and silent, with the strip's action provided by adults swirling in consternation over her eating habits. *Henrietta* was not so much a commentary on childhood or children's perspectives (McCay's kid strips seldom were) but rather was a comic examination of an obsession and its farcical possibilities.

The penultimate jewel in the crown of McCay's work for Bennett was *Dream of the Rarebit Fiend.* With this strip—which ran from 1904 to 1911 in several daily formats, until 1913 in a Sunday-page format, and for years thereafter via similar titles and premises—McCay firmly established the motif of unconscious and subconscious thoughts. He addressed both daydreams and nightmares and in them discovered a mother lode of comic possibilities.

Ironically, *Dream of the Rarebit Fiend* featured no one regular character as a rarebit fiend, and sometimes a gastronomic treat other than melted cheese was

Dream of the Rarebit Fiend was McCay's best-known dream feature after *Little Nemo.* It began as a black-and-white daily strip in the *New York Telegram* around 1903 and continued to appear as a color Sunday page in the *Herald* even after McCay switched to Hearst with *Little Nemo.* The strip was always signed with the nom de plume Silas. *(Facing page)*

A typical McCay central character whose character was devoid of personality, Sammy Sneeze left mayhem in his wake every week—never speaking but always sneezing. It was McCay's principal color strip until *Little Nemo in Slumberland,* when it became a one-color comic on the interior of the *New York Herald*'s Sunday funnies. Behind the comic obsession and the graphic mayhem lies a superb sense of composition, design, detail, and perspective . . . as in all of McCay's work.

what induced the bizarre dream. In the absence of continuing characters there was, however, an invariable theme: the strip (which could run anywhere from six to thirty-two panels) would open at the beginning of the vision, and, panel by panel, the story line would grow stranger. In the last panel the dreamer would awake, vowing to himself or his spouse to quit ingesting the demon rarebit.

In a structural sense, McCay established interesting and plastic conventions. Readers did not know whether the opening panels showed "reality" or a dream; there were no delineated symbols. The ambiguity was both purposeful and protean in effect. In the last panel the strip's internal reality would assert itself, and the reader would view the dreamer from middle distance. With no change in drawing style, lettering, or panel borders and no explanatory caption, the point of view would shift from inside the dreamer's thoughts to outside his body. In those tradition-free days of comic-strip expression, McCay made assumptions about his reader's perceptions, and readers, evidently, made assumptions easily about the comic strip's inherent mastery of time, space, and factors of continuity.

As striking as *Dream of the Rarebit Fiend* was, the strip turned out to be a mere sounding board for (and eventually corollary feature to) McCay's magnum opus, *Little Nemo in Slumberland*. Making its debut on the *Herald* color section's back page of Sunday, October 15, 1905, *Nemo* utilized brilliant hues and tones (*Rarebit Fiend* usually was in black and white), and experimented with unorthodox composition and panel arrangements (*Rarebit Fiend* unfolded in a standard gridwork of image frames).

Little Nemo's major attraction, however, was its audacious theme. Nemo was the son, approximately six years old, of a rather prosperous and certainly pedestrian urban couple. Nemo himself, in a fashion now typical of McCay's heroes, was remarkably nondescript; he was bereft of the personality characteristics that already were virtually prescribed for any comic-strip lead, and he was perpetually the victim, not the master, of the events in his dreams. This was not the result of neglect or faulty development by McCay; it was central to his larger thematic goal to structure major characters in this way. Even Nemo's name reveals the essence of his personality and role in Slumberland, for in Latin the boy's name means "no one." Each week Nemo was the player in a dream—as in *Rarebit Fiend,* presented mid-action to the reader—and just at the moment of climax, whether delightful or frightening, he would awake. Sometimes he fell from bed, often his parents would stir him, and usually his physical position mirrored that in the last moment of his dream.

The boundaries of Nemo's Slumberland were limitless, as were those, seemingly, of McCay's imagination. In the weekly full-page dream sequences, Nemo grew large and grew small; he was transported through the air to behold marvelous vistas; he cavorted with all manner of bizarre creatures—animal, human, and admixtures of both. Slumberland was a land, and its King was named Morpheus. Nemo sometimes sought the King and was sometimes protected in his adventures by the King. Likewise the beautiful Princess was variously an object of desire and quest to Nemo, and sometimes she was a surprisingly banal companion. Among other acquaintances were Flip, a cigar-smoking leprechaun type who appeared as a menacing figure but eventually became a disruptive associate; Impy, a silent, benign cannibal inherited from *Tales of the Jungle Imps;* and Dr. Pill, an intrusive quack.

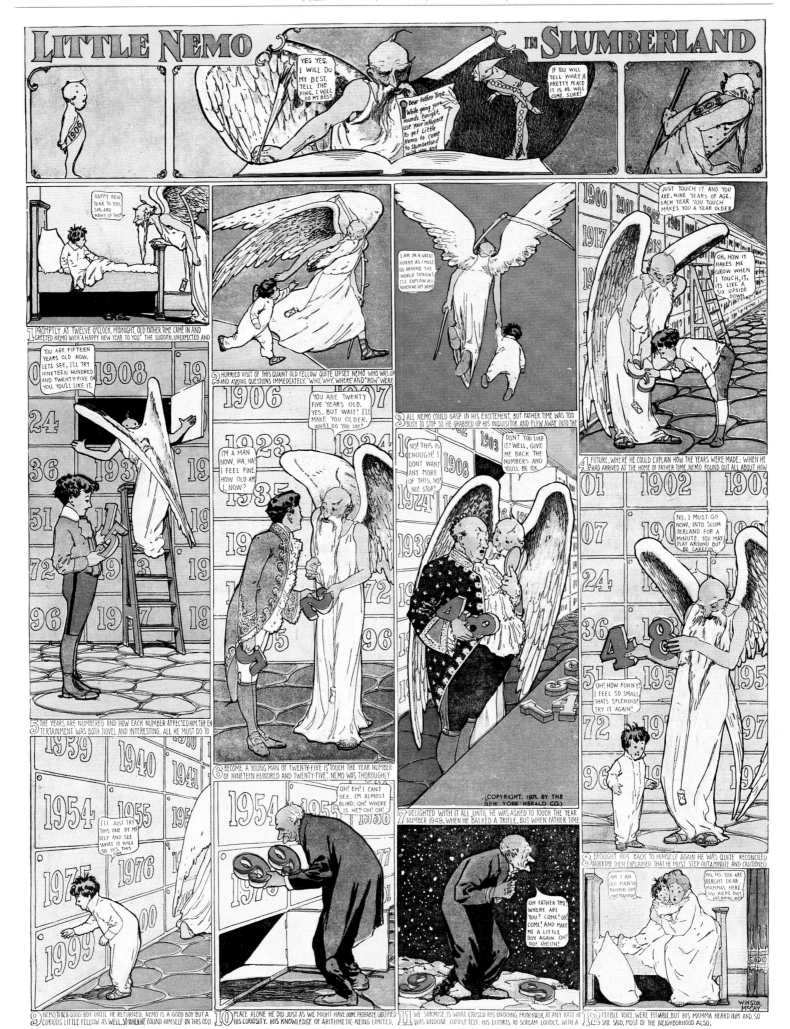

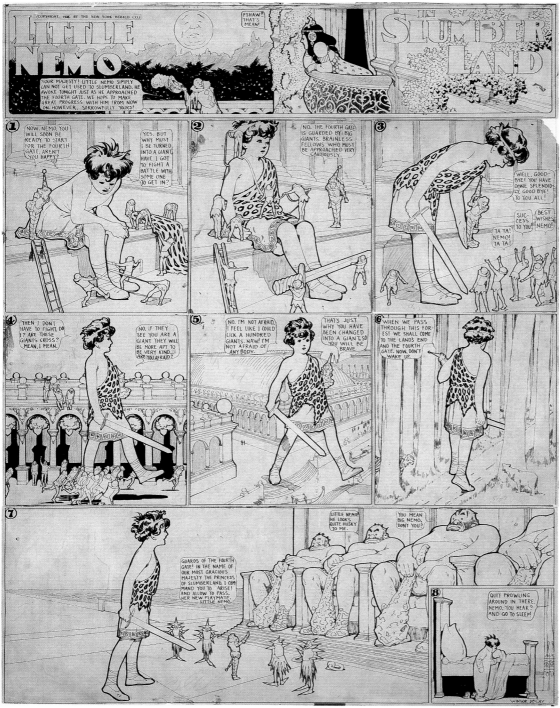

McCay employed all the best techniques of art nouveau, including heavy outlines around flatly detailed figures and infrequent use of solid blacks. This style may also have been influenced by McCay's childhood art instructor, who worked in stained glass. McCay let color do a lot of his work in finished pages, as can be seen by comparing the original art, reproduced at left, with the printed page at right.

The external beauty of Slumberland—as McCay invested his art with breathtaking panoramas and ornate decorations—was a cruel lie, for it promised wonder but usually revealed trouble that bordered on terror. Nemo's goals were forever elusive. His friends were, without exception, insipid or selfish. And when, at rare moments, genuine joy was within Nemo's fragile grasp, McCay would have the boy awake, full of regret.

Historians have routinely overlooked the underlying vein of disappointment and cruelty that established *Little Nemo*'s premise and fueled its adventures during its early years. Understandably, the superficial brilliance of Slumberland's settings could easily lead to mistaken impressions; certainly Nemo himself always trusted the image to be reality. But ultimately McCay's world was as sterile—full of grandeur but sterile—as the world depicted by his contemporary, illustrator Maxfield Parrish.

Winsor McCay's *Little Nemo in Slumberland*, for October 14, 1906. The dramatic effects of this sequence largely are due to the dynamic panel arrangement, the progressively larger image frames, the gradually brightening colors, and a transition from tension, danger, and violence to serenity—and then Nemo's rude awakening, as always. *(Overleaf)*

Possibly the most celebrated Sunday page of all time is Nemo's walking bed episode, from the July 26, 1908, *New York Herald* and syndicated newspapers in America and Europe. Once again the panels grow as the adventure heightens. McCay enlivened the sense of animation by extending a common background through panels 13 and 14. *(Page 85)*

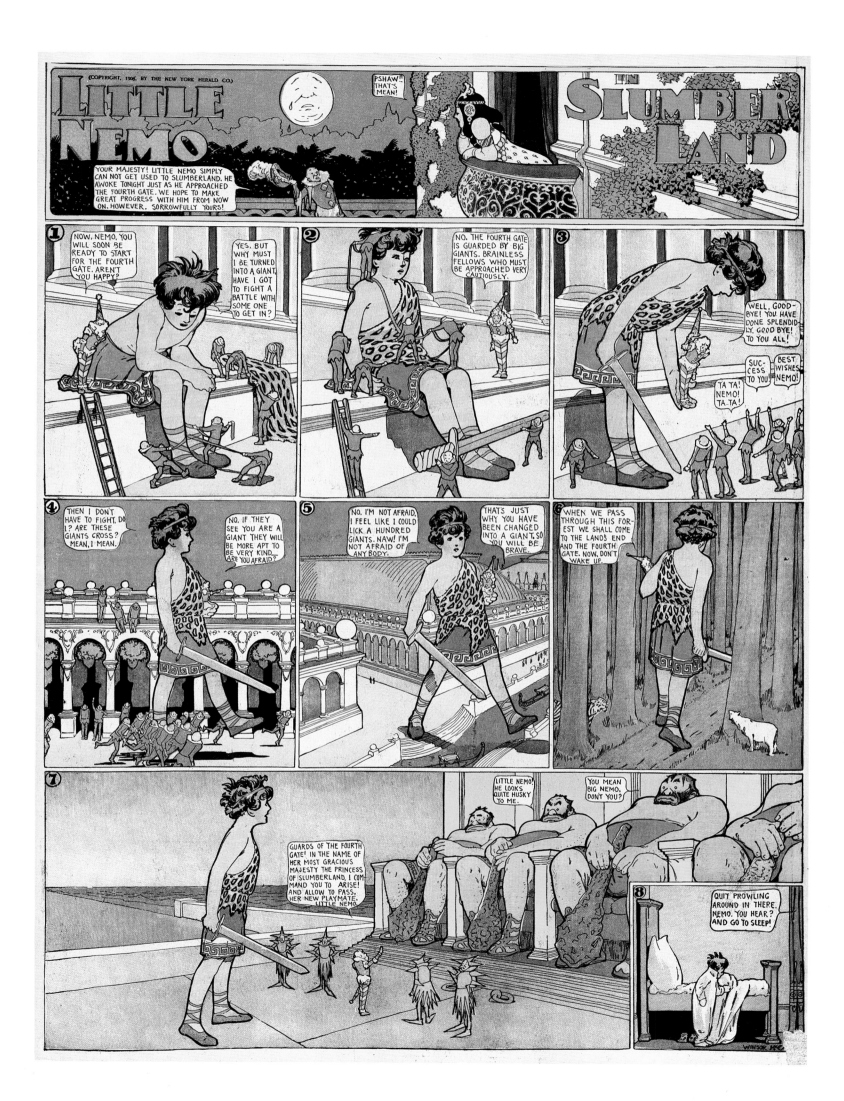

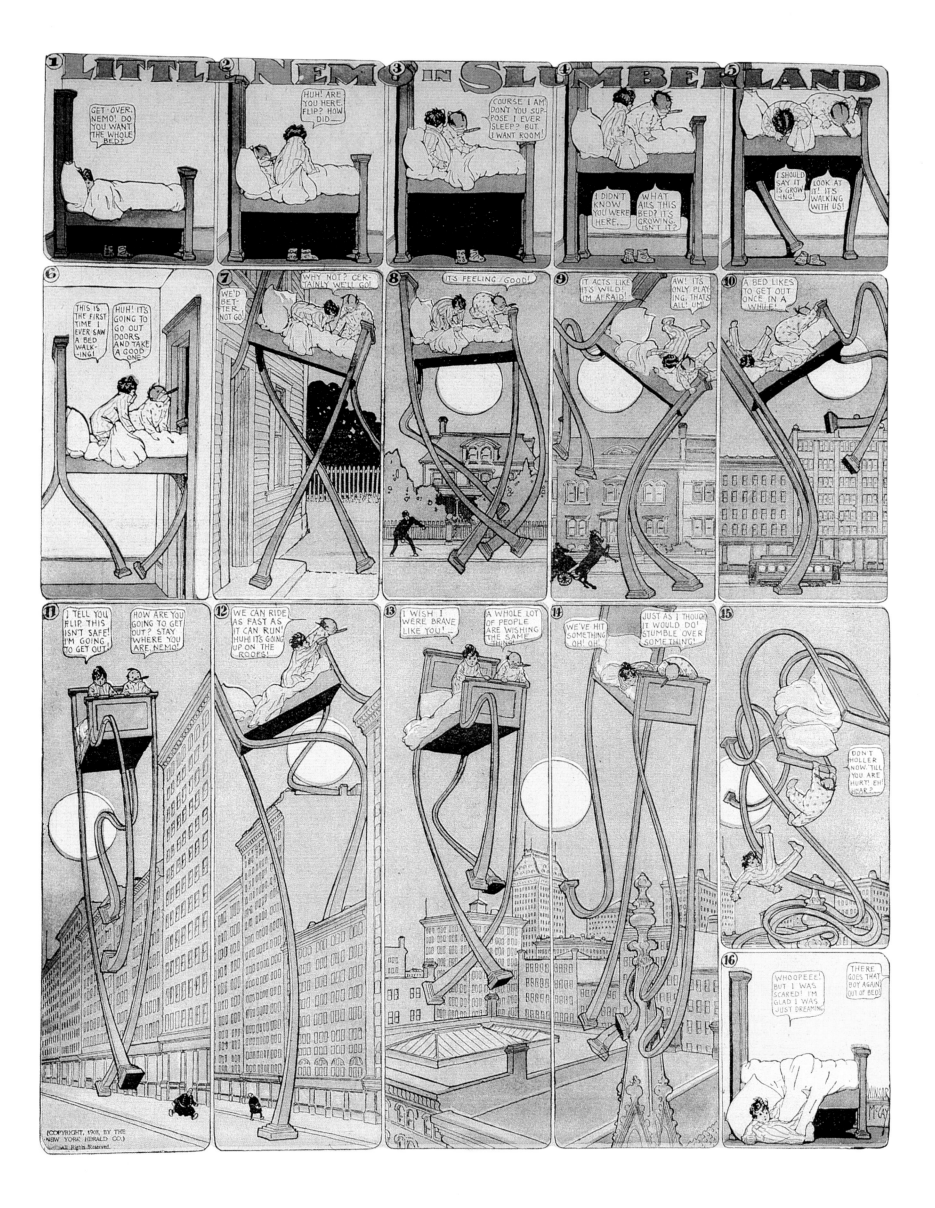

Several *Little Nemo* pages perfectly typified McCay's interplay of hope and disappointment, beauty and anguish. In a Valentine's Day page Nemo finally meets a group of pretty girls, and instead of fleeing or vanishing, they appear willing to be his sweethearts. When Nemo happily escorts one, to his intense sorrow she is transformed into a life-sized two-dimensional Valentine card. In another page, a New Year's Day commemoration, Nemo encounters Father Time and is taken to a Hall of Time, where the boy can open doors labeled with each year and remove numbers that correspond to his age at that future date. In each succeeding panel Nemo grows before our eyes to the age he would be in the years he samples—altogether a clever thematic device, once again joining fanciful speculation to the plastic properties of graphic narration. But in a cruel denouement, when Nemo knocks on the door that would make him ninety-nine, the transformation becomes permanent as the setting disappears, and McCay draws the aged and infirm Old Nemo helpless and desperate in a bitter snowstorm.

Eventually McCay caused Nemo to become a bit more sophisticated but hardly more in command of his environment. The year 1908 was the high point of *Little Nemo*'s graphic and conceptual virtuosity. Cruel fate finally yields to pure graphic abandon when Nemo, Flip, and Impy, dressed as policemen, find themselves in a prolonged adventure lost in Befuddle Hall, an endless mansion where the laws of gravity are routinely broken (the trio walk on ceilings through one episode and along walls in the next), where mirror images proliferate wildly, and where staircases stretch into infinity. It seemed that McCay was able to summon all of his early affections from sideshow and dime museum days and adorn them in the elegant trappings of Slumberland.

Also occurring in 1908 was one of the most impressive continuities in the history of the comics. In an abrupt redirection of *Little Nemo*'s tone and substance, Nemo himself lost his helpless innocence and assumed a character, if not a personality. He became a Christ figure and visited Shantytown. For once the pages of *Little Nemo* did not shine with marble palaces and lush gardens, but rather depicted squalid slums and decaying streets. Nemo, dressed in elegant raiment, visited tenements and healed the sick; he caused the lame to walk; and he redeemed the earth, transforming blighted landscapes into mansions in Paradise. On Easter Sunday he brought a dying girl to life. In all, McCay also accomplished the miracle of elevating a creation that clearly was a masterpiece to new heights of significance, excellence, and fantasy. Strangely, after 1908, Nemo the hero returned to his standard vacuous persona, and the strip itself abandoned the newer preoccupations.

Little Nemo, especially its first five years, can be compared interestingly with a contemporary strip, *The Kin-Der-Kids* by Lyonel Feininger. By 1906 the German-American cartoonist had been drawing political and social satire for nearly two decades and was induced by the *Chicago Tribune* to create a comic strip. For less than a year—after which time he devoted himself to pursuits that made him a pioneer in the Cubist and Expressionist movements—Feininger drew a fantasy strip about a band of youngsters and their trip around the globe one step ahead of malevolent relatives. Feininger's artwork clearly betrays the evolution toward Cubism and abstraction, and his images are wonderful concoctions of angularity and distension. Whereas Feininger's fantasy epic took place in the real world but was drawn in severely idiosyncratic fashion, McCay's world, by

In 1908 McCay had Nemo, Flip, and Impy visit Befuddle Hall, where reality played tricks on the characters—and readers—as the laws of nature, gravity, and perspective were broken week after week. Perhaps that is why McCay clad his heroes in silly policemen's outfits during this sequence: they were powerless to enforce any laws in Befuddle Hall.

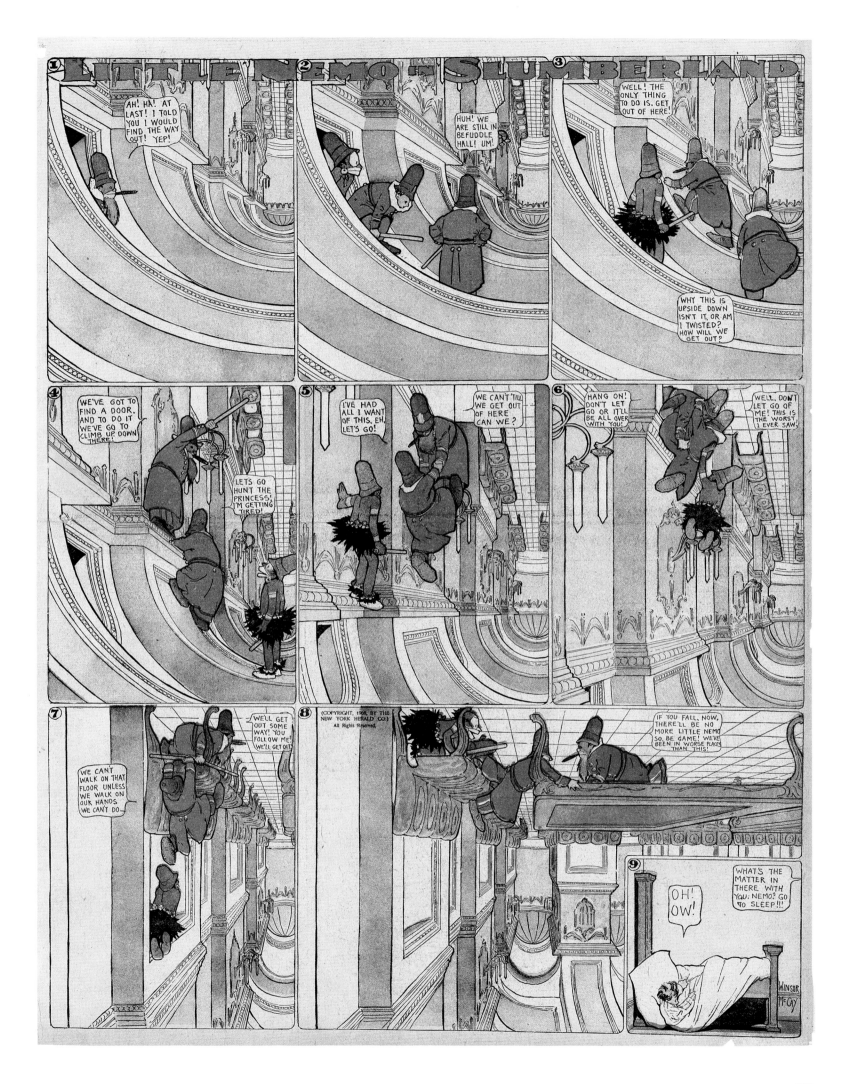

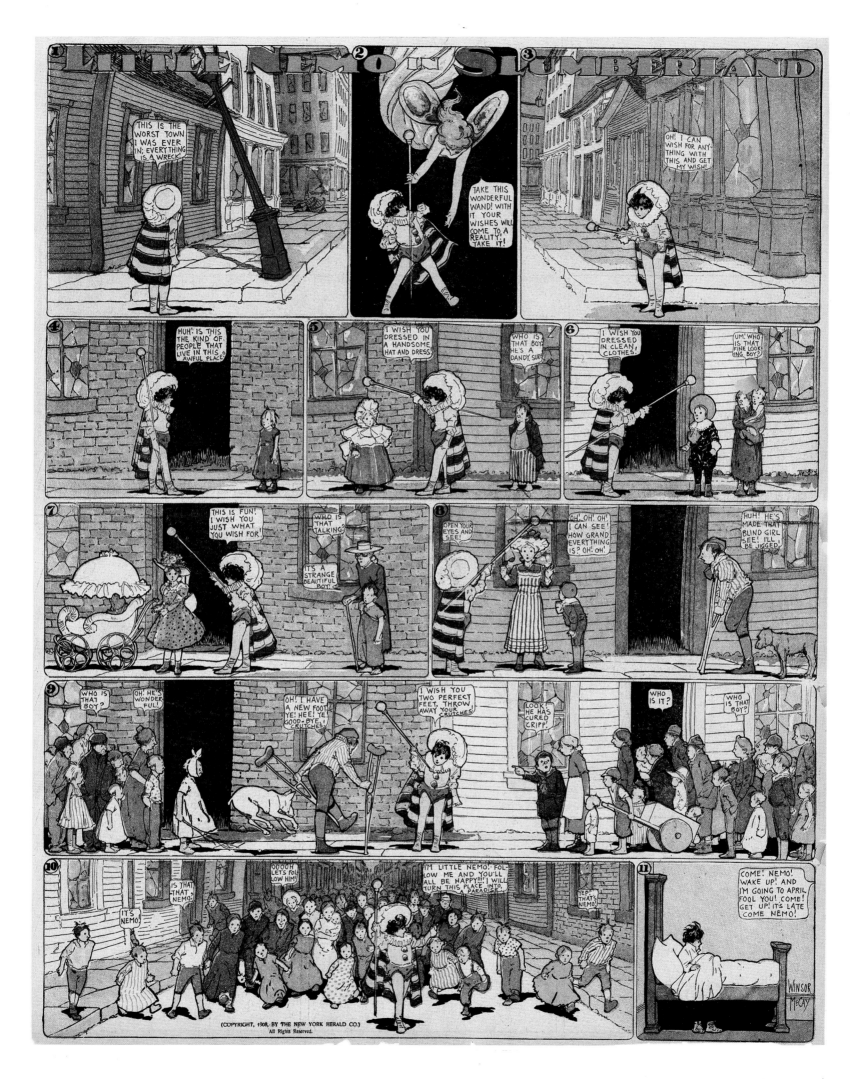

Another classic *Little Nemo* episode also appeared in 1908: Nemo in Shantytown. It was out of character for the title figure and the strip itself, as McCay invested the usually passive Nemo with active powers. Also there was a heavy dose of Social Realism during this sequence; McCay reflected current trends in literature, journalism, and politics (this was the Muckraking Era), as well as the graphic arts.

definition a dreamland, was realized in exacting authenticity; perspectives, anatomy, architecture were all academically correct. The juxtaposition of dragons and city skyscrapers—two of McCay's most utilized props—only enhanced the otherworldly aspect of the dreams that lulled and plagued Little Nemo.

The Kin-Der-Kids was not the only competition to *Little Nemo* in the category of fantasy comics. George McManus, years before *Bringing Up Father,* created *Nibsy the Newsboy in Funny Fairyland;* Harry Grant Dart drew the impressive *Explorigator,* about a band of children and their interplanetary balloon ship; Frank King, before *Gasoline Alley,* drew *Bobby Make-Believe.* Ed Carey chronicled a bizarre role reversal in *Dad in Kidland,* and William J. Steinigans created *The Bad Dream That Made Bill a Better Boy.* Gustave Verbeek drew two memorable features, *The Incredible Upside-Downs of Little Lady Lovekins and Old Man Mufaroo* (where pages were designed to be read forward and back, upside down and right side up) and *The Terrors of the Tiny Tads.*

There were other fantasy strips, but *Little Nemo* was the most accomplished and the most successful. There was a reprint book of *Little Nemo* adventures and a lavish musical on Broadway, with music written by Victor Herbert. There also were postcards, playing cards, a game, and articles of children's apparel inspired by Nemo and licensed by McCay or the *Herald.*

The cartoonist's relations with his showcase newspaper had become strained by 1911, however, and contributing factors undoubtedly included financial matters, McCay's growing interest in the new field of animation, and overtures by the ever-present William Randolph Hearst. In addition, the *Herald* conducted a search for new comic strips in 1911 and awarded the $2,000 prize to John Gruelle, workhorse of the World Color Printing Company studio, where he was drawing several comic strips he inherited from George Herriman. Gruelle, who later created the immortal *Raggedy Ann* series, developed a fantasy strip for the *Herald* called *Mr. Twee Deedle,* about a beneficent fairy who transported two children to realms of fancy or pastoral scenes. The stunningly conceived and rendered strip, hailed by the public for its moral tone, was a graphic masterpiece. In the course of its success, it pushed *Little Nemo* to the monochromatic interior pages of the *Herald's* funnies. By 1911 McCay's strip had lost much of its élan, and whether the cartoonist groused over *Twee Deedle's* success, or the paper's editors rudely neglected an established star in favor of a new celebrity, is unknown.

Whatever the motivation, it is clear that by 1911—after five amazing years of *Little Nemo*—McCay was doing spectacular work routinely but was actually growing routine. The cartoonist's discovery of animation, reportedly sparked by an old-fashioned flip book brought home by his son Robert, increasingly absorbed his time and, more significantly, his creative enthusiasm. Drawing every detail of thousands of images himself, McCay produced his first animated cartoon around 1911: a hand-colored film of *Little Nemo.* The animation was preceded by a filmed segment featuring celebrities like cartoonist George McManus and comedian John Bunny daring McCay to fulfill the gargantuan task of delivering the thousands of sequenced drawings needed to produce an animated cartoon. The production was distributed by Vitagraph and was soon followed by the comical *How a Mosquito Operates.*

In 1914 McCay produced his animated masterpiece, *Gertie the Dinosaur.* Although the cartoon was perforce less experimental in technical terms than

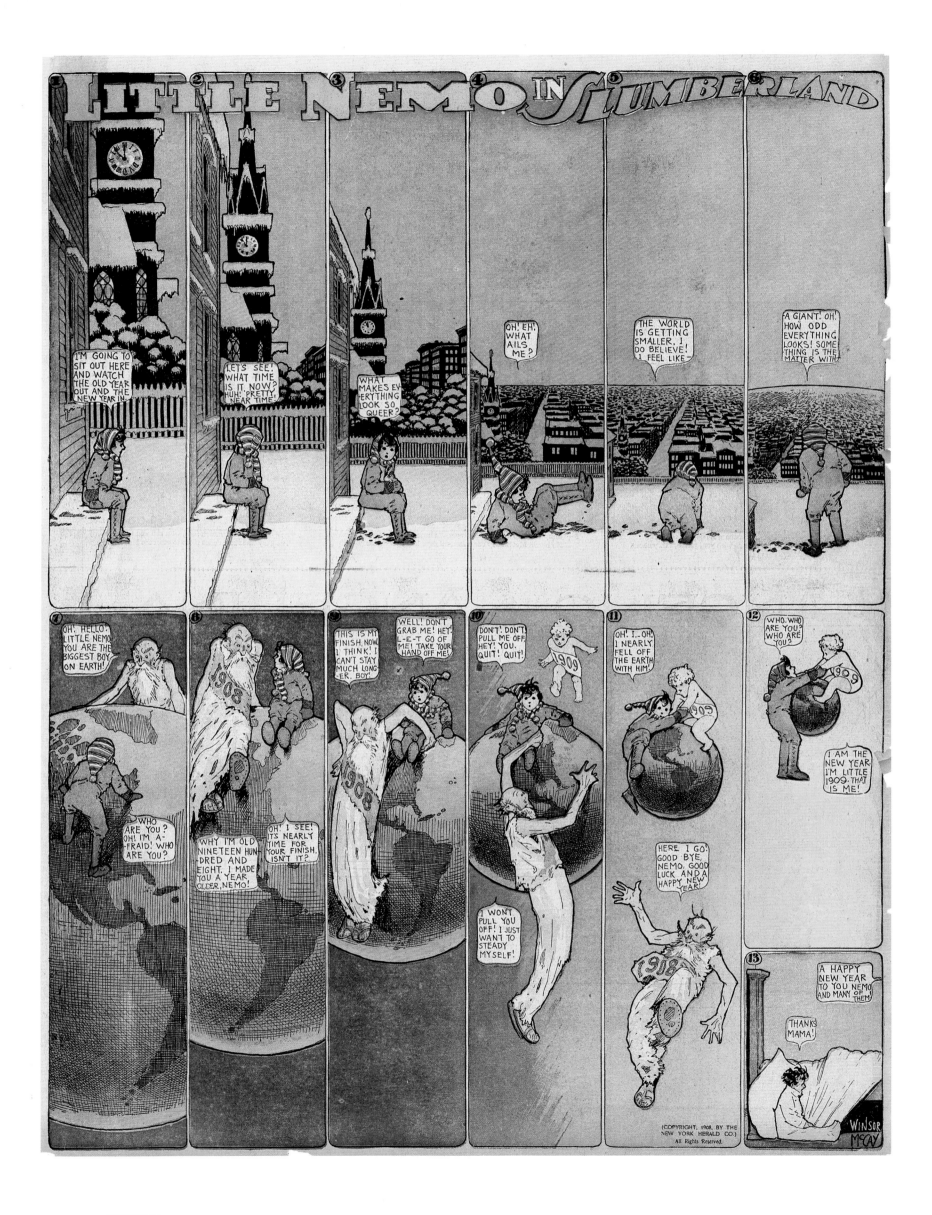

his two previous productions, it was more innovative. Gertie was a trained dinosaur who walked to center "stage" in a prehistoric setting and performed tricks; giving the commands was Winsor McCay himself, who toured with the animated film to various American cities. He stood next to the projection screen, spoke to Gertie at the proper moments, and even appeared to toss objects to her.

McCay's performance was an extension of a lucrative sidelight he had been pursuing since 1906 on the vaudeville stage. Billed variously as America's most famous cartoonist and the world's fastest sketch artist, McCay dazzled audiences with lightning-quick chalk talks, sketches, caricatures of audience members, and sermons on paper like "The Seven Ages of Man" from Shakespeare's *As You Like It.*

Vaudeville appearances, with an occasional exception, ceased around 1914, but McCay's interest in animation continued into the 1920s. Another major production was the incendiary propaganda cartoon *The Sinking of the Lusitania.* Other titles included *The Centaurs, Gertie on Tour, Flip's Circus, Bug Vaudeville, The Pet,* and *The Flying House,* which was a 1921 reprise of *Rarebit Fiend* devices.

In 1911 McCay joined the procession of comic artists who with seeming inevitability went to work for William Randolph Hearst. The denizens of Slumberland moved with their master, but—as in the cases of the Yellow Kid and Buster Brown—the title of the famed creation could not. So McCay launched a Sunday page for the Hearst papers called *In the Land of Wonderful Dreams,* and it starred Nemo, Flip, Impy, the Princess, and Dr. Pill, carried over from the *Herald* (which was wise enough not to attempt to replace McCay). Unfortunately, what also carried over from the *Herald* was the staleness that had recently overtaken *Little Nemo,* and *In the Land of Wonderful Dreams* was a rather dull and less colorful version, sometimes shrunken to a half page. It died after two quiet years.

McCay's career with Hearst blossomed after Nemo's faded, however. The artist became chief editorial cartoonist for the large Hearst chain, and his cartoons were syndicated to additional outlets. Technically he was illustrating the florid editorials of Hearst editor Arthur Brisbane, and recent critics have implied that McCay grudgingly provided decorations for the brittle homilies and that the assignment deprived the world of *Little Nemo.*

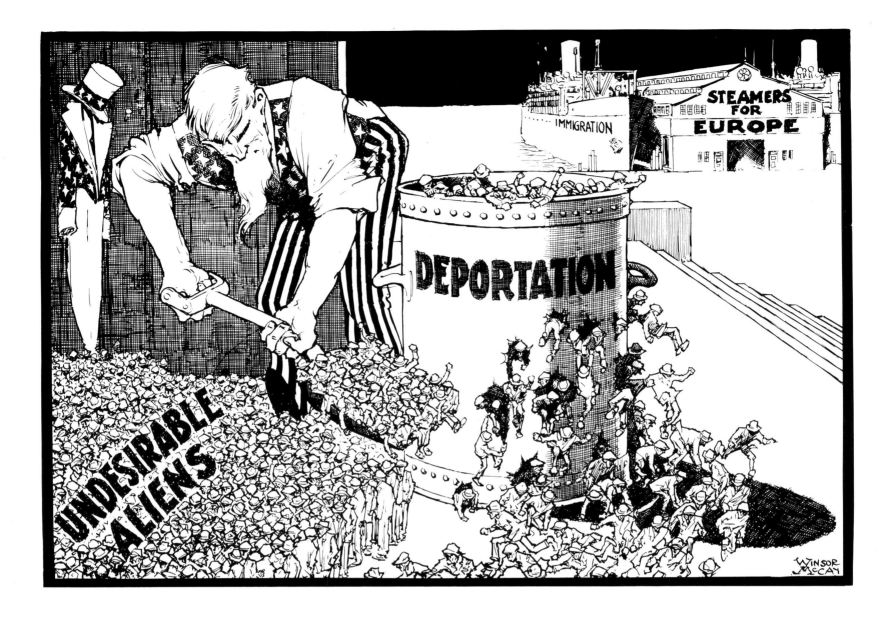

A review of McCay's editorial work does not bear out this analysis. For one thing, McCay had contracts throughout his career, but he was not a slave to Brisbane or Hearst; other newspapers or syndicates would have secured his services, and he could have earned a living from vaudeville and animation by devoting more time to those fields. Furthermore, the *Nemo* epic had been strikingly flat for a full five years, half of its life span, yet when McCay commenced drawing editorial cartoons, he invested them with a renewed sense of verve and excitement. Finally, in the mid-1920s, when McCay returned to the New York *Herald-Tribune* and resurrected *Little Nemo* (once again in rather pallid fashion), he had the chance to abandon the field of editorial cartooning but chose to continue in it for his new paper and its syndicate. Eventually McCay outshone Brisbane on the Hearst papers. He selected the topics and wrote the capsule observations; Brisbane followed behind, as it were, and expanded on McCay's written and drawn statements.

There has never been an editorial cartoonist like McCay at his full powers. He was not a political cartoonist, in that he seldom commented on partisan affairs or politics. His drawings—which again could be called sermons on paper—were enormous pictorial allegories, sometimes filling one-half or two-thirds of a newspaper page. His themes, like those of Dürer and Goya before

McCay could also be topical, but his subjects usually concerned broad issues rather than partisan politics or individual politicians. Obviously this practice did not preclude strong statements from the cartoonist. Through the years his attitudes ranged from opposition to the Spanish-American War to admiration of Benito Mussolini.

him, were universal, and his intention was to exhort, warn, and teach through his cartoons. If the dream strips earlier in his career were nonobjective fantasies, then the earnest editorial cartoons were visionary parables trying to bring old lessons to new generations. In politics McCay was a "staid old conservative Republican" (in the estimation of his animation assistant, John Fitzsimmons), but behind the drawing board McCay was like an Old Testament prophet; his amazing sense of perspective—conceptual this time, as well as graphic—propelled his readers to higher planes. His subjects ranged from puny man's conceit in the face of eternity, to the evils of drugs, to the scandal of child abuse.

McCay's major activity at the time of his death in 1934 was editorial cartooning, although he did not completely abandon comic strips. For Hearst through the years he developed more than a dozen daily strips—most of them, predictably, dealing with dream subjects—including *Midsummer Day Dreams, It Was Only a Dream,* and *The Man from Montclair.* These strips ultimately evolved, as critic Judith O'Sullivan has noted, from dealing with nightmares to wish fulfillment, and his images prefigured the Surrealism of twenty years later.

For all of McCay's many contributions to the comic strip and American cartooning, perhaps the most enduring—and most obvious—are the graphic statements he made. The newspaper comic was born of color, but *Little Nemo* was the first strip to fully utilize the enormous potential of the surprisingly sophisticated technology of color presswork in those days. Newspaper color today cannot approach the subtleties of McCay's day (both metal engravings and the craftsmen who worked on them are virtually obsolete), and few cartoonists after McCay even attempted his pyrotechnics. His pen-and-ink style reflected the modes of contemporary poster artists and the art nouveau movement: heavy outlines around foreground figures; little detail within those figures; negative

McCay's editorial cartoons could be categorized as grand statements, news commentary, or exhortations, themes that were probably his favorites. Sometimes filling half a newspaper page, these detailed, powerful cartoons were sermons on paper and reflected McCay's convictions and concerns.

WHERE IS OUR COURAGE?

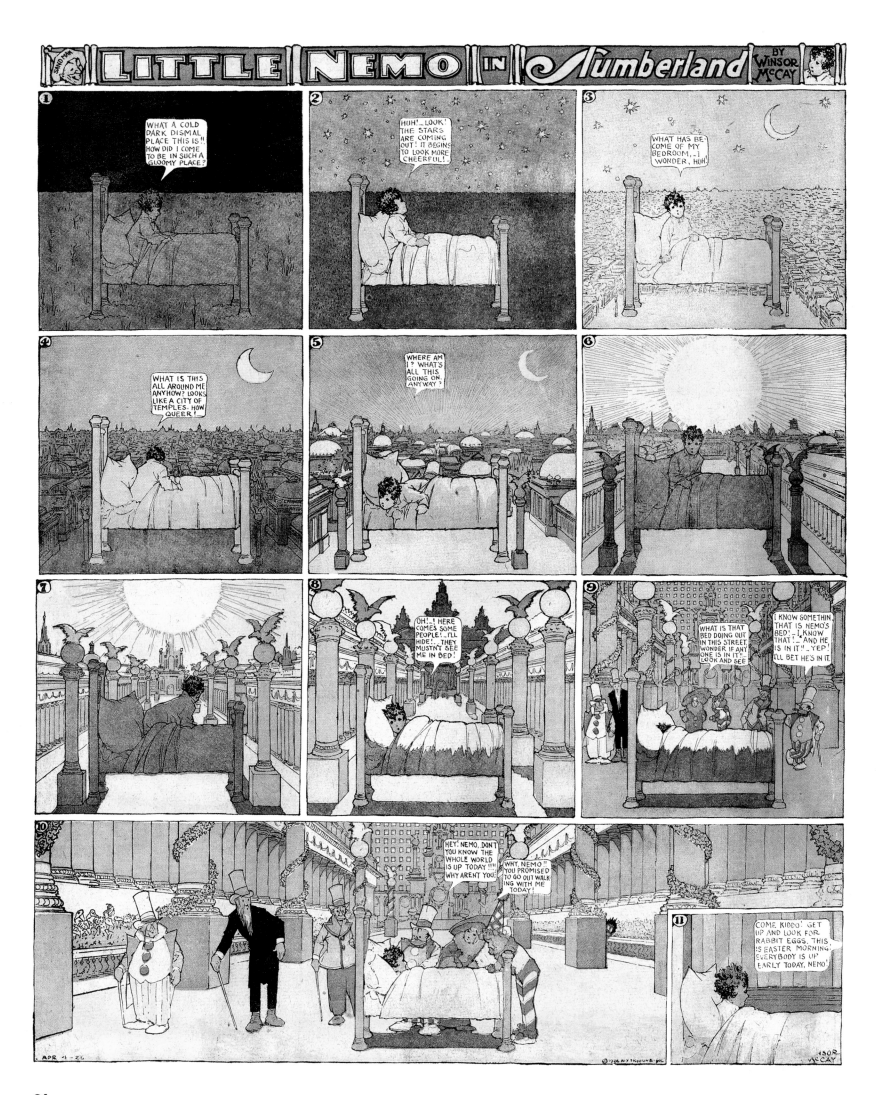

Gertie, Winsor Mc-Cay's animated dinosaur.

white space juxtaposed with selected background elements delineated in severe detail. His use of color was bold, calling on bright primaries, striking contrasts, and subtle pastel shades—the mauves and olives of his era.

McCay had a technical idiosyncrasy that has seldom been noted. In the midst of the exacting accuracy, flawless perspective, and detailed authenticity of props and settings in *Little Nemo* were clumsily drawn and sloppily lettered speech balloons. Frequently the dialogue did not fit the balloon (most cartoonists pencil in the lettering first and draw the balloons to conform), and McCay squeezed his lettering at the bottom or even twisted it around the side of the balloon. It would seem that he was merely leaving a thumbprint. Such effects were perhaps subconscious signs to the rest of us that a mortal produced *Little Nemo*.

The dream master, Winsor McCay wore his cartoonist's smock as proudly as a poet would wear a laurel wreath. But he was both, after all, and much more—an explorer of the widest boundaries of the universe and eternity, and of the minutest recesses of the pixilated imagination. And the maps he charted were on the comics page.

In a rare *Little Nemo* page from 1926, Nemo never leaves bed in his dream (or is it a dream?) because this time the environment is animated and the bed remains static. This page is from the third incarnation of Nemo's adventures. Both premise and graphic verve (including the startling use of color) could still inspire McCay to produce memorable strips. *(Facing page)*

5

Although George Herriman is the most celebrated comic-strip artist of all time—and by common agreement the greatest—his best-known strip, *Krazy Kat,* has been praised by people who have never seen it. In fact, few readers in his own day knew it firsthand because *Krazy Kat* ran in a limited number of newspapers—in direct, inverse proportion to its acclaim then or now. Very few readers understood it at the time, or even to this day.

Herriman was a cartoonist of almost pathological shyness. Gracious, withdrawn, and a bit gentle, he was a vegetarian and animal lover, a man who suffered migraine headaches and would slip away at parties only to be found washing dishes, an activity during which he claimed he could think best. Yet *Krazy Kat* is perhaps the most idiosyncratic and personal of all comic strips, confronting the reader and baring a fiercely individual vision; Herriman, the tentative personality, thought nothing of boldly climbing out on all sorts of artistic limbs. He seemed genuinely embarrassed at being paid handsomely for what he did ($750 a week during the Depression) and once attempted to refuse a raise from his boss, William Randolph Hearst.

GEORGE HERRIMAN

1880-1944

George Herriman is one of a handful of cartoonists who did comic strips almost exclusively, yet somehow produced more than a comic strip. He used the conventions of the strip form, inventing some nuances and stretching conventions to inspired limits, and infused his pages with more than humor: poetry, whimsy, irony, fantasy, wordplay, and, in his art, surrealism and bold colors, unorthodox compositions and thematic motifs. *Krazy Kat* was the creation of a rare genius who happened to express himself via the comics.

The story of George Herriman as one of America's great comic-strip artists is more than the story of *Krazy Kat*. It is little known that prior to *Krazy Kat* (and even collateral to most of its life) Herriman was a journeyman cartoonist. Even less appreciated—overshadowed, regrettably but understandably—is the high level of quality and the wealth of output of his many other comic-strip creations.

George Joseph Herriman was born in New Orleans on August 22, 1880. There has been debate, if not controversy, among Herriman scholars concerning facts about the cartoonist's birth and ancestry. His family has cited French lineage, particularly from Alsace-Lorraine, which would account for the Germanic character of the surname. However, his birth certificate lists his parents as "colored," perhaps because of the admixture of Creole blood through several Herriman generations in Louisiana—a possibility the cartoonist granted—or perhaps because dark-complexioned people were so classified then, as they are in South Africa today. The cartoonist possessed kinky hair (leading to the canard that he refused to be photographed without his hat) and supposed he probably was part Negro. In any case, Herriman was not free of the then universal practice of depicting blacks in a stereotypical fashion in panel cartoons and early strips.

Herriman's father was a middle-class entrepreneur who was engaged in several shop-owning activities; after moving his family to Los Angeles around 1886, he became a baker. Young George forever after considered himself an Angelino but evidently never considered himself a baker. As soon as he was old enough to assist his father in the shop, he was old enough to be discharged for practical jokes like salting the doughnut batter and planting a dead mouse in a loaf of bread.

The young Herriman attended schools attached to St. Vincent's College in Los Angeles and at the age of seventeen sold a sketch to the *Los Angeles Herald,* where he became an assistant in the engraving department at two dollars a week. Herriman was very reticent about biographical details, but according to Roy L. McCardell, his sometime literary collaborator, Herriman engaged in some colorful activities over the next few years, including a hobo-style railroad journey to New York and employment as a sideshow barker and billboard painter at the Coney Island amusement park.

What can be documented is that Herriman began cartooning with a vengeance in 1901. He sold gags to *Judge* magazine, the most humorous of several humorous weeklies, and to the *New York World,* arguably the most important paper in America. His drawing style at the time was at best untutored and full of native humor—and would be called amateurish except for the sparks of real innovation, if not genius, in his case. Amid the captioned cartoons in *Judge*'s pages he drew strips and utilized speech balloons; in his strips for the *World* he eschewed the panel borders that other cartoonists were adopting as standard elements of structure. His work from the start was filled with animation, ridiculous asides, eccentric characters, and bold color. Later in that important first year, Herriman also contributed to the Philadelphia *North American*'s color supplement and to the McClure Syndicate.

Nineteen-oh-two (in such pixilated fashion he would often date his work) was likewise a busy year for the young cartoonist. He returned to Los Angeles to marry the sweetheart of his youth, and back at the *World* he inaugurated some of his earliest comic-strip series: *Musical Mose,* starring a minstrel-type black; *Professor Otto and His Auto;* and *Acrobatic Archie.* Soon *Two Jolly Jackies,* about a pair of hapless sailors, became the featured front-page strip on the *World's Funny Side* section each Sunday—Pulitzer's answer to the strips by Opper, Dirks, and Swinnerton in the Hearst papers. It was a weighty responsibility and honor for the young cartoonist.

Resting on neither laurels nor deadlines, Herriman in 1903 also drew Sunday page series for two organizations outside the *World*: *Lariat Pete* for the McClure Syndicate and *Major Ozone's Fresh Air Crusade* for the World Color Printing Company of St. Louis. Around the turn of the century, these firms began preprinting comic sections for subscribing newspapers, enabling smaller journals to boast of their "own" colored funnies each week and enabling cartoonists like Herriman to gain national exposure.

For all of Herriman's enormous output in the space of a few creative years, his work can be seen as simultaneously diverse and amazingly consistent. His inventiveness continued unabated, and he created new comic series with such ferocity that other cartoonists inherited them in a flurry as he advanced to others. Certain creative wellsprings were apparent even in Herriman's early strip work, and they could be seen as prefigurations of later themes, except for the fact that from the earliest episodes his themes were developed and mature.

The most significant wellspring was the comic device of the personal obsession. During the first fifteen years of strip history, almost every feature was a one-premise strip: the Katzenjammer Kids played pranks; Maud the Mule kicked; Foxy Grandpa foiled his grandkids' ambushes; Buster Brown created mayhem; and so on. Most of these devices revolved around universal themes or occurred in merely variable settings.

What Herriman pioneered was the character bedeviled (or blessed) with intensely personal, even myopic, crusades and visions. Major Ozone, for instance, was the personification of the crank who pursues his faddist ideas at the expense of other characters' peace, comfort, and sanity. He opens windows to let in fresh air, and freezes his intended beneficiaries instead; a similar gesture aboard a passenger train results not in salubrious breezes but a surfeit of grimy soot, and Major Ozone is invariably trounced by his ungrateful neighbors. In like fashion Professor Otto elevates the motorcar from a fad (which it was, in those early days of bold tinkerers and joy riders) to a menacing juggernaut. To Archie, acrobatics were not a pastime but a passion. The device of the personal obsession allowed Herriman to stretch normal eccentricities familiar to readers to absurd lengths. In so doing he opened vast opportunities for comic personalities and plots.

In 1904 Herriman moved to Hearst's *New York American,* but not to draw strips. Mostly he drew sports cartoons, but in making the switch, he became probably the most widely disseminated cartoonist of his day. Carl Anderson (later to draw *Henry*) was the only cartoonist also drawing for the magazines, Hearst, Pulitzer, McClure, and World Color Printing in such a concentrated period of time.

Working for the World Color Printing Company must have been particularly

T he comic obsession carried to its hilarious extensions by the master of the comic-obsession motif, George Herriman. *Prof. Otto and His Auto* was an early and important strip—running front page on the *New York World's* supplement—by the young cartoonist. Many newcomers would tend to "tighten up" and draw stiffly under such responsibilities, but Herriman seemed to revel in graphic informality; note the elements breaking the panel borders, the long ending scene, the absurd premise, depictions, and dialogue. (*Overleaf*)

A very young George Herriman was the featured cartoonist on the front page of what was arguably the nation's most important newspaper in 1903, the *New York World.* His *Two Jolly Jackies* featured the graphic insouciance that would become a hallmark of Herriman's work. (*Page 101*)

FUNNY SIDE

PROF. OTTO AND HIS AUTO
(How He Cured the Millionaires' Auto Club of Running People Down.)

FUNNY SIDE

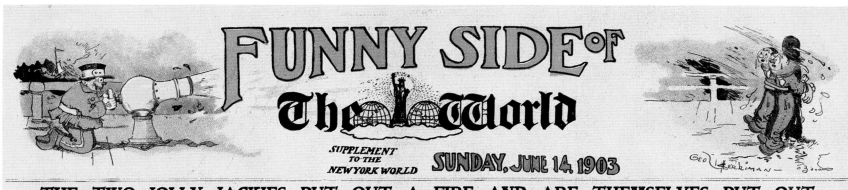

THE TWO JOLLY JACKIES PUT OUT A FIRE AND ARE THEMSELVES PUT OUT

satisfying to Herriman. Not only was he free to experiment with themes and titles, but he was not obliged to hang his hat in St. Louis. WCP's cartoonists mailed their work to the headquarters, and Herrriman was to freelance from New York while working for the dailies, and from Los Angeles, where he returned in 1905.

For World Color Printing, Herriman drew *Bud Smith, the Boy Who Does Stunts,* another obsession-tinged creation, and later merged it with *Grandma's Girl. Rosy Posy, Mama's Girl* was a seemingly innocuous children's strip but featured a promise of things to come—talking animals on the periphery of panels and plot line. *Daniel and Pansy* prefigured *Krazy Kat* all the more; it was an all-animal strip (starring, of all things, a kangaroo and a pig) whose characters were later revived in *Krazy Kat.*

Perhaps Herriman's most remarkable strip for WCP was *Alexander the Cat. Major Ozone* was probably his funniest strip to date, but *Alexander* was his most sophisticated. Already having proven himself as a master of the comic obsession, Herriman turned to urbanity. It was a daring turn for his work and growing reputation (and he was to extend such thematic explorations in two marvelous strips of the 1920s), as well as a decided departure from comic strips of the day, most of which were based on slapstick and basic farce. Most surprising of all, in terms of Herriman's work before and afterward, is that Alexander was a cat-as-cat, never speaking dialogue or asides nor displaying human traits.

Charlie and Leila are the suburbanite couple who own—or are owned by—Alexander the Persian cat, and the setting is domestic, with none of the creeping surrealism already happily infesting the panels of Herriman's other strips. Besides finding creative release in such a premise, Herriman was very possibly mirroring the warmth of his own domestic tranquility at the time (*Alexander* ran in 1909 and 1910); his marriage was happy and had produced two daughters.

Through the first decade of the century, the cauldron of Herriman's imagination bubbled and boiled unabated. Besides experimenting with themes, he also pioneered several formats, and the work was no less remarkable, even if it has been largely lost to history. In 1904 the *New York Daily News* (no connection to today's tabloid) had featured a Herriman daily strip, *Home Sweet Home.* For Hearst's *New York American,* Herriman had drawn elaborate sports cartoons in tandem with the master of the form, TAD Dorgan, and in Los Angeles in 1906-1907 he drew political cartoons of Byzantine complexity for the *Times.*

The *Times* did not keep Herriman long. He returned to the Hearst fold by joining the *Los Angeles Examiner* in 1906, and he was never to leave Hearst's regular employ again. It was during his four years on the *Examiner* that Herriman mined new ground in the field of daily strips. Previously there had been experiments and short-lived daily comic strips, including Herriman's own *Home Sweet Home* in New York; probably the most successful was George McManus's *Newlyweds* in the *New York World.* So successful was *Newlyweds,* with its boxy daily showcase, that in 1907 a reprint book was offered for sale. And on November 15 of that year, up the coast from Herriman, a young cartoonist named Bud Fisher introduced Mr. A. Mutt to readers of the *San Francisco Chronicle*'s sports pages; the strip became a daily fixture and eventually evolved into *Mutt and Jeff,* the first truly successful and sustained daily strip.

Typically, George Herriman was in the thick of these experiments. Less than a month after Fisher's *A. Mutt* appeared, Herriman offered *Mr. Proones the Plunger* to the public for two weeks. Curiously, perhaps, Proones was a racetrack roustabout and gambler just like Mr. Mutt. Strains of the old obsession tune were also heard with Herriman's next daily entry, *Baron Mooch,* starring a character maniacally devoted to free tickets, free lunches, free anything. The short-lived pretty-girl strip *Mary's Home From College* prefigured later strips dealing with daughters and their suitors, notably *The Dingbat Family* and *Now Listen, Mabel,* as well as titles by other cartoonists.

Most remarkable was a Herriman daily strip in 1909 and 1910 that comics historian Bill Blackbeard, when he unearthed examples in musty newspaper files, termed a Rosetta Stone for *Krazy Kat*. The strip was *Gooseberry Sprig,* starring a tophatted duck who had previously visited the corners of various Herriman panel cartoons and short-run strips. Under his own title he led a cast of animals engaged in ditsy dialogue and burlesque metaphysics in a rural setting. It was ground that would be explored in *Krazy Kat*—the marginal style of character introduction, the talking-animal cast, the sparse settings, the off-center concerns of plot. Clearly *Krazy Kat* was not a fortuitous aberration in the cartoonist's lifeline.

But the Kat was not yet ready to make his appearance.

Herriman once more made the transcontinental trek when he was summoned to join the staff of Hearst's major outlet, the *Evening Journal* in New York. During his first week among old cartooning friends he created *The Dingbat Family,* which made its debut on June 20, 1910. The Dingbats were an odd family, midway in personality between the cartoonist's domestic and dippy characters of the recent past, and once again Herriman used the comic appeal of bizarre obsessions. A family, never named and never seen, moves into the apartment above the Dingbats, and their activities, noises, and improbable visitors drive the Dingbat family to distraction. Eventually, yielding to the lure of creative possibilities, Herriman retitled the strip *The Family Upstairs,* and its comic variety was hilariously displayed until 1916.

But there was something going on downstairs, too. As Herriman had done in other strips in his brief but crowded past, he occasionally filled the bottoms of *Dingbat* panels with miniature comic animals. They could play the role of a Greek chorus or engage in their own farcical adventures, and soon they earned

Mr. Proones Dreams of Landing a Winner.   *By George Herriman.*

LARIAT PETE MAKES TEN DOLLARS FOR HIS NEPHEW

ROSY POSY---MAMMA'S GIRL

SHE TEACHES "DOG" A NEW STUNT

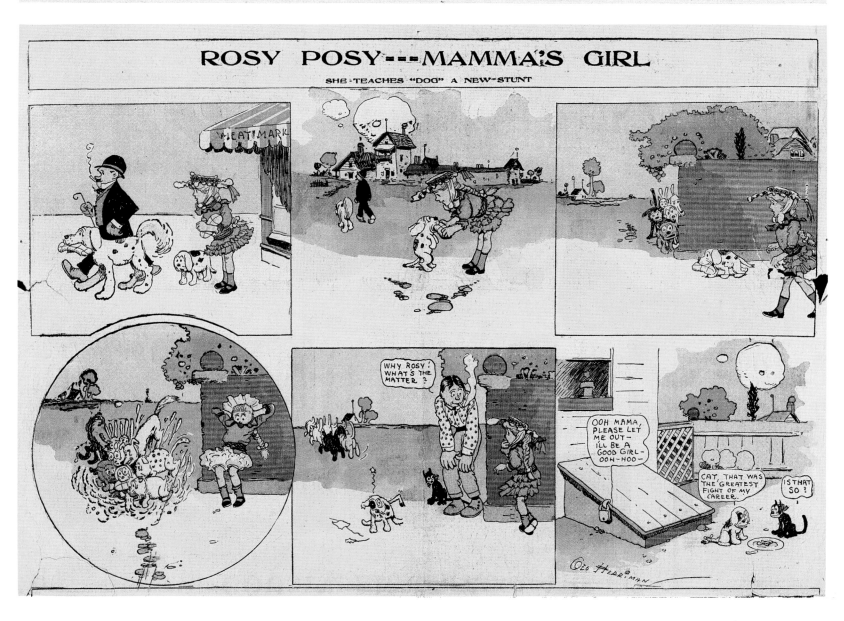

MAJOR OZONE'S FRESH AIR CRUSADE

Baron Mooch---He's Leading a Regular Dog's Life
By Herriman

Mary's Home From College
By Herriman

Gooseberry Sprig Goes in for Aquatics
By Herriman

The Family Upstairs—Ignatz Mouse and Krazy Kat Are Sent Below
By Herriman

Four early daily strips (1908–1910) by George Herriman. All were mature in terms of Herriman's humor and structure, but were experimental in their themes, which the cartoonist revived later in his career. *Baron Mooch* was a prototypical *Baron Bean*; *Mary's Home From College* prefigured Herriman's domestic comedies like *Us Husbands*; *Gooseberry Sprig* foreshadowed the animal cast of *Krazy Kat* (many of the characters in *Sprig* would later populate Krazy's Coconino County); and *The Family Upstairs*, which evolved from the *Dingbat Family* and spawned *Krazy Kat*, was also a domestic comedy.

The *Dingbat Family* began as a daily strip about the comic trials of an average family but evolved into a saga of comic obsessions. The Dingbats became increasingly preoccupied with the noises, visitors, and mysteries in the apartment of the family upstairs—which eventually became the title of the strip. Meanwhile, below, surprising things were taking place.

107

EVENING CAPITAL NEWS

BOISE, IDAHO, SATURDAY

DEC. 18, 1909

ALEXANDER $500 REWARD TO CATCH HIM-- CAN YOU?

their own dialogue balloons. Gooseberry Sprig had graduated to his own strip, and so would the cat just south of the Dingbats. But first he became a Kat.

Befitting the casual manner of presentation, the cat's little activities were at first light in tone. *The Dingbat Family* was comedy, and *Krazy Kat,* as the substrip came to be called, was nonsense. The Kat was dumb, but a wise fool, as he turned phrases of the day around and skewered logic. The usual antagonist was a mouse, of course, but any antagonisms were the result of dialogue, not natural tendencies. And invariably the mouse would visit the Kat's head with a rock or a brick. Later this device was to be seen as a comment on displays of affection, but at the beginning it was, plain and simple, a slapstick prop of comics and stage comedy. In a playful parody of a comic-strip cliché, the cartoonist varied the sound effects of the flying bricks with "ziz," "zip," "zup," and other silliness. In fact, for the Kat's first few years, the strip-under-a-strip (and then under its own marquee) was a literate version of *Mutt and Jeff,* with comic exchanges and slapstick payoffs.

More intellectual things were at work, however. Herriman's wordplay grew more sophisticated, the musings of Krazy grew more philosophical, and the appeal of the feature became more mature. Even though Herriman's work appeared in the sensationalist Hearst press, readers discovered Herriman's emerging literate fancy. In 1912 the Sunday chain offered a *Herriman Joke Book* featuring the first expanded episodes of *Krazy Kat,* and by 1913 *Krazy Kat* became an independent strip. While Dingbat humans pursued their obsessions, the growing cast of *Krazy Kat* (including the former solo stars Gooseberry Sprig and Daniel and Pansy) evolved their own. In 1916 Herriman was given a Sunday-page format for the Kat, but not in the color sections. Hearst constructed his *City Life* section— a sophisticated arts supplement—around Herriman's *Krazy Kat.* It was reported that President Woodrow Wilson refused to miss an episode, even reading *Krazy Kat* to cabinet meetings. And in 1917 an article in *Cartoons* magazine, for perhaps the first time in comic-strip historiography, termed a cartoonist, namely George Herriman, a genius of the comics page.

Clearly many people, not the least of whom were Herriman and Hearst, sensed something special in *Krazy Kat.* Yet the cartoonist's parallel activities continued. When *Family Upstairs* ended, *Baron Bean* immediately commenced. Its star character (whose name was a pun on "barren bean," or empty head) was a type more familiar to earlier twentieth-century America than our day. The nation was awash with gentlemen on their uppers, and daughters of the "400" were susceptible to impoverished European nobility and often willing to trade the family fortune for a title.

In the Baron's case we are not quite sure whether he actually had a title or had appropriated one; he was less the *poseur,* however, than the self-deluding dreamer. He assumed he was entitled to the world's homage, but for all his sincerity and purposefulness, his field of vision was never wider than lunch counters and small-town politics. In a very real sense the Baron was a modern-day Don Quixote, and Herriman even provided him with a descendant of Sancho Panza: Grimes, the street-wise sidekick who stuck with his master through thin and thinner.

The strip was unlike *Krazy Kat* in its low-life preoccupations, unlike *Major Ozone* in its examination of comradeship, and unlike *Alexander* (and later

domestic sagas of Herriman) because the Baron never identified with the everyday challenges to the common man. It was a wonderful strip, wonderful in its essence and in its virtuosity.

In 1922 yet another masterpiece flowed from the ink in George Herriman's magic pen: *Stumble Inn*. To contemporary readers familiar with the British television comedy *Fawlty Towers*, Herriman's *Stumble Inn* will strike a familiar chord. Uriah Stumble was the innkeep, and Ida was his wife; the moocher Joe Beamish (a character in several earlier strips) and house dick Owleye rounded out the regular cast, and thereafter the strip overflowed with bizarre and eccentric guests.

Stumble Inn ran in Sunday episodes until 1926 (and for a brief period in double-tiered dailies as well) and was succeeded by the most domestic of Herriman's gentle family series, *Us Husbands*. It was a neighborhood strip, an early-day *Blondie,* concerned with household chores, bills, and married couples' occasional games. Such strips proliferated in the 1920s, when in America a virtual exodus took place to the promised land of the suburbs. It is remarkable that Herriman, with all his other specialties, could also produce a sustained, year-long sympathetic portrait like *Us Husbands*. (TAD Dorgan, the raffish sports cartoonist, turned a similar trick during the same period with his tranquil Sunday page *For Better Or Worse.*)

One more creation occupied Herriman's attention before he worked on *Krazy Kat* full time. *Embarrassing Moments* was a one-panel daily feature that had bounced around among Hearst cartoonists for years. Herriman inherited it between 1928 and 1932 and turned the endless succession of social gaffes into his very own property, of course. He introduced a hapless victim named Bernie Burns, who became his last human character; even his now infrequent freelance work, like illustrating Don Marquis's *archy and mehitabel* classics, featured animals alone. (Herriman was of a caliber that virtual offhand work would achieve legendary status, as happened with the Marquis collaboration.)

Krazy Kat was a daily strip from 1913 until Herriman's death in 1944, but its weekly version changed format considerably through the years. Inaugurated as a black-and-white page, it appeared briefly in color in the early twenties and had a full run as a colored tabloid Sunday page between 1935 and 1944. The premises, themes, and, yes, obsessions of the strip are more elusive than its chronology, and properly so. *Krazy Kat* evolved from a sophisticated humor strip to a humorous commentary strip, with Herriman commenting on life and love.

Maybe. There are many ways to view *Krazy Kat,* and it has been analyzed

A daily-only feature, Herriman's *Baron Bean* ran from 1916 to 1919. At the same time *Krazy Kat* was running in the Hearst and syndicated papers. The Baron's freeloading schemes and impossible dreams were accompanied by classic bits of double-take, like hats spinning in unpredictable fashion over surprised characters' heads.

Herriman's last assigned feature was the daily panel *Embarrassing Moments*. It was a standard gag cartoon that probably struck many chords among readers, but Herriman's trademark lettering and illogically placed quotation marks preserved an individuality.

Embarrassing Moments

TOO LATE, THE NEAR SIGHTED "COLONEL" WHO WON'T WEAR GLASSES, FINDS OUT THAT HE'S SALUTED A DOORMAN, THINKING HE WAS A "GENERAL".

exhaustively. It has been portrayed as a variation on the eternal triangle of tragic romances; as a grand statement on freedom versus authority; as an allegory on innocence meeting reality; and, of course, as a comic cacophony of obsessions. The strip had a Joycean affinity, especially in its high/low wealth of language. Herriman is supposed to have once responded to these analyses with the astonished reply that he merely drew a comic about a cat and mouse.

Throughout the 1920s the Sunday pages were replete with words—coming from Krazy, the narrator, the incidental characters—and fragrant with a type of prose-poetry to make those words like sweet librettos. Krazy could be ethereal, Ignatz cynical, and Offissa Bull Pupp the hard voice of reality. Other leading characters were Joe Stork, purveyor of progeny and other sorts of blessed intrusions, and Kolin Kelly, brickmaker. The pages could be sparse, with huge white spaces and lonely images, or crowded, with hundreds of words, scores of characters, and dozens of busy panels.

Codified during the twenties were two final elements that ensured *Krazy Kat*'s immortality: the setting and the brick. Herriman was introduced to the Southwest after the turn of the century by the ailing cartoonist Jimmy Swinnerton, who was sent there to be cured or die (he wound up living to ninety-nine), and Herriman was enchanted. It was particularly the striking desert of Arizona— with mesas rising from nowhere, absurd-looking cacti, and silent, unearthly joshua trees—that appealed to Herriman, and Coconino County (Herriman was not one to let that juicy name escape) became the locale of *Krazy Kat,* although it was actually some distance from the most picturesque landscapes.

The brick became as significant as the "real" characters. First used as a prop to deliver the "pow," it became a central element as the lyrical pages of the 1920s gave way to a renewal of Herriman's trademark obsessive theme. Thereafter Herriman frequently elevated his meditations-on-paper to the abstract, in terms of composition and motif—playing endless variations on the relationship between Kat, Mouse, and Pupp, and on the role of the brick. The theme, as critic Gilbert Seldes wrote, became greater than the plot. The brick in Coconino was like the apple in Eden, an agent of both disruptive and bonding impulses. Krazy was androgynous (sometimes male, sometimes female, sometimes flipping gender within a strip), but always in love with Ignatz. Not only did the mouse reject the affection, he tried to obliterate the possibility by aiming bricks at Krazy's head. The Kat, meanwhile, only saw such aggression as signs of affection, and in later years the brick-throwing act became a literal tryst. All might have gone well if not for several impediments, including the fact that Ignatz was married (his sons were named Milton, Marshall, and Irving) and that cosmic law and order invariably asserted itself in the form of Offissa Pupp. The dog had an abstract devotion to justice but an amorous devotion to Krazy, who, in his/her innocence, never suspected any tender aspect of Pupp's interruptions.

Krazy Kat's greatness, however, transcended the whimsy of its premise. Herriman's poetic gifts had been evident in earlier titles, but the dialogue in this one—particularly Krazy's—was inspired. The Kat spoke in a singular patois of phoneticisms, slang, Yiddish, Spanish, Tin Pan Alley patter, and other verbiage we can term Herrimanesque, a gumbo of speech patterns the likes of which the cartoonist might actually have tasted in his New Orleans past.

The props in *Krazy Kat* became Herriman's visual trademarks. There were

Herriman's two new strips of the 1920s were creations that would have assured him a place in comic-strip history. But unfortunately *Stumble Inn* and *Us Husbands* were short-lived, drawn as adjuncts to the well-established *Krazy Kat*. (Overleaf and page 113)

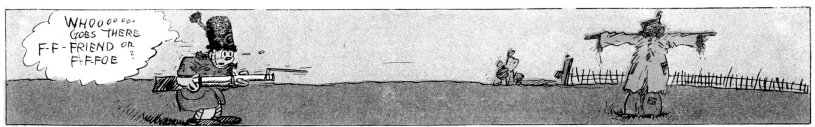

Stumble Inn
Registered U. S. Patent Office

Us Husbands

113

the mesas, of course, but they changed from panel to panel. So did other items like trees—which sometimes grew from tiny Navajo-decorated pottery—and the moon itself. Herriman's moons revealed, for instance, that a quarter-moon has a large slice taken from it, as the cartoonist plainly delineated by hanging one as if by a string in front of a mesa. Day would change to night and back again through any given strip, and skies would sometimes be graced with plaids or herringbone patterns.

George Herriman's layouts were as orthodox as his premises, dialogue, backgrounds, and props. From his earliest days as a cartoonist his inclination was to view the perimeters of his allotted space in terms of possibilities, not restrictions. In addition to changing from enormously large to incredibly minute scales from week to week, Herriman forever experimented with symmetry and asymmetry in panel arrangement; with a rythmic flow of large and small frames; and with dropped panel enclosures or circular borders. When he had color, he

This early (1920) *Krazy Kat* appeared four years after the debut of the Sunday-format page. For years the *Kat* Sundays ran in black and white in the interiors of Hearst's *City Life* supplement aimed at more literate readers. And through the teens and twenties Herriman constructed these pages as short stories—multipaneled, witty, with extensive captions, and very often poetic. The daily strips revolved around gags with Kat, mouse, and brick, but these Sundays dealt with the larger world masquerading as the Coconino Desert and its denizens.

used both complementary desert hues—earth colors—and wildly clashing primaries. For many years he would hand-design a different, and brilliant, *Krazy Kat* logo for each week's Sunday page and sometimes place it in the middle or at the bottom of the page.

In later years, when Herriman's pen lines grew scratchy and almost abstract, shadows grew up behind figures and props, lending the appearance of a backdrop perpendicular to the ground rather than a distance fading to the horizon. Occasionally Herriman even pictured his characters on a stage—in random panels and with no relation to the story at hand—complete with footlights and side curtains.

All of these elements combined to result in a unified relationship between Herriman's language and structure. Motifs were echoed not only in seemingly disparate visual artifacts, but in composition, decoration, lettering style, logo design, speech patterns, depictions, and even shading. Any cartoonist who can

The casual quality of
Herriman's line and the loose atmosphere
in his universe belie a strong standard
of composition in *Krazy Kat*. In this
1928 page the corner panels are all balanced with black skies (even to a small
cloud counterbalancing a patented
Coconino moon); the center decorative
panel provides unique graphic respite;
and the outside center panels feature
angles to the mesas—even to the shading
lines—that complement each other. Indeed, nothing was haphazard in Herriman's work.

master one element, or join two, in the act of figuration can produce significant works of art. Yet the humble Herriman—almost as if by instinct—gathered, molded, and propelled the stuff of comic immortality.

When George Herriman died, *Krazy Kat* was appearing in only thirty-five newspapers, but William Randolph Hearst was the faithful reader who counted most. His patronage ultimately put the heritage and quality of American letters in his debt; other publishers, especially today, would have rudely closed the curtain on the saga of the enchanted mesa. The Kat's popularity was limited not because readers were hostile—few readers understood *Krazy Kat*—but because most were too impatient to like it. In all of comic history, it was the strip that demanded the most attention—not necessarily sophistication, as is usually assumed—on the part of the readers.

Stephen Becker wrote in *Comic Art in America:*

When Herriman died in 1944 his editors knew better than to
search for a successor. Here, if ever, was a marriage of
the man and the material. It was poetry—i.e.,
thought—that made *Krazy Kat* great; and no other human being
could have been expected to think like George Herriman. In
the truest sense of the word he was a genius. Between him
and the universe of men there was a kind of love affair, and
the allegory he gave the world was unique. With him the
world took on a new dimension; without him it was reduced to
reality. There will be no more *Krazy Kat,* and we are all of
us the losers; but how much we have gained because he
existed at all!

It has been tempting through the years to give Herriman a surrealist label, but such a simplification obscures proper consideration. His contributions to American comic art were vastly greater than even *Krazy Kat* itself; and although he utilized surrealist modes, they were representational, not elemental. George Herriman's entire output was not surreal or ironic or even merely humorous; it was fanciful.

Fancy is an artistic commodity in short supply this century. George Herriman showed us not only that whimsy, playful caprice, charmed sensations, gentle impressions, comic obsessions, and wit *can* underpin a comic strip, but also that the comic strip may be our last and best refuge of such expression.

At the end of Herriman's career (this page appeared exactly one year before his last), *Krazy Kat* became more abstract than ever. Here the large panels bear no contextual relation to the simple four-panel gag, but their symbolic relationship to the entire premise of the strip is overarching. Their statements, their placements, are anything but ad hominem.

6

It is remarkable that few students of the comics have noted the relationship between the comic strip and the theater. The strip's panel, the theater's stage, and the movie's screen are virtually identical image frames, although the cartoonist is granted the most plastic of the three forms for telling his story.

Through the years a number of comic-strip creators have found the similarities irresistible, using theatrical devices for comic purposes. Cartoonists from Winsor McCay to George Herriman to Walt Kelly transformed the usual two-dimensional environment of their strips into three-dimensional worlds as on the stage. Panel borders have become stage wings; characters have talked to readers apart from the dramatic continuity (removing the "fourth wall"); figures have chatted about finishing their day's work when readers got to the last panel. Of all the great comic-strip artists, however, no cartoonist dwelt more on theatrical references than E.C. Segar; no other cartoonist so consciously intertwined the conventions of stage and cinema with those of the comics, or did it so cleverly and joyously.

E. C. SEGAR

1894-1938

Elzie Crisler Segar was born in the Camptown section of Chester, Illinois, on the banks of the Mississippi River, on December 8, 1894. His grandfather had settled in the Midwest and found work as a distributor of olive oil, of all things, foreshadowing Olive Oyl, the star of the very first *Thimble Theatre* by young Elzie years later. When he was twelve, Elzie secured a job at the local opera house, and when it was transformed into a motion-picture theater, his chores included changing the posters, drawing show cards, playing the drums in the pit (the "orchestra" being a lone piano) and eventually running the projectors.

So proud was Segar of his work as projectionist of the flickering images and shadow stories that he had MPO—Motion Picture Operator—tattooed on his forearm. And so enamored was he of the telescoped tales that could amuse and thrill audiences that he regularly re-created movie plots outside the theater, drawing comic-strip versions in chalk on the sidewalk. Segar seemed to be practicing (however subconsciously) for his later career, but according to locals, he must have been making all sorts of mental notes; the manager of the opera house, Bill Schuchert, was a dead ringer for the character who was later known as Wimpy.

Segar's penchant for drawing led him to subscribe to the W.L. Evans Correspondence Course in Cartooning. Mail-order lessons proliferated in the early part of the century, and the Evans course was second only to the Landon "school" in teaching the proper method of depicting wrinkles, frowns, sweat beads, and those little shadows that always lurk beneath cartoon characters' shoes.

In 1916 Segar moved to Chicago, where, according to legend, an interview with the legendary R.F. Outcault led to employment on the Chicago *Herald,* although Outcault was not a resident of the city, and the paper was not his outlet. However, there must have been influence employed by someone, even though the job was not prestigious (as comics historian Bill Blackbeard has noted, the *Herald* was sixth in a field of six) because at that stage of his career, E.C. Segar was possibly the worst working cartoonist in America. Clearly he was also the luckiest. The *Herald*'s owner, James Keeley, formerly of the *Tribune,* was anxious for independent success, and in 1916 he signed a contract that seemed sure to add luster to his paper's pages: *Charlie Chaplin's Comic Capers* was an officially licensed property depicting the misadventures of the most visible and popular character in America. Keeley had Chaplin, and by some working of fate—because talent must have played a subsidiary role—Segar had the Chaplin strip.

Once more the movies and the comics were intersecting in Segar's career. Although two of the era's great comedic talents were involved, the results were insipid at best. Segar's drawings were vapid, his gags weak, and construction flimsy. The strip is a bizarre footnote in Chaplin historiography—killed within a year, it was surpassed by another, unlicensed, strip by the excellent Ed Carey— and is even only a footnote in the Segar chronology, although a more revealing one. The cartoonist obviously had to approximate the characteristics that endeared. Chaplin to masses of Americans, so his reliance on simple slapstick (and the absence of the Tramp's appeal to sympathy) reveals that Segar was an enthusiastic amateur and that Chaplin's persona had not yet matured. The gag situations were routine vaudeville wheezes, with no apparent attempt to exploit the Tramp's emerging traits, and often the Chaplin character was even the straight man to other characters' gags.

The most arresting feature of Segar's Chaplin was the Tramp's voice; the cartoonist gave him a voice, even though in the early days of silent movies, all characters were silent. Chaplin the actor had not yet developed his pantomimic aspect, so Segar gave him a voice; cartoonist Carey, in his version *(Pa's Imported Son-in-Law),* drew Chaplin mute.

Charlie Chaplin talking? In a time when all movies, and movie stars, were silent, a comic strip could logically make all of them talk. Segar, in his first daily strip, from 1917, went a little further with the Tramp's persona by transforming him into a straight man, which definitely was not part of the screen character.

By 1917 Segar's strip itself was mute, and he developed another strip, actually an outgrowth of his earlier Chaplin efforts. Barry the Boob was the star of the new strip, and the War to End All Wars provided the setting. Like the Chaplin strip, it had slapstick gags and weak art and paled further in the *Herald*'s comic section alongside a surprising pair of talented newcomers, Billy DeBeck and Frank Willard (later to draw *Barney Google* and *Moon Mullins,* respectively). Another *Herald* comic strip of the late teens, drawn by a succession of artists, was a parody of movie serials called *Movies,* starring Haphazard Helen.

Movies was not the only contemporary strip that borrowed from or parodied stage or motion-picture conventions. C.W. Kahles in 1906 had created *Hairbreadth Harry,* which cleverly satirized cliff-hangers while also pioneering the continuity strip. Not only did Kahles run loose story lines from week to week, but he also combined the narrator's voice with those of his characters. Harry Hershfield worked in a similar fashion on two early classics, *Desperate Desmond* and *Dauntless Durham of the U.S.A.,* which were replete with the stock villains and hoary clichés of road shows and nickelodeons.

The curtain fell on *Barry the Boob* when the Chicago *Herald* folded in 1918, but the event was hardly calamitous for Elzie Segar. William Randolph Hearst bought the newspaper, and the cartoonist found himself transferred to the staff of a leading paper, the *Chicago American.* He was soon drawing not a strip but—significantly—a unique cartoon feature that was concerned with the theater. *Looping the Loop* was a thin vertical hodgepodge of current events in the Windy City, usually centered on theatrical doings and visiting celebrities. The quality of Segar's artwork was not critical because the tiny images could hardly be more than stick figures, and his narrative talents were not tested by the vignette structure. During this time Segar matured as an artist and humorist, and *Looping the Loop* brought him his first success, evidently attracting the personal attention of Hearst and his New York staff.

In 1919 Segar was summoned to New York to join the staff of Hearst's *Evening Journal.* Rarely were cartoonists lured away from the Hearst stable, but in that year Ed Wheelan moved to the fledgling George Matthew Adams Service. Segar's assignment was to replace Wheelan's feature with a similar strip. Perhaps predictably in Segar's case, the comic prescription was for a daily parody of stage melodrama! Wheelan's strip, *Midget Movies*—at the Adams Service it became the long-running classic *Minute Movies*—dealt with a cast of paper actors who assumed roles in various strip stories. Wheelan even "cast" himself in a studio role, as the strip was "presented" by Wheelan Pictures, Ink. His various players consisted of characters with names like Dick Dare, Ralph McSneer, Blanche Rouge, Fuller Phun, and Hazel Dearie, who were introduced in iris shots as each story commenced.

Thimble Theatre made its debut in the *Evening Journal* on December 19, 1919. Like its alliterative forebear, it featured a cast of players whose comic-strip names were presented as if on a marquee or a playbill, along with their "character" names for each day's episode. Each of those episodes was titled and—in an apparent nod to the cliff-hanging device of stage and screen—the next day's strip title was previewed. The players on the very first day consisted of Olive Oyl (as Lizzie Lampshade) and Harold Hamgravy (as Jed Simpson); soon Harold became Ham Gravy, Olive's suitor, and a villain named Willie Wormwood entered and eventually departed from the tiny stage. At first the glorified stick figures resembled the serviceable figures in *Looping the Loop,* and the boxed strip (two panels stacked in each of three tiers) parodied stage melodramas and movie serials in a respectable though hardly outstanding manner.

E. C. Segar, however, proved to be a cartoonist who was never content with the quality of his work; he doggedly improved his drawing and writing through the early years, and during his later period of enormous success he was increasingly innovative. After a couple of years of *Thimble Theatre* parodies, Segar did not abandon the premise but rather expanded it, building on the opportunities inherent in the formula. If stage and screen stories could be more than vignettes, then *Thimble Theatre* could have longer tales, and Segar thereby became a pioneer of the daily humorous continuity strip. As his dramatic structure allowed the possibility of incidental characters—and characters who could focus, reflect, or embody the action within a plot—Segar was able to parade a host of memorable figures across his comic-strip stage.

In these two areas, story line and character development, Segar ultimately proved to be a master. In his art he was not, although his drawings did develop to a level of delightful competency. The literary—and the dramatic!—component of comic-strip expression, however, can more than compensate for pedestrian artwork and reminds us that the form is not exclusively visual. His character designs and comic sets were amiable and never distracted from his masterful— and forever expanding—architecture of sophisticated story lines and personalities. Nevertheless, Segar would occasionally display some jarring visual element; for instance, he had a habit of drawing running figures with their left arms and legs simultaneously thrust forward.

Thimble Theatre hit its stride not only when the stories developed length and breadth and when the characters grew more interesting, but when Segar's premise subtly changed from parody to farce. Comic melodrama became the strip's fare, and a new character—Olive's brother, Castor Oyl—became a new type in the comic pages: an unrepentant lowlife and schemer. Castor was a roustabout, like such fellow comic-section denizens as Barney Google and Moon Mullins, but those two would never have fixed fights or bribed trainers, as Castor did. Happy Hooligan's brother, Gloomy Gus, was a moocher, but he did not steal coins from blind men's cups, as Castor did. The diminutive rascal was thoroughly amiable in his rascality—indeed, he reveled in it—and such a character type was new to the comics.

As Castor's activities broadened, so did his acquaintances, and *Thimble*

The original major players in *Thimble Theatre* were Castor Oyl, his sister, Olive, and her boyfriend, Ham Gravy. Note the theatrical or cinematic motif of the titled episode and the "leader" for the next day's installment. *(Above)*

Segar—now with his distinctive signature—had a hit with *Looping the Loop* in the *Chicago American* in 1918. Local events, more than his own characters, were the stars of the strip. *(Facing page)*

Early on, Segar betrayed an affinity for the prize ring, fisticuffs—or the gamecock equivalent—and comically florid narrative. *(Below)*

Theatre soon had a varied troupe of players. The most significant among them prefigured later, more famous characters, revealing that Segar's career was one of organic growth as he constantly experimented with themes and premises. For instance, in 1923 and 1924 Castor acquired a gamecock named Blizzard, who possessed nearly invulnerable strength and whose prowess led Castor to all sorts of competitions and gaming situations. At the end of the decade, Bernice the Whiffle Hen appeared in the strip, and her powers were more magical: by rubbing her head, Castor could foretell the future (and again was led to more sporting and gambling activities). It seemed only a logical next step to the creation of the famous Jeep, the orchid-eating creature of the fifth dimension. Today Jeep is remembered from Segar's work during the 1930s—after Popeye came on the scene and the strip was widely circulated—but his two predecessors were no less vital or versatile as characters. Actually, sequences during Blizzard's presence in *Thimble Theatre* are some of the most deliciously vulgar (in the true sense) and humorously violent in comic-strip history.

Likewise Popeye himself, whose entrance onto *Thimble Theatre*'s stage marked a turning point not in Segar's creativity but in the public's notice, was prefigured several times. Segar introduced a pop-eyed strongman named Hogan, who was simple, honest, and virtually indestructible, and whom Castor thrust into the prize-fight ring. Then Castor centered a new variety of schemes around the fighting prowess of a runtish strongman named Battling (Batt) McGnat, who also possessed a pop-eyed visage. When Popeye made his appearance, he was, of course, a sailorman, but Castor transformed him, too, into a prizefighter

for a couple of years. Segar as a cartoonist was obviously interested in perfecting comic devices and situations, not in rushing his paper actors across a stage spouting one-liners.

Popeye's debut was inauspicious, suggesting that Segar intended the sailor to be an incidental character. By 1929 the stories in *Thimble Theatre* had grown epic in length if not always in scope; one Sunday adventure, for instance, lasted more than two years. Popeye popped up in the middle of a lengthy adventure that saw Castor taking the Whiffle Hen to the mysterious Dice Island. Castor's objective was to use Bernice to foretell the immediate future at the gaming tables, and among his many obstacles was just reaching the dank haven. Popeye appeared in a dockside encounter that has become the comics' most famous riposte: "Hey there! Are you a sailor?" "Ja think I'm a cowboy?"

Popeye was hired to do twelve jobs on Castor's boat. He proved a resourceful ally when things grew dangerous and seemed indestructible, although he survived his initial brush with death only through the Whiffle Hen's magical powers. Popeye became romantically involved with Olive Oyl. He spoke in absurd malaprops, but always honestly, and made the faux pas a way of life. Despite an appearance as comely as a sailor's knot, he was generous, pure, and innocent. Popeye seized America's attention.

The bundle of comic contradictions in which Segar presented Popeye was classic; the sailorman was a descendant not only of Hogan the Fighter and Batt McGnat but of Paul Bunyan and Davy Crockett. No mean accomplishment among many was bringing Olive Oyl back to the daily *Thimble Theatre*. Castor had virtually taken over the dailies, and the Sunday page, launched in 1925, mostly

Thimble Theatre

POLLY AND HER PALS

Paw Sees Through the Whole Thing

JERRY ON THE JOB

Trapped

DUMB DORA

Her Head Always Registers Zero

THIMBLE THEATER

"Gobs" of Work

VANILLA AND THE VILLAINS

The Bugle Call

ABIE THE AGENT

Poor Women!

127

centered around a plump Olive and her boyfriends, chief among them being the hapless Ham Gravy. Popeye pushed him from the scene, and the relationship—sometimes tender, usually cockeyed—between Popeye and Olive became one of the strip's many propellants.

Segar and his editors discovered that Popeye was an incidental character who was not incidental to the public. For a full decade before Popeye's entry on January 17, 1929, *Thimble Theatre* grew in élan and comic virtuosity but remained an obscure feature seldom published outside the Hearst chain. (Once again William Randolph Hearst was key; *Thimble Theatre* was unprofitable, but Hearst proved to be the one fan who mattered.) After Popeye's entry, *Thimble Theatre*'s client list increased until it was one of America's most popular comic strips. For all the sailorman's popularity, however, the title of the strip remained the same.

Segar continued the elements of farce melodrama with a hilarious vengeance, consciously appropriating the clichés of stage and screen. He introduced new stories with buildups satirizing overblown movie trailers. He identified his characters as actors in a play, occasionally depicting the entire cast on a stage. Sometimes, in a narrator's voice, he parodied cliff-hanging promos. Once he ballyhooed an upcoming continuity: "More hot stuff than any mystery since the birth of fiction!!!" Best of all, considering his immense talent for characterization, he soon populated *Thimble Theatre* with a proverbial cast of thousands.

In an abrupt shift from the strip's comedy, the Sunday *Thimble Theatre* in 1933 embarked on a macabre suspense tale titled "Plunder Island." It was a long episode, lasting almost eight months, and featured a galaxy of singular characters like the murderous Sea Hag and the bizarre Alice the Goon. The Sea Hag became Popeye's nemesis, reappearing through succeeding years, and the Goon was so ghastly—she was an alien creature, naked except for fur, who spoke in oscillating lines—that young readers reportedly had nightmares from reading *Thimble Theatre*. The Goon eventually mutinied against the Sea Hag and became a sympathetic character.

Swee'Pea entered Popeye's life in a box, and after some custody problems that represent Segar's deference to pathos amid hilarity (he had finally caught up with Chaplin), the "orphink" became the sailor's juvenile sidekick. Bluto was one of many bone-crushing bad guys and appeared in *Thimble Theatre* for only one short episode. However, his character was appropriated by the story department at Fleischer Studios, and he became Popeye's permanent antagonist in hundreds of animated cartoons through the years. (Popeye became the comics' biggest merchandising success before *Peanuts;* animation was the most visible and, eventually, the most disappointing spin-off.) Eugene the Jeep became a fixture, as did Glint Gore, Tinearo, Joe Bilge, Prof. Kilph, Jabbo, Toar, Fadewell, Oscar, King Blozo of Nazilia (in a political satire of the 1930s), and, after editors reportedly requested that Popeye's rough edges be smoothed, the rakish Poopdeck Pappy. Like Bluto, the spinach-for-strength device was confined mostly to the animated cartoons, but grateful spinach growers erected a statue in Crystal City, Texas, in honor of Popeye, who saved their businesses during the Depression.

Thimble Theatre's most memorable character—outshining even Popeye—indeed, one of the comic strips' great creations, was J. Wellington Wimpy. He first appeared in the strip as a nameless, intermittent character, usually a referee

Segar's greatest dramatic sequence was the Sunday Plunder Island story of 1933–1934. There was humor, certainly, but mostly it was a chilling adventure of mysterious characters, deadly turns, and suspense.

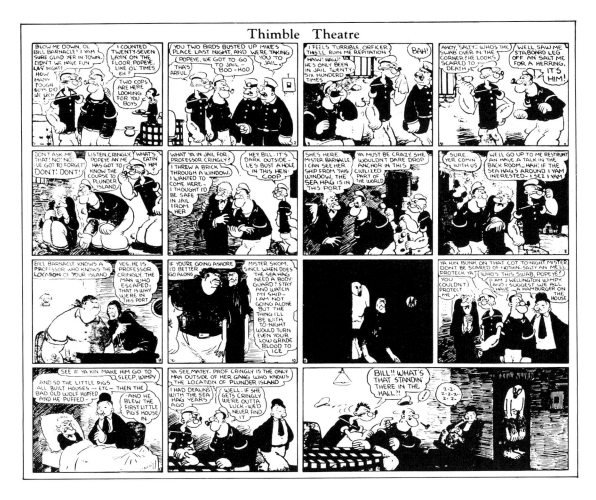

Most of the "adventures" in *Thimble Theatre* were of the farcical variety. The 1930s saw, in the comics, the widespread use of the humorous-continuity mode. Plot lines ran for months, with gags at each day's finale, and—in Segar's case—wildly delineated character types and absurd situations.

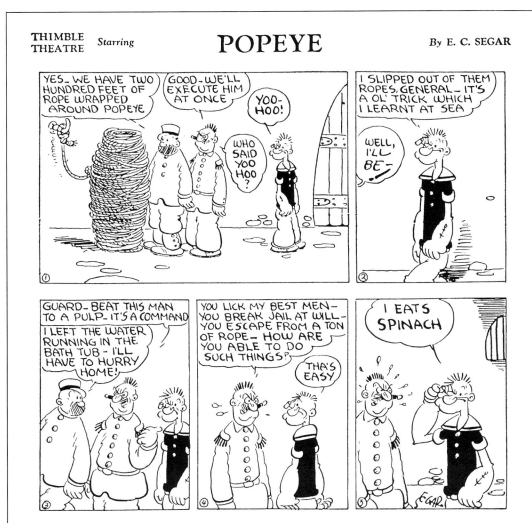

Here, for the first time on any stage, you see all the famous characters created by E. C. Segar for his hilarious comic "THIMBLE THEATER, Starring POP-EYE."

In this special drawing Mr. Segar has gathered his fantastic troupe together with appropriate atmosphere, so that his hosts of fans can recall the ludicrous personages who had their day in he spotlight, before POPEYE lumbered upon the stage and stole the show—to such a tumult of applause and guffaws that he has become a national comic idol.

But let the inimitable Segar recall some of the members of his cast in his own words:

"Olive Oyl was the first character to be born to 'Thimble Theatre.' Ham Gravy came about a minute later. I was eating a banana at the time and he was born with, or rather marked with, a nose not unlike that fruit. When ideas were scarce I could usually get up something on his beezer such as—'Is that your nose, or are you eating a cucumber?'

"Castor Oyl came next. He invented coal that would last forever. It was FIREPROOF. He also invented 'non-parkable chewing gum' and 'safety dynamite'—it wouldn't explode.

"After a while, with no characters between, came Bernice, the Whiffle Hen, hatched from an egg found in Africa by Castor's uncle. There are no male Whiffle Hens. The males are Whiffle Roosters.

"POPEYE arrived when Castor needed a sailor for the ship he'd bought. It was a perfectly good ship —not a hole in it except in the bottom where they wouldn't show. Castor saw a man leaning against a piling and called: 'Hey, are you a sailor?' The man answered, 'Ja mnk I was a cowboy?' It was POPEYE, and those were his first words. POPEYE kicked at having to do the work of the whole crew, but Castor fixed that. Says he: 'I'm only the captain, just one man, while you're first, second and third mate and the whole crew. You should feel proud.' POPEYE saw the logic and was okay."

in one of Popeye's prize fights, but soon he began to take on identifiable personality traits. He started to show corruption in his role as referee and would solicit bribes from the boxers, from folks in the audience, from anybody at all. Wimpy, and E.C. Segar, took off from there. Castor Oyl was eclipsed; never before or since in the comics has there been a character to rival Wimpy in outright, lowdown venality—or, ultimately, disarming appeal.

Wimpy was hardly a villain, and he never displayed the malevolence that Castor Oyl delighted in exercising, but perhaps it was due to lack of drive. Besides being worthless, corrupt, and disloyal, Wimpy was lazy. He was a placid island in the ocean of mayhem that Segar depicted in his boxing-ring sequences. His persona deepened and matured, however, when Segar shifted him to the lunch counter at Rough-House's cafe, where he graduated to being a moocher and a pest. Wimpy became a constant source of consternation to Popeye, his sometime defender, and of murderous impulses to the victimized cook and

The dramatis personae of *Thimble Theatre* are shown in this newspaper promotion piece from 1931.

Elzie Segar's *Thimble Theatre* was indeed a stage, even after its parodies of melodramas ceased. Seldom changing the point-of-view from middle-distance, Segar provided only the sparest of background props. His technique was manifested in inventive characterizations, like the rough but good-hearted Popeye, and the baseless scoundrel Wimpy, one of the most memorable figures in comics history. When no hamburgers were present, J. Wellington Wimpy proved capable of shameless scheming in pursuit of baked potatoes as well.

customers like George W. Geezil (who spouted comic Yiddish epithets like "You is flies in my zoup!").

In this character E.C. Segar maintained the comic-strip tradition of the comic obsession. Wimpy's two most evident compulsions were hamburgers and a proudly personal form of corruption, although he had other faults, such as mendacity, a desire for foul intrigue, and a joy in betrayal that was almost congenital. On the positive side, it must be noted that Segar bestowed upon Wimpy a unique form of universality: he would betray *anybody*. Avarice was not the darker side of his nature; it was his very soul. Wimpy was at once wimpy (another of Segar's contributions to the American language, *jeep* and *goon* being two others) and stubborn.

As a base fellow, Wimpy traveled in good company, for he shared traits with fiction's greatest rascals. Like Dickens's Micawber, he specialized in pretense and pomposity and affected flowery prose; both characters subscribed to the dictum that "something"—in Wimpy's case a hamburger would be sufficient, thank

you—"will turn up." Like Papageno in *The Magic Flute*, Wimpy was cowardly, unreliable, and selfish; one of his favorite invitations was "Let's you and him fight." Like the fat hypocrite Tartuffe, who resembled him physically, Wimpy mixed disloyalty with innovation; in one episode the Sea Hag bribed him with a hamburger to deliver Popeye's severed head, and Wimpy tried to negotiate for his big toe instead. In the movies, W.C. Fields's pettifogging persona and use of elegant monickers mirrored the Wimpy of *Thimble Theatre*.

As if Wimpy's actions were not enough—hugging some disgusted stranger, hopping atop the lunch counter, "borrowing" a starving man's hamburger—

Most vulnerable to Elzie Segar's jibes were members of his own cartooning profession—or, perhaps, himself in caricature. Several times through the years cartoonists were lampooned in *Thimble Theatre*.

The casual asides of Segar's characters were often funnier than the premises or main dialogue. Wimpy's conscience is clear only when "they cannot prove my guilt"; Popeye hates "dishonest crooks."

Segar adorned his classic character with some of the most memorable catch phrases in comics history. Thereby the cartoonist defined Wimpy's personality, infused his strip with more flavor, and provided a collection of one-liners that determined *Thimble Theatre*'s place in the consciousness and affections of its readers: "Thank you too much" . . . "I would gladly pay you Tuesday for a hamburger today" . . . "Come up to my house for a duck dinner; you bring the ducks" . . . "Will you join me in a lunch on you?" . . . "Would you happen to know where I might find one hundred thousand dollars?" . . . "Pal of mine" . . . "Nice weather, isn't it, we're having?" . . . "You must have me confused with somebody; my name is Jones, I'm one of the Jones boys" . . . "I'll have pickles, onions, and lettuce both on mine, please" . . . and so on.

Elzie Segar was the beneficiary of a syndicate system that sustained his unnoticed work for ten years, but he may have been victim of the system as well. In his early forties Segar developed leukemia, and according to cartoonist Jules Feiffer (who wrote the screenplay for the 1970s *Popeye* movie), Segar signed a deathbed contract revision that left his family without estate benefits. In the years after Segar's death in 1938, the syndicate's creative handling of the strip seemed even more reprehensible. Not only did it overlook mishandling by animation studios, but it allowed the strip itself to wither and die at the hands of available cartoonists. Routine handlers included Doc Winner, Tom Sims & Bela Zaboly, and Ralph Stein; brighter moments were provided by Bud Sagendorf (who had once assisted Segar) and Bobby London, former underground cartoonist who now draws the daily *Thimble Theatre*. Today Popeye and friends appear in only a handful of newspapers in America.

Yet the enduring appeal of Popeye, Wimpy, and Olive proves that a cartoonist can establish a significant presence in American culture—not only in the field of entertainment, but in belles lettres as well. E.C. Segar was devoted to dramatic and cinematic traditions, but did not allow the devices of parody and satire to become his own comic obsession. He fashioned a universe of memorable characters, a collection of sophisticated story lines, and a remarkable—for one cartoonist—variety of plot structures that went beyond parody and satire to include farce, melodrama, pathos, and even surrealistic absurdities.

All in a comic strip? About as likely as a theater the size of a thimble.

7

The cartoonist who is arguably the most gifted graphic artist in this book is certainly the least celebrated. Cliff Sterrett was a professional cartoonist for fifty-five years and devoted himself to one comic strip for all but nine years of that career. That his strip, *Polly and Her Pals*, was successful for forty-six years and that it ran, at its height, in more papers than *Krazy Kat* (for it is George Herriman with whom Sterrett must be compared) testify to his acceptance during his career. But Sterrett was never a major star in his chosen profession—even the reclusive Herriman received more attention—and he has been virtually ignored by historians. Cliff Sterrett was born of Scandinavian ancestry in the town of Fergus Falls, Minnesota, on December 12, 1883. He was educated in public schools there and in nearby Alexander and, like most cartoonists in this book, remembered drawing anything and everything from an early age. When he was eighteen years old, he moved to New York City, where he was enrolled at the Chase Art School for two years of study.

CLIFF STERRETT

1883-1964

On his twentieth birthday Sterrett secured a position in the art department of the *New York Herald*, where at first he executed border designs, decorations, and custom lettering for feature stories. He worked side by side with other cartoonists on the paper, including Winsor McCay, and eventually created four daily strips for the *Herald's* sister paper, the *Telegram*. All four—*Ventriloquial Vag*, *When a Man's Married*, *Before and After*, and *For This We Have Daughters*—ran simultaneously, but by 1911, when they were flourishing,

BEFORE AND AFTER

The genesis of Cliff Sterrett's countless dissections of domestic life and strife appeared in the *New York Telegram* in 1911.

daily cartoonists in New York were expected to maintain several running features. Rube Goldberg, on the *Mail*, was creating a sensation, and an example for his fellows, by maintaining several categories, themes, and characters.

At the end of 1912 Sterrett was hired away by the talent-hungry William Randolph Hearst, for whom he drew a variation of *For This We Have Daughters* called *Positive Polly*. The strip featured mother, father, family cat, and comely daughter Polly. The first Sundays were titled *Polly!* but daily and color versions eventually became known as *Polly and Her Pals*.

The theme of the strip was supposed to revolve around Polly, her boyfriends, and their social life. In this sense *Polly* pioneered a genre that was to be common, especially in the 1920s and 1930s: the "pretty girl" strip. There had been a few

Early *Polly* pages were like short stories, with elaborate setups and copious dialogue. Until very late in his career, Cliff Sterrett was given a full newspaper page on which to tell his tales. *(Facing page)*

Polly—Ashur's Clothes Drive Pa to Desperation

Gibson Girl types in the funnies before Polly (Gene Carr's *Lady Bountiful* is a prominent example), but Sterrett's strip was the first that dwelt on the social type and dealt with courtship.

Except, as soon as Sterrett established the genre, he demoted it. Polly was independent, leggy, and maintained her share of suitors, but gags on that theme became just one category among many in *Polly and Her Pals* through the years; in fact, Polly eventually was featured far less than her pals; that is, her family and relations. Paw Perkins became the de facto star, and episodes usually centered on his office affairs, card-playing cronies, and domestic squabbles.

Other cast members included Maw, whose common sense provided counterpoint to Paw's occasional stunts but whose strong will accorded opportunities

The short-story mode of the teens gave way in the 1920s to a streamlined form of storytelling in *Polly and Her Pals*. Many of Sterrett's gags became pantomimic, and it was at the time of this page (1927) that the cartoonist adopted surrealistic visual elements. *(Facing page)*

Eventually fantasy and allegory entered Polly's world—or rather Paw's world, for he and Kitty became the real stars of the strip. This remarkable Sunday ran on March 3, 1935.

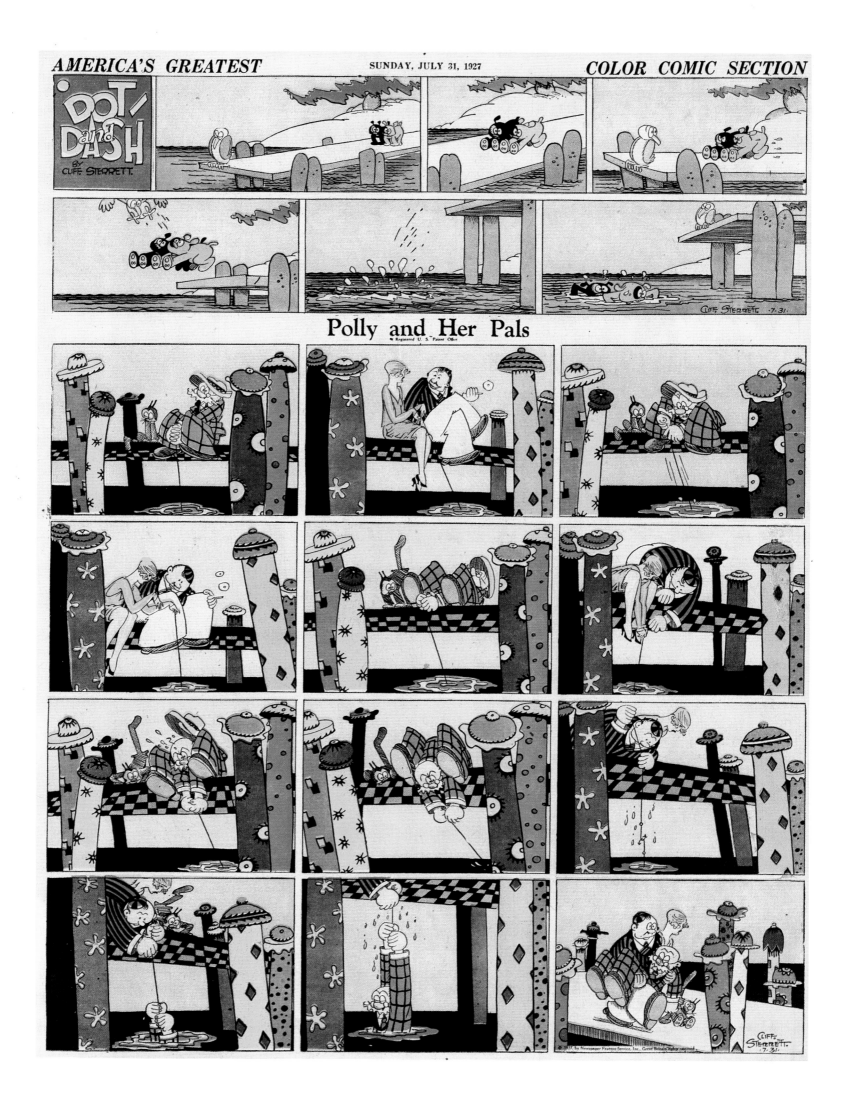

Polly and Her Pals

Polly--Ashur Has a Striking Idea.

for humor on her own. Ashur Earl Perkins was a scheming and dim-witted nephew. Carrie, a sister-in-law whose visit never ended, always had her brat, Gertrude, in tow for household mayhem. Whether in the Perkins's urban household or on rural retreats, the Oriental servant, Neewah, was Paw's constant foil. And then there was Kitty, a one-cat Greek chorus whose pantomimic reactions alone revealed turns in the plot.

In the middle 1920s syndicates started to require their cartoonists to divide their Sunday pages into unequal portions and to create a second strip on the top third of the newspaper page. (These "top strips" were mainly devised so that newspapers could boast of having, say, thirty-two comics each Sunday instead

Polly and Her Pals

The cityscapes in *Polly* were as distinctive, and as impressive, as *Krazy Kat*'s desert landscapes. (Above)

The cityscapes in *Polly* were as distinctive, and as impressive, as *Krazy Kat*'s desert landscapes. *(Above)*

Even when the gags revolved around Polly herself, the focal point was Paw and Kitty. *(Left)*

In *Dot and Dash* both theme and art could be surreal, but in *Polly* Sterrett cleverly mixed conventional—and hilarious—comedic situations with his individualistic artwork. *(Facing page)*

When Sterrett hit his stride with his unique graphics, nothing on the landscape was safe from portrayals by his pixilated pen—and it seemed that nothing on the landscape failed to conspire against Paw. *(Overleaf and page 145)*

of sixteen on the same number of pages.) Sterrett's contributions over the Sunday *Polly* were *Damon and Pythias* and later *Dot and Dash*, each being pantomime bits starring animals. Then—just as he had derived *Polly* from *For This We Have Daughters*—Sterrett dusted off the premise of *Before and After* and created *Sweethearts and Wives*, later called *Belles and Wedding Bells*, sometimes subtitled *And So They Were Married*. Basically the theme was romance after the blush fades from the rose. Polly's—or mostly Paw's—comic trials continued underneath each week, and in the dailies Sterrett enjoyed constructing humorous continuities. Thus *Polly and Her Pals* continued, appearing in fewer papers through the 1940s and 1950s, until it ended in 1958.

The cartoonist made it difficult for us to explore his life and work further. Unlike some of his fellows, he did not leap from feature to feature during his

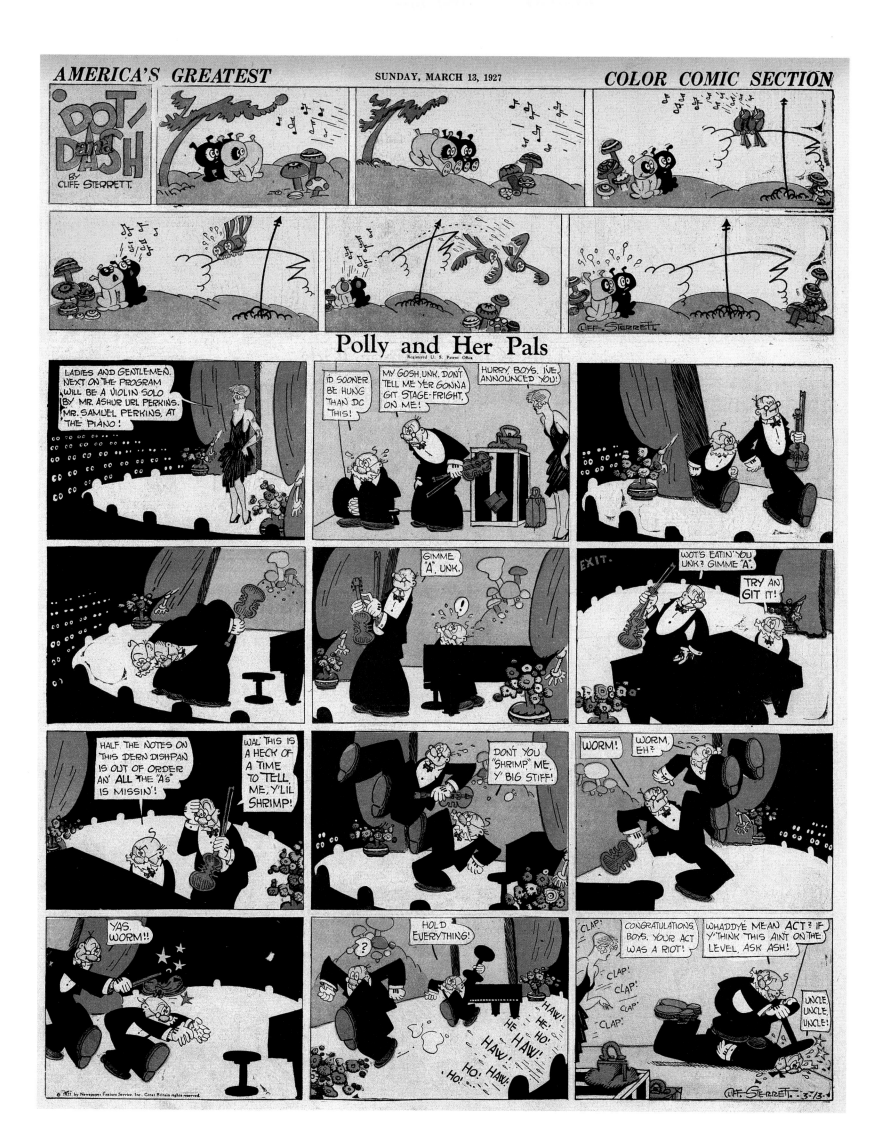

Polly and Her Pals

Polly and Her Pals

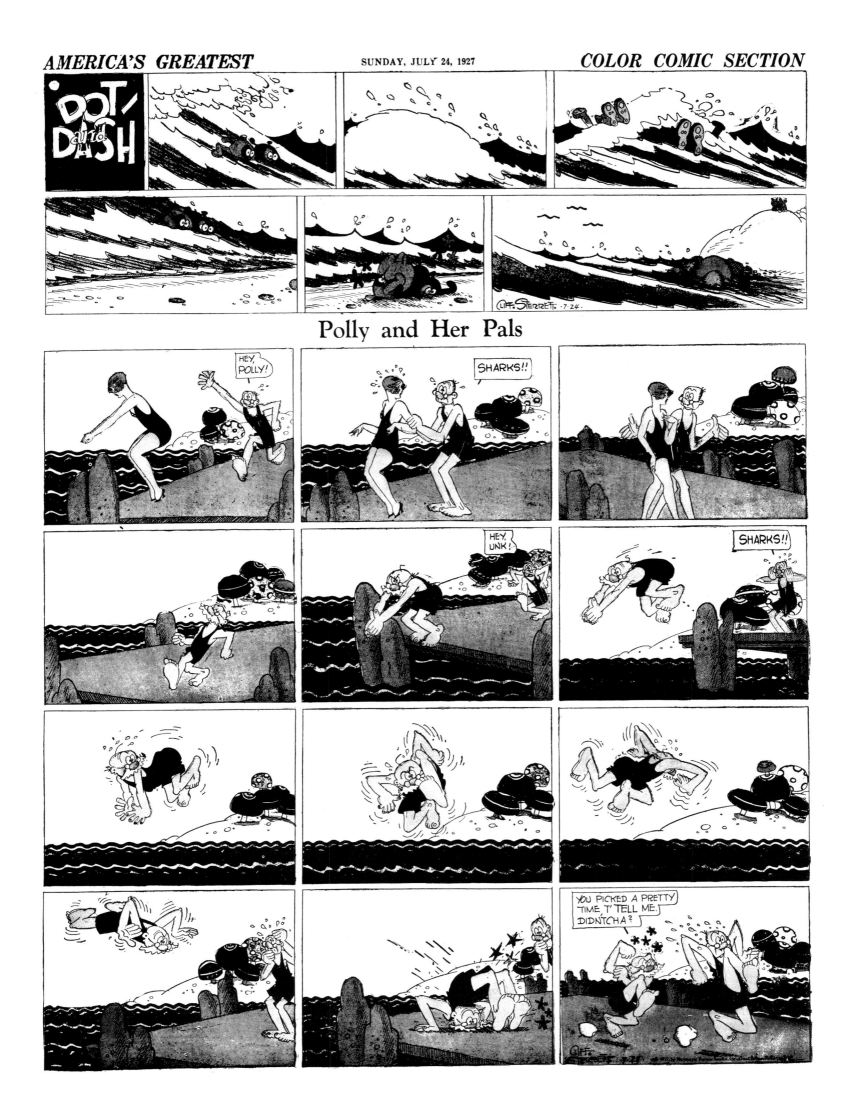

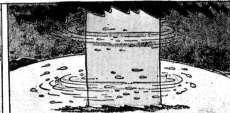

Polly and Her Pals

145

As Sterrett's artwork grew more abstract, his use of comic-strip conventions grew purer. In this page—without captions or balloons—readers can take for granted the proper passage of time between panels, can sense the moods and thoughts of Paw, and can share the exasperation of Paw, however exaggerated his situation is depicted here. In another cartoonist's hands the unorthodox visual elements might trip the reader's eye while advancing through the panels, but Sterrett integrated everything in his universe masterfully. *(Facing page)*

career, and he granted few interviews—sadly, it is not likely that many were requested of him. Little is known of his personal life. It seems he was a saddened man at the time of his death in 1964, having been predeceased by his wife and two children (his son, Paul, had been a composer and arranger of some repute, noted for his ability to play fourteen instruments and for his collection of vintage musical instruments).

It seems that Sterrett suffered from rheumatism and had periods when he did not draw his wonderful strip; it was in remarkably good hands during the

Polly and Her Pals

late 1930s and early 1940s, with Paul Fung on the dailies and Vernon Greene on the Sundays. Sterrett helped establish Ogunquit, Maine, as an artists' colony and for many many years spent half his time there among cartoonist friends like Rudolph Dirks, Gus Mager, Walt Kuhn, and Peggy Bacon. Rudy's son, John Dirks, remembers Sterrett as an amiable man and avid string-bass player who instigated impromptu musical ensembles at the colony.

Although *Polly* had its followers—perhaps cult would be a closer description—it was seldom merchandised or licensed. There was no *Polly* movie serial or radio show, and there are no *Polly* collectibles turning up today at antiques shows. Nevertheless Sterrett's classic strip earned its niche—quietly secure in the funny pages of its time and in comics history today—by dint of its graphic brilliance and Sterrett's astonishing creative audacity.

In visceral terms, Cliff Sterrett did things no other comic-strip artist ever did, or did so consistently. His panel arrangements, his colors, his striking lines, his playful treatment of reality, his teasing of readers' perceptions (a trick that can be done better in the comic strip than in any other medium, save perhaps animation)—all were handled in startling, innovative fashion week after week. Sterrett challenged the very landscape and won, as trademark images in *Polly* became patterned cityscapes, angular staircases, checkerboard house fronts, pixilated flowers and potted plants (Vern Greene recalled liking to draw Sterrett's flowers better than his characters), and so forth. There is no evidence that Sterrett followed any trends in any of the fine or popular arts (on the other hand, there is little evidence of any sort about him). Nevertheless his world seemed designed by cubists and his interiors borrowed from *The Cabinet of Dr. Caligari*.

Sterrett's artwork evolved, and—as happened with other comic strips through the years—*Polly* was actually several different strips. In the beginning the artwork was broad, almost crude; the balloons wordy; and the episodes like short stories. Construction was complicated, but Sterrett was definitely concentrating on story lines. By the early 1920s his artwork had become streamlined. Angular lines softened, backgrounds became simpler, and dialogue was more economical. In an apparent process of distillation, during his most brilliant period between 1927 and 1935, Sterrett drew many pantomimic Sunday pages. Some angularity returned to the artwork, and with it the unorthodox points of view, bold colors, generous utilization of comic-strip signs and symbols, and universal abstractions.

These abstractions were not only in the story lines so much as in the manner by which Sterrett depicted his scenes. George McManus, in *Bringing Up Father*, could "spot" large areas in black and devise visual abstractions, but his purpose was almost always decorative. Sterrett used black masses, observed painter Bernard Karfiol, to "represent a summer sky or midnight, a dark room or a surface of ice. In the [black-and-white] daily strips they lend a body and color to the *Polly* compositions that stands them out from a page full of comics. In the Sunday page they lend wealth to the colors, making them sparkle and sing." (Although Karfiol's observations were written for King Features promotion, they are nonetheless valid.)

Sterrett and *Polly* have been compared with Herriman and *Krazy Kat*. Both cartoonists dealt with abstractions, unconventional imagery, and even surrealism. It takes nothing from Herriman's achievements and contributions to note that Sterrett scaled similar artistic heights but set a path for himself that was

inordinately more difficult than Herriman's. In *Krazy Kat*, the universe was Herriman's to change or redesign or redirect at whim, and in fact readers expected the Kokonino landscape to change constantly. *Polly and Her Pals* indulged in similar imagery but in an extremely conventional setting and conservative theme. *Polly* was always an urban family strip. Gags were about bills, boyfriends, and missing collar buttons, not implied metaphysics.

Sterrett is clearly of Herriman's rank or above—except that superlatives are futile when assessing the handful of cartoonists who possessed a singular vision of life and reality and to whom God granted a special genius for relating that vision to us through comic strips.

Emerson said, "Great geniuses have the shortest biographies." Cliff Sterrett left few conventional footprints, but his comic-strip legacy is enormous and astounding.

8

As noted in the chapter on Elzie Segar, the continuity comic strip did not originate in the 1930s; it merely proliferated at that time. Loose, almost exclusively humorous continuities were present from the birth of the art form. The Yellow Kid embarked on a protracted trip around the world, as did Happy Hooligan and the Katzenjammer Kids. Little Nemo's dreams often continued from week to week, as did the adventures of Feininger's Kin-Der-Kids. The escapades of Mutt and Jeff, as well as their political lampoons, were informal continued episodes, and weeks-long stories can be found in such strips as Herriman's *Baron Bean*. All these ex-

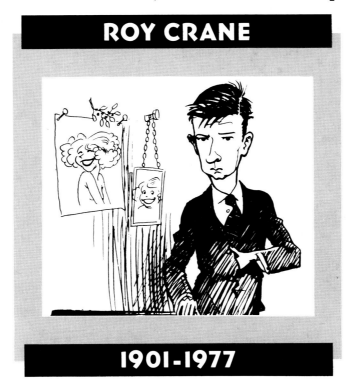

ROY CRANE

1901-1977

amples occurred be-fore 1920, and all stand apart from the group of strips that satirized theater and the movies, whose structure necessi-tated the continuity format. But virtually all were primarily humorous, leading to the question, Why did the comics take all of thirty years to develop the adventure genre? There are numerous possible answers, including the fact that the comics were intended primarily as children's entertainment and that the movies were becoming more mature. Certainly by the 1920s there was a need for thematic diversity, a need filled by Roy Crane. Although his individual approach presents no clues to the lack of adventure themes before the mid-1920s, it represents the exploration, experimentation, and vitality of such themes afterward.

Royston Campbell Crane was born in Abilene, Texas, on November 22, 1901, the only son of a local judge, and was raised in nearby Sweetwater. He evinced an early talent for drawing and at one time was encouraged by his father—at fifty cents per week—to keep an illustrated diary. The young Crane drew for his high school newspaper and held various local jobs. He dropped out of two colleges, Hardin-Simmons and the University of Texas (where his cartoons were picked up by the national magazine *College Humor*), and attended the Chicago Academy of Fine Arts for a few months. His teacher there was Carl Ed, who was drawing *Harold Teen* for the Chicago Tribune Syndicate.

Probably the most important part of Crane's training then took place. He became a hobo, riding the rails around America with another Texas boy, Les Turner, likewise an aspiring artist, then took a job as a seaman on a freighter. His work was as eventful as the rough seas he seemed to attract. (Once, stranded in Antwerp, too long on shore leave, he managed to catch his ship in England, only to nearly founder in storms crossing the Atlantic.) Very possibly it was his firsthand experience with somewhat exotic adventures that later fueled his creative wanderlust.

Disembarking in New York—it was 1922—Crane sought a more placid existence and secured a position in the art department of the *New York World*. It was the type of job held at one time by almost all of the day's successful new strip artists. In addition to doing spot drawings and decorations, the twenty-one-year-old cartoonist was invited to pencil the nationally popular Sunday page *The Man in the Brown Derby* for H.T. Webster, the famous creator of the classic Casper Milquetoast character. For Webster the arrangement allowed more time at bridge and golf; for Crane it was a chance to cut his eyeteeth on technique and deadlines. In his spare time he sold cartoons to *Judge* magazine (although he was never paid) and worked up samples for comic features of his own.

Crane's submissions were received with tentative interest by the Newspaper Enterprise Association, a syndicate that offered newspapers complete packages of features, including comics, instead of separate properties (it operates today on the same basis). The art director was a man named Charles N. Landon, remembered years later by Crane as a pipe-voiced man who favored selected sartorial elegance like celluloid cuffs and spats. Landon asked Crane if he had had any cartoon training, and the young man cited his stint at the Chicago Academy and the Landon Correspondence Course. During the teens almost every aspiring cartoonist subscribed to one of the many mail-order courses.

It so happened that the course's founder and the syndicate art director were one and the same man—a situation that was not coincidental. Through the years Landon had scooped up talent he discovered through his weekly lesson sheets, and it did his "school" no harm to list, in its advertisements, a surprisingly large number of graduates who swiftly secured professional assignments. Roy Crane, having somehow escaped Landon's eye the first time, was added to his list of conquests in 1924, when a new strip, *Washington Tubbs II,* was announced as one of NEA's bright new offerings.

In point of fact, *Wash Tubbs,* as the strip was soon called, was bright but hardly new. Crane was somewhat mystified that Landon mandated a theme about a shop clerk in humorous situations, because NEA had just introduced such a strip by George Swanson, called *Salesman Sam*. Either Landon was head-over-heels dippy for such a premise, or he wanted "Swan" and Crane to fight it out for the turf. Crane considered the turf hardly worth fighting for; from the start he yearned to do both continuity and adventure. Even while Landon continued

Roy Crane's foreign locales were the comic equivalents of Dean Cornwell's exotic illustrations in the magazines of the 1920s and 1930s. To the inviting artwork, however, Crane added the perfervid voice of the narrator. The splash lettering and exclamation points could practically be heard as well as read.

to impose the general-store setting, Crane sneaked in a mystery about strange voices from the stockroom and missing money. Within a year he was able to free Wash from the confines of small-town commerce. Things were never the same in *Wash Tubbs*—nor in the entire world of comic strips.

The first adventure sequence begins with Wash daydreaming about the South Seas, just as Crane himself, situated at NEA headquarters in Cleveland, was doing. A fortune-teller reveals to Wash that there are sunny islands and buried treasure in his future, and soon all the ingredients are in place. Crane's first adventure story was a foretaste of many to follow over the next few years, with colorful locales, beautiful girls, cliff-hanging mysteries, menacing bad guys, and lots of action. The formula was nothing new, really—countless dime novels and swashbuckling movies had plied the deathless themes—but it was new to comic strips and therefore seemed astonishingly fresh.

Crane brought a new sense of vitality to the comics in the way he constructed a strip. First, there was an overwhelming sense of fun in his work. Characters frequently reveled in their joy (and, similarly, villains were villainous to the nth degree), and there was a great deal of animation in his panels, with figures running and jumping out of borders, often right toward the reader. Crane's drawing style, which matured quickly, was a combination of the comic and the straight. His anatomical renderings were sure—and his women were particularly comely—but a simple, supple line kept the graphic effect essentially comic; in the beginning, at least, Crane constructed comic strips in the style of a humorous cartoonist, not a serious illustrator.

The cartoonist's own personality was a vital component of the strip also. Going a step beyond the melodramatic captions in *Hairbreadth Harry* and *Thimble Theatre,* Crane made the voice of *Wash Tubbs*'s captions more breathless than satiric. Captions, and to a lesser extent speech balloons, abounded with oversized words, open block lettering, and exclamation points.

This method of lettering, which Crane pioneered in the comics, fused the visual with the narrative. In Crane's hands, letters did not merely combine to form words. The very style of lettering suggested a mood; their display revealed a voice; even their size conveyed actual emotions. Previously in all of literature, sentences and paragraphs served these ends, but Crane made letters and individual words into *visual* elements that functioned in thematic and narrative ways. Pictures and words henceforth could serve cross-purposes, and new purposes, in comic strips.

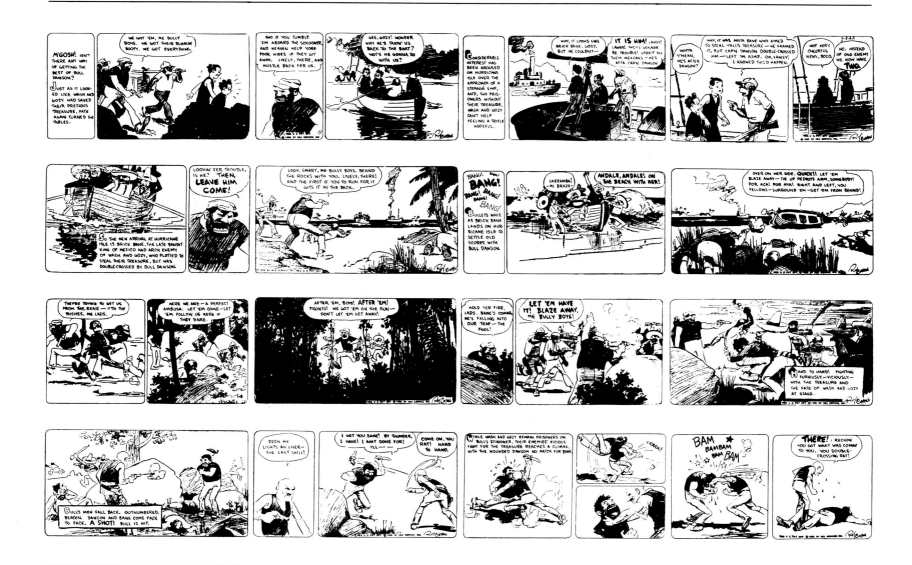

In his efforts to expand on this technique, Roy Crane also became the father of the sound effect in the comics. Onomatopoeia was strangely absent before Crane; flashes would be seen but explosions not heard. Sometimes cartoonists would indicate noise by stars or even exclamation points, but it took Crane again to fuse the physical imagery of words with their sounds. If sweat beads and motion lines could be symbols, why not the graphic approximations of sounds?

Why not, indeed. As always, Roy Crane raised the level of his experimentation to lofty heights. His sound effects remain the most distinctive in the comics, even after generations of other cartoonists. Charles Schulz recalls that when Crane drew a plane crashing into the water, it did not go "splash" but "ka-wump," with a juicy exclamation point. There were plenty of sound effects like "pow" and "blam" and "zing," but one of the most famous in *Wash Tubbs* was "lickety-whop!" which was onomatopoeia with a dose of moral suasion.

There was an élan to *Wash Tubbs* that made it the most extroverted of strips. Part and parcel of its movement, noise, and other enthusiasms was unrestrained physical adventure. For all its good humor, the strip's fights were the most brutal of any in the comics. The violence in, say, *Dick Tracy* or *Little Orphan Annie* was actually brief and very grim—quick dispatch often accentuated the grimness—and in a larger sense the overall mood in those strips was

A comic-tinged realism, joy unconfined, and brutal violence—Roy Crane combined the best of several worlds in creating his comic strips.

incipient violence. The overall mood in *Wash Tubbs,* conversely, was of good humor—even in the fights. They were rough-hewed, and sometimes featured actions (like kicks in the groin) that other comics never portrayed. But Crane infused his fights with a form of joyous physicality, and his readers would sometimes witness a brawl that lasted two weeks. Punching, kicking, wrestling, rolling, cheering from the sidelines, always with the narrator's voice providing colorful commentary—it was enthusiastic; it was fun; it was an adventure.

Many of these memorable fights did not have Wash as a combatant. He was diminutive and earnest, but no hero. With his oversized glasses he seemed to be a short Harold Lloyd, and comics historian Ron Goulart has noted how Wash seemed to reflect the type of 1920s leading man that Lloyd epitomized. He

Roy Crane can be seen as the father of the modern adventure strip, but his early preoccupations were, ironically, of rapidly anachronistic costume melodramas. In one stroke Crane depicts the horrors of war and comical overstuffed generals of silly kingdoms. But the world—and comic strips—would soon change.

needed sidekicks for his adventures around the globe, and for a while Crane provided a skinny fast-talker named Gozy, but ultimately he was too much like a tall Wash Tubbs and too glib to provide decent counterpoint.

In 1928 another sidekick presented himself. *He* was a brawler, a good guy with a very shady past, a character who was destined to take over the strip. Captain Easy was a true soldier of fortune—the adventurer that Wash Tubbs

*R*oy Crane's women were among the prettiest ever to be drawn in comic strips.

*A*nd his villains were among the meanest ever to appear in comic strips. Bull Dawson, the constant nemesis of Wash and Easy, was a classic character, the manifestation of evil.

himself always dreamed of being. Crane had found the perfect combination. The mock hero was teamed with the authentic, the cut diamond with the rough, the picaresque with the real.

Wash's early adventures always had a sense of the picaresque about them, and Crane's cartooney style nestled the violent fights and brutal villains in settings that seemed to come from Anthony Hope novels or Victor Herbert operettas. When Captain Easy established himself as a character, the story lines eventually became more realistic, as did Crane's drawing style. Crane began to experiment with the very paper he drew on, employing for a while in the late 1920s the grained board that editorial cartoonists used. He applied grease crayon to the paper's surface, creating moods through tones, shades, and textures never before seen in comic strips.

In the 1930s Crane experimented further, with a new paper called Craftint, a drawing board that contained invisible patterns made visible by chemicals applied with a brush or a pen. Crane seized upon the duoshade pattern that contained both parallel lines and mechanical crosshatch. Masterfully, he began achieving stunning effects with Craftint, depicting depths of perspective and evocations of atmosphere through hazy background renderings.

As Roy Crane was capturing the attention of his peers, Captain Easy was stealing the show from Wash Tubbs. In 1933 he was given his own Sunday page—without Wash—entitled *Captain Easy, Soldier of Fortune.* The settings were the same exotic locales, but Easy, the lantern-jawed, hook-nosed loner, eschewed the comic touches that Wash Tubbs provided. (The pair continued to co-star in the dailies, and in the 1940s the strips were united as *Captain Easy* daily and Sunday.)

Always looking for more worlds to conquer, Crane explored wondrous graphic possibilities in the *Easy* Sunday page. He chose bold primaries as his colors and made full use of his patented splash lettering. He ignored the conventions of page design and drew vistas and panoramas galore. Given a full newspaper page to work with, Crane fashioned unorthodox panel shapes, circular frames, dropped borders, and huge vignettes sometimes filling half the page. He used balloon placement, patterned panel design, and colors to lead the reader's eye through his compositions. Each Sunday his comic strip was not just a succession of panels but a unified statement, as impressive in its whole as in its parts.

Then in 1937 a change occurred that ruptured Roy Crane's love affair with the Sunday comics page and quietly infected much of the creativity that was, up till that time, the hallmark of many color comics. The syndicates adopted a practice that enabled them to offer their Sunday pages in convertible formats—full pages, half pages, and sometimes (increasingly) third pages. They required their strip cartoonists to design pages with panels that were expendable, whole rows that could be dropped with no offense to the remaining story line. Worst of all in Crane's case, the cartoonists had to use a template to design their pages. So that a newspaper could convert a full-page strip to a half page, the panels had to have a standard dimension—usually little boxes. The verve disappeared from comics like *Captain Easy,* whose spirit had been reflected in its design. The strictures were ostensibly due to paper shortages, but clearly were devised instead to accommodate advertisers, and Roy Crane was disgusted.

He surrendered the Sunday *Easy* to his assistant—his boyhood friend Les

Following (on pages 158, 159, and 161) are the opening pages of the first *Captain Easy* story, done in 1933. Roy Crane in this period proved himself an absolute master at establishing a story line and setting, varying the multiple points of view, moods, and premises and designing an interesting graphic architecture of his Sunday page via floating captions, accented panel borders, and unconventional frames.

CAPTAIN EASY
SOLDIER OF FORTUNE
by ROY CRANE

SEVEN CENTURIES AGO GHENGIS KHAN AND HIS HORDE OF SAVAGE MONGOLS OVER-RAN ALL CHINA.

IT WAS HIS BOAST THAT WHERE ONCE HIS FOOT HAD TROD NO BLADE OF GRASS EVER GREW AGAIN.

TIMID YANG PU LI, GOVERNOR OF THE RICH PROVINCE OF GUNGSHI, SICKENED OF SUCH BLOODTHIRSTY CONQUESTS.

BY HIS ORDER, THE MOUNTAIN TRAIL TO THE OUTER WORLD WAS DESTROYED.

AND FOR SEVEN CENTURIES, THE PROVINCE OF GUNGSHI HAS REMAINED HIDDEN, ALMOST FORGOTTEN, BEHIND THE SNOW-CLAD PEAKS OF CENTRAL ASIA.

THIS LOWLY TRAMP WILL GATHER A FEW CHOICE PEBBLES FOR POCKET CHANGE.

EVERY FEW YEARS, SOME DARING TRADER RETURNS WITH AMAZING STORIES OF STREETS PAVED WITH GOLD....

AND FEROCIOUS GIANTS TWELVE FEET TALL!!

MEANWHILE, CAPTAIN EASY, HERO OF THE RETREAT FROM JEHOL, IS TRYING TO GET OUT OF THE CHINESE AIR CORPS.

IT'S THIS BLASTED INACTIVITY OF LATE, SUH! I CAN'T STAND IT!

THE EAGLE PREFERS THE PERILS OF THE DISTANT HEAVENS TO THE COMFORTS OF A SHELTERED CAGE, EH?

EXACTLY, SUH, EXACTLY.

AND YOU, O RECKLESS YOUTH, WILL FLY TO THE LOST PROVINCE AS A SPY OF CHINA.

EASY'S GENERAL IS DELIGHTED...HE TELLS OF THE LONG LOST PROVINCE OF GUNGSHI, AND HOW CHINA, STRIPPED OF MANCHURIA, IS ANXIOUS TO REGAIN IT.

GREAT! WHEN DO I START?

AT ONCE! BUT I WARN YOU, MY FRIEND, THE MISSION IS EXTREMELY DANGEROUS.

NEXT WEEK: THE LOST PROVINCE OF GUNGSHI.

CAPTAIN EASY
★ SOLDIER OF FORTUNE ★
EASY by ROY CRANE

TWO THOUSAND MILES TO CHINESE TURKESTAN, ALMOST TO PERSIA, EASY FLIES. THE COUNTRY GROWS WILDER AND WILDER.

CURIOUS DESERT PEOPLE WHO HAVE NEVER BEFORE SEEN A PLANE, CROWD AROUND HIM AS HE REFUELS FOR THE FINAL HOP.

THEN OVER SNOW-CLAD MOUNTAINS FOUR MILES HIGH, AS A SPY OF CHINA, INTO A LAND UNSEEN BY WHITE MEN SINCE THE DAYS OF MARCO POLO.

SUPERSTITIOUS PEASANTS THERE ARE HORROR-STRICKEN AT HIS ROARING APPROACH.

MORE THAN ONCE HE IS FIRED UPON

FISHERMEN, ON AN INLAND SEA, LEAP OVERBOARD IN TERROR.

AN ENTIRE CITY IS THROWN INTO A PANIC.

EASY, EAGER TO EXPLORE THIS STRANGE AND HOSTILE CITY AFOOT, FLIES OFF IN SEARCH OF A SAFE LANDING PLACE.

HOLY MEN, THINKING THAT A DRAGON DEVIL HAS COME TO DESTROY THEM, BEAT HUGE DRUMS TO FRIGHTEN HIM AWAY.

WOMEN AND CHILDREN LIGHT BONFIRES AND SHOOT FIRECRACKERS. SCREAMING WARRIORS CLATTER THEIR SWORDS ON EVERY ROOF TOP. THE DIN IS TERRIFIC!

© 1933

NEXT WEEK: EASY'S PLANE IS DESTROYED.

Turner, by then a respected illustrator—and concentrated once again on the daily adventures. Late in his life Crane wrote, "If I had it to do over, I'd never do a Sunday. It's the straw that breaks backs." He was referring to the grind of doing seven strips a week, but he was always bitter about the creative playground that was taken from him.

It possibly was his old creativity and wanderlust that prompted another departure in 1943. This time the departure was from NEA and *Captain Easy*. Like so many comic-strip masters before him, Crane was lured to the Olympian confines of the Hearst organization. For King Features—and for ownership of his creation and editorial freedom—he developed a new comic strip. *Buz Sawyer* was the title and the lead character, a Navy aviator in the thick of World War II.

During the salad days of *Wash Tubbs*, the venal nemesis of Easy had been Bull Dawson, a chillingly believable villain, but for the most part, characters with names like Hudson Bey peopled places like the Kingdom of Kandelabra. With the approach and outbreak of World War II, however, such relics of classic romance adventures became instantly obsolete. Coping with a changed world, Crane had Easy join the FBI, then become a real captain in the service; Wash Tubbs, meanwhile, got an office job and married the boss's daughter. Eventually, however, Crane seemed to decide that if reality was the order of the day, he would create a brand-new adventure strip instead of gutting his old one.

Buz Sawyer was drawn more realistically than *Captain Easy* and certainly was less cartooney than *Wash Tubbs*. Buz was more handsome than Easy—and

Roy Crane was a master draftsman to begin with, but when he began using Craftint paper, he elevated comic art to new graphic and expressionistic heights. Textures, patterns, and photographic realism complemented his expansive storytelling layouts.

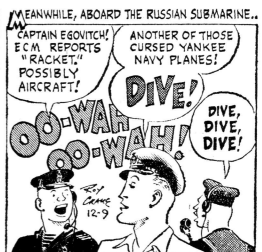

CAPTAIN EASY

SOLDIER OF FORTUNE

by ROY CRANE

HIGH ON THE FACE OF A MOUNTAIN, EASY FINDS A SAFE HIDEAWAY FOR HIS PLANE.

WHAT A BREAK! NOBODY WITHIN MILES

HE SURVEYS THE SURROUNDING PLAINS WITH SATISFACTION......

AND CHANGES INTO HIS DISGUISE, CONCEALING PISTOLS, DAGGERS, AND TEAR-GAS BOMBS ABOUT HIM.

FOLLOWING THE NARROWING LEDGE PAST NESTS OF SCREAMING VULTURES....

HE MANAGES, AT LAST, TO REACH THE FOOT OF THE PRECIPICE.

AND STARTS OUT AFOOT, A SPY IN A STRANGE AND MYSTERIOUS LAND, TOWARD THE WALLED CITY, TWENTY MILES DISTANCE.

WITHOUT ATTRACTING ANY ATTENTION, HE FALLS IN WITH A CARAVAN.

AND, WITH IT, SLIPS UNNOTICED THRU THE HIGH, FORBIDDING GATE OF THE CITY ITSELF.

HE IS DELIGHTED AT HIS AMAZING SUCCESS. BUT LITTLE DOES EASY REALIZE THAT THREE WAR SCOUTS, ATOP THE MOUNTAIN, HAVE WATCHED HIS EVERY MOVE.

NOR DOES HE REALIZE THAT AT THE VERY MOMENT, HIS PLANE IS A MASS OF CRUMPLED WRECKAGE.

NOR HAS HE ANY WAY OF KNOWING THAT THE HUGE ASIATIC, JUST BEHIND HIM, IS ONE OF THE SAME SCOUTS.

NEXT WEEK: THE GREAT MOGUL

clearly blander. A humorous element remained, however, in the person of Roscoe Sweeney. During the war the buddies fought together, but afterward Buz starred in the dailies, continuing to defend democracy, working for the CIA, traveling to locales like Vietnam. Roscoe took over the Sunday page, which was purely humorous—in fact, filled with broad slapstick.

Crane's *Buz Sawyer* was one of the finest of all adventure continuity strips. Its story construction was solid, and Crane maintained many of his finest traditions—raucous fights, taut suspense, and blaring headline-flavored captions. The strip's particular excellence, though, was in its artwork, which Crane continually refined to higher levels of illustrative panache. Invariably using Craftint, he depicted the bright glare of snowcapped mountains and burning deserts and the steamy environs of jungles.

Eventually Crane passed *Buz Sawyer* along to his assistants, writer Ed Granberry and Crane clone Hank Schlensker, who had each worked on the strip for years and who were to sign it as collaborators after Crane's death in 1979. An ulcer condition, and possibly creative burnout, finally slowed Crane's enthusiasm. Les Turner had inherited *Easy* and infused it with his own brand of adventure, alternating between the rough-and-tumble, romance, and inspired farce.

The humor that always underpinned *Captain Easy* was absent from the adventurous *Buz Sawyer*. So Roy Crane preserved his affinity for the comic in the Sunday version of *Sawyer*, starring Roscoe Sweeney. Sweeney had been Buz's Navy sidekick—and comic relief—in the initial Sawyer episodes during World War II.

The evocation of a presence, whether in high-adventure action scenes or exotic locales, continued to be Crane's forte through the years. Additionally, he was the master of the caption in comic strips; running text could be mundane or superfluous, but Crane—whether comic and breathless in *Wash Tubbs* or savage and taut in *Captain Easy* or grim and documentary in *Buz Sawyer*—made the narrator's caption vital in a manner that other cartoonists didn't achieve.

It was World War II, as well as the Cold War that followed, that changed the direction of Roy Crane's work. Many comic strips suffered during the 1940s because their characters and themes were sublimated to the war effort—a noble cause but one that did violence to the special and, it was proved, fragile worlds the cartoonists had created. After cartoon characters had fought in the anti-Nazi underground, it seemed forever impossible for them to say (as Wash Tubbs once had), "Oboy! Oboy! We're off to Pandemonia for adventure!" And perhaps it was equally impossible for newspapers to offer such fare to a postwar new world facing the grim prospect of an atomic age. *Buz Sawyer,* for all its simultaneous solidity and verve, became a recruiting poster for the military, whereas *Wash Tubbs* had been a travel poster for imaginative romance.

Because of the times he lived in, Roy Crane had at least two cartooning careers, two "periods," and he varied his approaches constantly. No one drew a better picaresque adventure strip, and no one drew a better international-intrigue adventure strip. In his remarkable career he was a master not only of storytelling but of the art form, developing expressive techniques and a whole dictionary of conventions and signs for future strip artists to employ and somehow, if they can appropriate a measure of Crane's innovative genius, build upon.

9

On the most superficial of levels, it can be said that there were other cartoonists who drew with more verve and whose strips exuded a more visceral élan or virtuosity. Yet Harold Gray, in *Little Orphan Annie,* mastered every element of comic-strip construction and expression as no one else before or since. Behind the flinty, idiosyncratic façade of Annie's black-and-white world (a description that applies to both the graphic and thematic elements) was a strip as vibrant, innovative, and worthy of study as any in the history of the

HAROLD GRAY

1894-1968

comics. For decades *Little Orphan Annie* dominated readers' polls in spite of frequent criticism of everything from Gray's stolid artwork, to his political views, to the ways in which "Daddy" Warbucks treated his de facto ward. Many critics missed — although millions of readers, perhaps by instinct, did not—the superb sense of craft that permeated *Little Orphan Annie.* One of the major traits that set Harold Gray apart from his contemporaries was his solitary individuality. Milton Caniff's work on *Terry and the Pirates,* for instance, could serve as a textbook on comics technique, and indeed a whole generation of cartoonists adopted his conventions, but for all of Gray's quality and popularity, he left no "school" as his legacy. Like George Herriman, Walt Kelly (*Pogo*), and a select group of geniuses, Harold Gray seized the opportunities afforded by comic-strip expression and fashioned an intensely personal statement.

Harold Lincoln Gray was born on January 20, 1894, on his parents' farm in Kankakee, Illinois. He grew up there and on a farm near Chebanse, Illinois, and on another farm in West Lafayette, Indiana. Not far from the last homestead was Purdue University, from which Gray was graduated in 1917 with a degree in engineering. Another Purdue alumnus was the unofficial dean of the midwestern school of cartooning—specializing in gentle humor and homespun themes—John T. McCutcheon of the *Chicago Tribune*, and in 1917 young Harold Gray sought his advice. McCutcheon recommended Gray for a job on the *Trib*'s art staff, but since there was no available opening a position as cub reporter was offered and accepted.

His eye on the prize, Gray soon moved into the art department, working on all manner of newspaper assignments—decorations, photo retouching, and the like—interrupted only by six months as a bayonet instructor during World War I. In 1920 he worked as a freelance illustrator but then capitalized on a *Tribune* association and became assistant to Sidney Smith, creator of the wildly successful marital farce and sometime melodrama *The Gumps*. Gray worked on the animated cartoons starring Smith's characters and also lettered and drew backgrounds for the newspaper strip.

The heady atmosphere of the *Tribune* art department, and more likely the heady news of Smith's million-dollar contract signed in 1922, prompted Gray to submit his own strip concepts to "Captain" Joseph Medill Patterson, cousin of *Tribune* publisher "Colonel" Robert McCormick and publisher of the *Trib*'s cousin newspaper, the New York *Daily News*. Patterson's Tribune-News Syndicate was challenging Hearst with such popular features as *The Gumps, Harold Teen,* and *Winnie Winkle*.

According to legend, one submission intrigued Patterson: a strip about a little gamin that would provide both laughs and tears. Little Orphan Otto—so goes the story—was the character's name, and Patterson offered one adjustment: "He looks like a pansy. Put skirts on the kid." And thus Little Orphan Annie (with a debt to "Little Orphant Annie," a poem by Hoosier poet James Whitcomb Riley) was born. Her coming-out was on August 5, 1924.

It seems clear that, at least in the beginning, *Little Orphan Annie* was designed as if by formula. Annie, as orphan, could easily evoke chuckles or sympathy as needed. Her situation enabled Gray to change her locale at will, with little investment in new characters or premises and less explanation. It was thought that if nasty "home" administrators and cruel foster parents would not take Annie in, readers surely would.

In the mid-1920s the comics were experimenting with new themes. *Wash Tubbs,* by Roy Crane, was certainly light in tone but was utilizing adventure. George Storm, in *Phil Hardy* and *Bobby Thatcher,* depicted kidnapping and rough violence. Other strips explored adaptations of classic literature and focused on Horatio Alger themes. With *Little Orphan Annie* Harold Gray occupied himself with melodrama. It had served *The Gumps* well for occasional story lines and was clearly popular with the movie-going public of the day.

In fact, Annie, who was evidently six to ten years old, bore a slight resemblance to Mary Pickford, whose stock-in-trade seemed to be vulnerable-orphan roles. She may have had Pickford's demure looks, but Annie also, from the first week, had a strong left hook (as Gray was fond of describing her essence and attitude). She was cast in pathetic situations, but Providence, friends, and grit—mostly grit—saved her time after time. Annie could outwit her "protectors," flatten

Annie was to escape many a situation, flee many an oppressor, and start walking along many unknown roads. But this early example (1925) finds her leaving "Daddy" Warbucks, and the cause is his shrewish wife. Warbucks, meant to be an incidental character, returned to the strip, but his wife never did.

bullies, climb down drainpipes, and escape into invariably dark and stormy nights. What preserved the pathos and ensured her ultimate growth into adolescence was her constant companion, the mute, cute doll, Emily Marie. In short order Annie lost the doll—and, as it turned out, her emotional adolescence—and acquired Sandy the dog, loyal companion and silent confidant.

She also acquired a friend. It seems probable that Gray and Patterson originally planned for Annie *never* to form permanent attachments, at least with humans; but comics, good comics, have a way of developing organically. The very first story finds Annie being placed in a mansion owned by Mr. and Mrs.

Warbucks. The wife is an icy snob, but Mr. Warbucks is a diamond in the rough—a henpecked regular Joe who, in spite of his apparent windfall of riches and his wife's social pretensions, walks around his opulent home in shirtsleeves and suspenders. He and Annie are kindred spirits, and after episodes revolving around divided loyalties and assorted faux pas, Annie moves on.

But she also moves back; the chemistry is compelling between the impoverished young orphan and the burly millionaire. Their relationship not only continues but matures in matters basic to the strip's premise. Soon "Daddy" Warbucks is not an empty-eyed recollection of Jiggs (from *Bringing Up Father*) but a friend, protector, inspiration, and touchstone. Eventually he assumes mythic proportions in the strip.

The oval, open eyes of Little Orphan Annie are an emblem of other conventions. One critic suggested that expressionless eyes obliged readers to provide their own emotions in different story situations. But, in fact, Gray infused the circlets with subtle expression and made much of little. In a larger sense the famous eyes were symbols of the bleak space they observed and in which Gray placed his characters in a spirit of foredoom; they also were part of a primitivistic aspect in the artwork of the strip. In the beginning *Little Orphan Annie* appeared crude, but soon Gray's visuals were to transform themselves into a gallery of icons. Indeed he was to become the comics' great expressionist, with every graphic element reflecting—even manifesting—moods, currents, and fears.

Into the early 1930s Gray followed a general pattern in which the daily episodes were continuities and dwelt on melodrama—mild adventures, escapes from various nasties, encounters with folks more impoverished or less resourceful than Annie—and the Sunday pages were usually unrelated humorous vignettes or attempts at such. The artwork *was* awkward at first, with clumsy backhand lettering, rough crosshatching, and a false sense of animation.

But influences were at work, and the simple formula was becoming obsolete in a way that Captain Patterson—and probably Gray himself, at the beginning—could not have envisioned. What at first seemed like wordiness took on the aspect of soliloquy and sometimes sermon or editorial. What could have devolved into endless stock situations or stereotyped relationships between Annie and her protagonists or antagonists blossomed into hyperrealistic encounters and exchanges. Gray's artwork matured into a leaden though handsome style that reflected both his prose and his overarching premises. Gone were the stories of the 1920s in which Annie befriended baby bears and miniature elephants and briefly became a movie star; in the 1930s she met smugglers, avaricious plutocrats, and venal labor agitators.

What also changed, of course, was America. In the 1930s the Depression was exacting its cruel toll on millions. Gray had used his strip for observations on life, responsibilities, conduct, and similar topics, and his views were consistent with an old-school, native American philosophy whose tenets included the Protestant work ethic and mind-your-own-business. The Depression did not change Gray's philosophy; it merely intensified his mission to proclaim it. It also animated and accelerated the structure of Gray's work, for during the 1930s *Little Orphan Annie* adopted its definitive form—a very different formula—wherein the totality of elements, both visual and thematic, served ends that were personal and philosophical—and were often attacked as merely political.

Who's afraid of Virginia Woolf? Harold Gray employed the device of the interior monologue from contemporary fiction and drama, where Woolf, Dreiser, Pirandello, and Joyce used it to great effect.

Harold Gray was no voice crying in the wilderness, no lonely crusader (he detested reformers and never saw himself in that role); America took his strip, and his message, to heart. Annie's homilies and examples of self-reliance and realistic optimism struck a chord with millions of readers who formed a fanatical and loyal corps of followers. He achieved something remarkable in the strip: a personalized creation in which his own voice obviously predominated, yet one that featured a succession of characters and situations so vivid as to move

169

Annie was indomitable. When the richest, most powerful man in the world lost his stuff, Annie redoubled hers. As Harold Gray molded his strip and his universe, Warbucks became mythic though mortal, but Annie became metaphoric—and eternal.

Critics decried a supposed plutocratic cast to the stories in *Little Orphan Annie*, but there were countless attacks on the moneyed classes and as many "sermons" on charity. They were messages America needed to hear in both the 1920s and the 1930s. *(Facing page)*

Harold Gray demonstrates that violence does not have to be florid nor tragedy graphically detailed to be effective.

adherents to tears and detractors to impotent fury over events in the "lives" of mere paper actors.

Annie's audience affirmed its loyalty by supporting a wide array of permutations. There were at least two *Little Orphan Annie* hit songs; several movies and movie serials; a very popular and long-running radio show sponsored by Ovaltine; many reprint books; a line of toys and games; and various mugs and decoder rings that survive today as collectibles. During the 1930s newspaper polls always placed the strip in the nation's top five, and often first, in popularity.

More permanent cast members appeared. As "Daddy" Warbucks was transformed from a mere rich man to the wealthiest (and most just) man on earth, and as his power became synonymous with righteousness, aspects both mythic and fantastic entered the strip. Mysterious factotums appeared in the persons of the Asp, a deadly Burmese, and Punjab, a giant Sikh possessing magical powers. One of the most intriguing characters in all the comics was Warbucks's friend Mr. Am, who claimed to have lived for millions of years. Am was the repository of a worldview that seemed variously wise, cynical, and pixieish, the result of his having seen countless civilizations rise and fall even before Eden. Am might have been the symbol of an up-to-date Santa Claus with his full white beard, or perhaps God himself (from the Old Testament name "The Great I Am"), or, most likely, Harold Gray himself at moments when even Annie would have trouble uttering his observations.

Al Capp, while an admirer of Gray's craft and techniques, once remarked that the figures in *Little Orphan Annie* had "all the vitality of Easter Island statues." The point has validity, but Gray knew, as a comic-strip expressionist, what he was doing. The stolid figures are functional reflections of the inevitable shadows, the omnipresent open doorways to inevitably dark rooms, the skies that, as critic Donald Phelps has noted, seem less like openings than oppressive ceilings. Deliberate figures and frozen backgrounds—which always seem like friezes rather than animated settings—set a mood. It is a mood of overall, and overwhelming, tension.

There are forces at work in Annie's world, and in Gray's as he saw it, and many of them are menacing and somber. These moods were stars of the strip as surely as Sandy was—and, like Sandy, they were constant companions and usually silent. The moods, seldom broken, were like black holes, absorbing all other moods and emotions, almost absorbing light itself. Gray did not trust society or organizations, and never conceded that human nature was capable of significant reform. If life held the promise of danger, then every aspect of everyday life in his comic strip would reflect it clearly.

Does Annie change locale? The cities and rural areas she graces seem like cold, interchangeable tableaux behind her, reinforcing her isolation. Do fights or gunshots come as denouements in continuities? Gray's violence is usually understated—off-panel, perhaps—a puff of smoke instead of a flashy, loud discharge, a fight, but with speedy dispatch. There is never the traditional release that such elements are supposed to bring to stories. The tension remains, still forbidding, and triumphant.

In this regard, Harold Gray and Roy Crane were opposites. Crane would draw a fight in *Wash Tubbs* that continued for two weeks; but Gray rarely drew two consecutive *panels* of violence. And Crane, the father of onomatopoeia in

the comics (*Pow! Bam! Whop!*), realized elements of violence differently from Gray, who usually made his violence silent—and grimmer—certainly uglier, even when justified. Both cartoonists were in command of their singular techniques, and both made significant statements.

Gray was also a master of characterization. His players were not etched in subtlety, as were the multifaceted players in, say, Milton Caniff's *Terry and the Pirates.* They were more like the characters in Chester Gould's *Dick Tracy,* either good or bad, and nuance was not attempted; Gray and Gould were expressionists, and their goal was to reflect their worldview through every element, from background props to characters' names and faces.

Harold Gray displayed an affinity with John Bunyan as he created and named characters. As in *Pilgrim's Progress,* characters' very names reflected their personalities, and their actions were predictable and consistent. Neither author lacked the skill to create more complex figures; rather, both utilized the literary device of personification and placed singular character types in a starkly delineated world, where they let their stories develop. Thus Gray was deliberate, not bankrupt, when he bestowed upon his characters such names as Mrs. Bleating-Hart, J. Preston Slime, Fred Free, Phil O. Bluster, Phineas Pinchpenny, and Miss Asthma. Like *Pilgrim's Progress,* the entire run of *Little Orphan Annie* can be seen as an extended morality play, with characters that personify abstract qualities, and story lines that are allegories.

Gray compares well not only to Bunyan, but to Dickens (whom he admired

This was the sort of sequence—and the type of justice—that evoked howls among Gray's critics and fierce loyalty among a greater number of supporters.

greatly) for richness of invention and a talent for dialogue; to Hugo for plot construction and the employment of obsessive motifs; and to Goethe for sympathetic observation.

Other special aspects to Gray's art and craft present themselves. Alone among all the cartoonists of all the periods in comic-strip history, he set for

Mature pacing, interior monologue, and composition. Gray was an artist whose black-and-white superseded his color work.

himself the seemingly impossible and almost ridiculous task of truncated, one-a-day episodic construction; with only occasional exceptions, each *Orphan Annie* strip represented a different day's action in the story line. This is a bizarre challenge to the handling of action, conversation, conflict, and running story line. Yet Gray met his own challenge, producing a comic strip that was structured and paced like no other—providing a unique sort of flavor to events via this remarkable technical feat that few of his contemporaries ever attempted.

If the locales in *Little Orphan Annie* seem interchangeable, nevertheless they do change, as Annie visits farms and cities, hovels and castles, tenements and jungles. In fact, Annie is an inveterate wanderer, and she leaves friends as often, and as easily, as she escapes enemies; likewise "Daddy" Warbucks routinely leaves her to pursue his latest challenge. Gray's overwrought critics, who always seemed to be legion, deplored Annie's rootlessness and Warbucks's alleged callousness, but in fact Gray was turning once again to literature for inspiration. The motif of the unending journey or the obsessive quest is a respected device as old as the *Odyssey* and the *Aeneid* and as fresh as *Huckleberry Finn,* whose river prefigures Annie's road. Her style was to visit, not stay; her goal was not riches but wages.

Gray frequently had the several characters central to his stories engage in soliloquies—and lengthy ones at that, for *Little Orphan Annie* was certainly the most wordy of strips. On a simple level Gray was providing readers with recapitulations. Some of his stories ran close to a year in length (the strip held records in this category), and readers needed reminders, perhaps; besides, they were bound to occasionally miss an episode. On a more sophisticated level, Gray was employing yet another device totally unique with him. Readers would witness the strip's action and know the "reality" of a given situation. Then Annie would provide her perspective. Soon, via stage whispers and soliloquies, the attitudes of the story's sympathetic character, the antagonist, and even incidental bystanders would be revealed. It was a remarkable manner of enriching a plot and infusing the fantasies and allegories with a genuine sense of realism. There was truth, and there were different versions of truth that animated each of the characters. Gray was exercising the comics' answer to Pirandello's techniques.

Gray's philosophy, for all the other factors that could be admired or debated about his work, was the most obvious preoccupation in *Little Orphan Annie,* or at least in the minds of liberal critics. When Warbucks dispatched kidnappers by a wink to his henchmen, civil libertarians howled. When he depicted union organizers as opportunistic thugs, papers were swamped with complaints. He caricatured a local bureaucrat, a ration board official in Fairfield County, Connecticut, and he seldom pictured a politician in a flattering light. For these efforts he was frequently assailed; *The New Republic* published an article by Richard L. Neuberger (later a U.S. senator) decrying Little Orphan Annie as "Hooverism in the Funnies" and later ran an editorial about the strip titled "Fascism in the Funnies." Ultimately the attacks were as numerous and about as effective as gnats while Harold Gray continued to produce his comic strip. But they are remarkable for their intemperance; after all, the object of the critics' wrath was only a comic strip. What the vituperation proved was that Gray was doing an effective job, that he was creating a real world that was strikingly compelling, that his ever-present commentary had notable resonance.

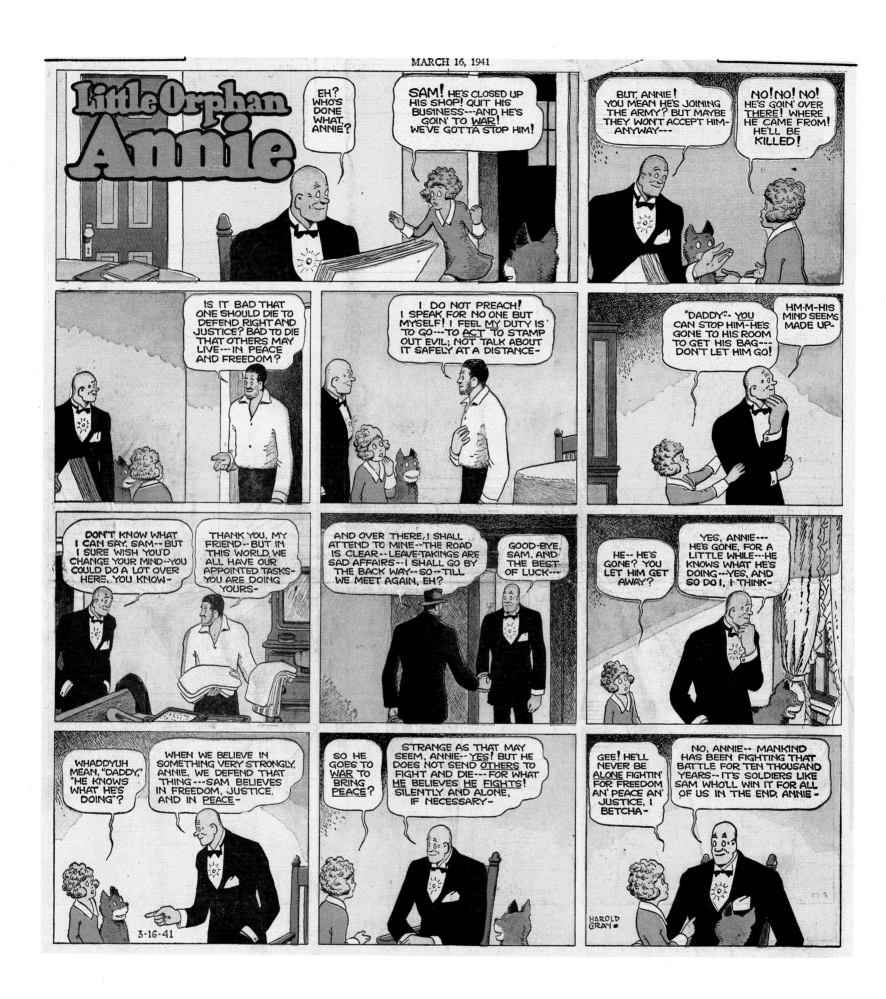

In the controversies surrounding *Little Orphan Annie,* many mistaken impressions abound. Because "Daddy" was wealthy, for instance, many critics have charged that Gray celebrated plutocracy and despised the masses. On the contrary, Warbucks was virtually the only man of means who was ever depicted favorably in *Little Orphan Annie;* Warbucks's peers were invariably hypocrites, swindlers, or shallow fools. And although common folk were often seen as dupes, Gray's real heroes were members of the *petite bourgeoisie*—shopkeepers, farmers, modest entrepreneurs, and sometimes factory workers. Union members were usually depicted as indolent types seeking security, and their appearance allowed Gray to preach about self-reliance and the dignity of artisans through diverse voices—including his own captions, the observations of Annie and others, and the self-indicting words of the unfortunate creatures. Even the very structure of the strip revealed motivations and actions as it unfolded.

Finally, as "Daddy" Warbucks became less human and more mythic, Annie herself became less of a child and more of a symbol. As the years passed, she socialized less with her contemporaries, until her mere presence among children seemed unnatural. When it did happen, it was either under duress (placed in a home, forced to attend classes); as an alien (rejected from the company of other

And the manner of dealing with wrongdoers and injustice continued into the Cold War years. Many saw politics in such sequences, but Gray—who had been consistent about matters like personal honor and governmental intrusion since the 1920s—considered it philosophy more than politics. *(Above)*

The only question asked more often through the years than the one about her blank eyes concerned the red dress Annie perpetually seemed to wear.

Critics thought Gray editorialized in *Little Orphan Annie*, but occasionally *Maw Green*—the Sunday companion strip to *Annie*—contained strong opinions of the cartoonist, including this one about cartoonists from 1936.

children for being too industrious or honest); or as an agent of charity. In this last scenario, her gifts were as often spiritual as material, as in a 1936 episode in which she delivers sustenance to a Depression-ravaged family but offers a palpably more beneficial sermon wherein Theodore Roosevelt is held up as a role model for the nearsighted son of the family she visits.

Such encounters with children were somehow awkward for Annie—or at least for her creator—and it can be presumed that as her strip companions grew in median age, so too did her average readers. What else changed was her basic role; eventually it was radically different from that assigned her by Patterson and Gray during the first steps of her eternal journey. In the beginning she was a vulnerable figure on three counts: she was a girl, she was young, and she was an orphan. Ultimately these traits not only softened but became irrelevant.

The remarkable aspect of Annie's personality was to be her invulnerability, not her vulnerability. Armed with honesty and guile—wits notably akin to her creator's—and that strong left hook, she prevailed in a myriad of dilemmas as surely as she has endured in America's consciousness through the years, even since Gray's death.

Harold Gray married twice but never had children of his own besides Annie. He was remarkably devoted to his comic strip, traversing the continent each year to scout locales, talk with common folk, and seek inspiration. He loved comic strips so much that for years he ghosted a second one, *Little Joe* (about a redhaired boy in the wild West), for his assistant and cousin, Ed Leffingwell, the only instance of a major cartoonist serving anonymously on a relatively minor strip. He died in 1968 and had plotted the death of Warbucks to coincide with his own and then the death of the strip itself. But his syndicate would not have it so, and a succession of hapless imitators desecrated Gray's memory with heartless pastiches. Eventually the syndicate reprinted classic Gray material before turning *Annie* (the new title, appropriated from the hit Broadway and Hollywood musical based on the old strip) into a brand-new strip. Today it is drawn admirably by Leonard Starr but bears little graphic and hardly more psychic resemblance to *Little Orphan Annie* by Harold Gray.

That is as it should be, for Harold Gray was a cartoonist who used his tools as no other cartoonist did. *Little Orphan Annie* was a strip that appeared, and offered itself to readers, as no other strip did. It was intensely personal, but it revealed the personality of a genius.

There had been continuity strips, and even strong elements of adventure, before Hal Foster started drawing comic strips, but approximately thirty-five years after the birth of the art form it was Foster who introduced illustrative techniques—and the sensibilities and standards of the illustrator—to the comics page. Realistic depictions and sophisticated compositions had been curiously absent before him.

The pioneering cartoonist was born Harold Rudolph Foster on August 16, 1892, in Halifax, Nova Scotia. He attended school only to the ninth grade and at age seventeen moved with his family to Winnipeg, Manitoba. He always liked to draw, and in later years quipped that he learned to draw fast because the weather in Manitoba was too cold to permit him to be free of mittens for too long. At the age of eighteen he drew illustrations for the catalogs of local merchants, the Hudson's Bay Company. By 1921 Foster had

HAL FOSTER

1892-1979

married a young woman from Topeka, Kansas (where they lived for a time before eventually settling in the United States permanently), and with Canada in the throes of a depression, he decided to visit Chicago with an eye toward work and study in art. So he and a friend bicycled the thousand miles. Before long, Mrs. Foster followed, for the young artist not only took instruction at the city's top schools but rose to become one of the region's most successful illustrators, working on everything from advertising art for exclusive shops to painted covers for *Popular Mechanics*.

It was Foster's advertising work that led to his career in the comics. In

In 1888 young Lord Greystoke and his bride of three months sailed from Dover on their way to Africa. He had been commissioned to investigate alleged atrocities on black subjects in a British West Coast African colony. Lord Greystoke never made the investigation; in fact he never reached his destination.

Arrived at Freetown, they chartered the Fuwalda, which was to bear them to their final destination. And here, Lord and Lady Greystoke mysteriously vanished forever from the eyes and from the knowledge of man. Two months later, six British war vessels were scouring the South Atlantic for trace of them.

Beyond sight of land, the Fuwalda's captain, with a terrific blow, felled an old sailor who had accidentally tripped him. The swarthy bully's brutality caused big Black Michael to crush the captain to his knees. This was mutiny. The enraged captain suddenly whipped a revolver from his pocket and fired.

Lord Greystoke struck down the captain's arm, saving Black Michael's life and thus forged the first link of what was destined to form a chain of amazing circumstances ending in a life for one then unborn such as has probably never been paralleled in the history of man.

With suspicion of organized mutiny confirmed, they hurried to their quarters. Even their beds had been torn to pieces. A thorough search revealed the fact that only Lord Greystoke's revolvers and ammunition were gone. An undefinable something presaged bloody disaster!

1928 an enterprising ad man who had worked with Foster, Joseph H. Neebe, secured the rights to serialize and illustrate *Tarzan of the Apes* for the newspapers. The 1912 Edgar Rice Burroughs character was already a popular favorite and had been in the movies for a dozen years; a comic-strip spin-off seemed natural.

Actually it did not seem natural to everyone. *Tarzan* illustrator J. Allen St. John was not interested in the adaptation, so Foster was the second choice. Then Neebe was unable to sell the idea to newspapers. Eventually he found a syndicate, the small Metropolitan Newspaper Service of New York, willing to distribute the adaptation.

This time newspapers bit, and *Tarzan* became a sensation. Foster's serialization was more of a picture story than a comic strip, the sixty daily episodes comprising illustrated vignettes above running typeset text. But his artwork was arresting, in the best drybrush, pulp-flavored style of the day, and there was a ready-made audience for the popular jungle hero. Ironically, on the very same debut day— January 7, 1929—another startlingly new strip bowed: *Buck Rogers*. This science-fiction continuity was not drawn realistically (as hard as cartoonist Dick Calkins might have tried) but, like *Tarzan*, was self-consciously different from other story strips. Among the few pathfinders up to that time were *Little Orphan Annie*, which featured melodrama; George Storm's *Bobby Thatcher*, which featured melodrama and action; and *Wash Tubbs*, featuring action and humor. Chaffin and Forrest's *Tailspin Tommy* was a baroque exploitation of the Lindbergh craze, and there were several Frank Merriwell-type strips, including *Frank Merriwell*, all hewing close to musty dime novels. There also had been sporadic comic-strip versions of literary classics, served up for young readers.

But *Tarzan* and *Buck Rogers* were something different—exotic, forthrightly adventurous, and popular in a way the others were not. They heralded a spate of adventure strips that changed the entire complexion of comic strips for a full decade and beyond.

Foster worked on just the first story serialization; Neebe intended to ask readers for their reaction about continuing *Tarzan*. He did not have to. The reaction was massive and enthusiastic. He did not have to ask Foster, either, for the artist saw the first story as a mere assignment, and one he was not particularly proud of. At that time he considered comics a step below advertising art, and he resumed his account work as Rex Maxon inherited *Tarzan*. In 1931, however, a Sunday *Tarzan* was launched, and Foster consented to draw it. "I was a little

Enter Lord Greystoke, enter a new type of comic strip, and enter Harold Foster into the comics. *Tarzan's* initial appearance (this is the introductory strip, January 7, 1929) looked suspiciously like the old-fashioned picture-stories.

For a strip he was never enthusiastic about, Harold Foster invested *Tarzan* with great visual excitement. He was compensating for a tendency toward book illustration caused by his reliance on captions rather than balloons.

offended to be asked to sell my birthright for a mess of pottage," he remembered about the *Tarzan* page, but it was the Depression and Foster thought, "Wouldn't it be nice to have a little bit of pottage right now?"

At first the Sunday *Tarzan* looked like his earlier dailies—handsome but merely illustrative, serving the lettered text below each picture. And then, although Foster did not turn to the use of balloons, he subtly began to integrate his own versions of comic-strip technique. He experimented with close-ups for emotional impact, and silhouette scenes for mood and tension. His characters developed personality. A flow developed between the panels constituting his Sunday page, maintained by elements like action or shading. He also began to rely on thick black shadows, a rather rare technique in colored Sunday pages.

Foster's *Tarzan* grew more vital and interesting, and Foster became an inspiration to other cartoonists, most notably the young Alex Raymond. In a sense, however, it was all in a losing cause—Foster harbored an aversion to Tarzan that he was unable to shed. As a matter of fact, almost everything about *Tarzan* was distasteful to him. He considered the premise silly; he disliked illustrating other writers' scripts; he thought the scripts handed him were inferior; and he was nurturing a quiet ambition to create and own a comic strip. The reluctant illustrator had been converted to an enthusiastic comic-strip cartoonist.

Fortunately for the retiring Foster, but not surprising to anyone familiar with William Randolph Hearst's never-ending talent-hunting forays, the legendary publisher by 1935 was seeking him out. He was invited to create a strip of his own desire and to own it completely, both rare offers of the day. Nevertheless, a sense of loyalty moved Foster to offer his new strip to United Features, successors to Metropolitan; they rejected it peremptorily. So Foster finally obliged the insistent and flattering King Features syndicate of Hearst.

Derek, Son of Thane was the submission, and in it Foster harked back to medieval legends and epic sagas. It was a period of history and literature that had always attracted him, and a favorite author/illustrator of his was Howard Pyle, who wrote of the Round Table. Foster also reckoned that the fashion in adventure strips was for exotic locales (like Tarzan's jungles) or the future (like Buck Rogers's worlds and those of his imitators); so he would look backward. Everything was set but the name, which was altered to *Prince Valiant*.

Val made its debut on February 13, 1937. For the first three months the strip—which was, and remained through the years, a Sunday-only feature— was one long flashback, establishing the premise, setting, and lead characters. In these episodes Val is an adolescent, and the stories tell of his noble family's desperate escape from their beloved kingdom of Thule. King Aguar, Val's father, vows revenge on the evil Sligon the Traitor, and seeks refuge for his family and few supporters on the coast of Britain. But half-wild natives attempt to drive them away, and after bloody confrontations a compromise is offered wherein the outcasts can settle on an island in the fens. There Val learns some skills while his father plots his return to the throne. Eventually Val encounters Horrit the Witch (who predicts a lifetime of "no contentment," a spell later to be broken by Merlin), Sir Galahad, and Sir Gawain.

By midyear of 1937 Prince Valiant was a young man (occasional captions having bridged, for instance, "the next year" spent "preparing for the destiny he feels sure is awaiting him"), with witches among his more mundane acquaintances. Over the first several years of the strip, Val visited a host of witches, giants, dragons, and sorcerers. He wrestled with Father Time, and he visited such unlikely places as Africa and North America.

All such was proper in a strip designed to be part fantasy, and as a matter of fact the "realistic" side of the strip—England of the Dark Ages, replete with costumes, armor, and architecture—was hardly realistic either. Foster strove for things to be genuine if not literal as he telescoped three hundred years of history into Val's life and times. The cartoonist had an eye for detail—it might have been closer to an obsession, as he frequently traveled to Europe on sketching and photography assignments—but he was weaving stories, after all, and the setting for his entire saga, the Arthurian legend, was just that—a legend.

In the early years of *Prince Valiant* fantasy was an important component, as seen in this full Sunday page from 1940.

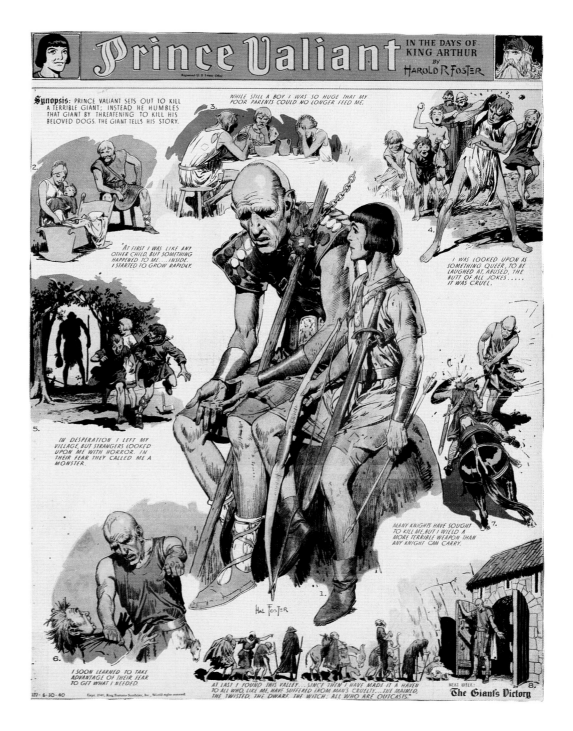

The point has to be made for two reasons: Foster's attention to minutia was so impressive that *Prince Valiant* had the flavor, if not the substance, of documentary. And then, bit by bit, the fantasy began to disappear, and *Prince Valiant* became a tour de force of not just heroics but of everyday life.

"Most of the castles in *Prince Valiant* are not authentic in that they are Norman castles," Foster once observed; "when King Arthur lived[!] there were mostly remnants of Roman fortresses that had been set up during the Roman occupation; castles were subsequently built during the Norman conquest. The picture we have of King Arthur is given by the Norman story-writers; it is they who fostered the legend. So you must dress the characters almost like Norman knights rather than Roman centurions—they are dressed in a way that *I* think they should be dressed."

A passion for such concerns and the slow, comic-strip-time aging of his character combined to move Foster toward a more human story. Val eventually married and fathered children and saw his son, Prince Arn, take on many of the

JOYOUSE GARDE
LAUNCELOT
SAVE THIS STAMP

Prince Valiant

Registered U. S. Patent Office.

IN THE DAYS OF
KING ARTHUR
BY
HAROLD R FOSTER

CAMELOT
THE ROYAL PALACE
SAVE THIS STAMP

SYNOPSIS: IN THE SHELTER OF A GREAT CAVE VAL MEETS A WITCH-WOMAN WHO GIVES HIM A POTENT DRINK AND A GRIM WARNING, WHICH HE IGNORES AND ENTERS THE ABODE OF "TIME."

"YOU DON'T BELIEVE THAT 'TIME' IS UNCONQUERABLE...THEN SHALL WE WRESTLE?"

THE STALWART YOUTH PICKS UP THE SENILE OLD MAN TO FLING HIM AMONG HIS DUSTY TROPHIES.

BUT THE ANCIENT CREATURE CLINGS TENACIOUSLY WITH WEAK, FRAIL HANDS, AS VAL STRIVES TO FREE HIMSELF.

HOW LONG THEY STRUGGLED IN THAT WEIRD, DIM PLACE VAL COULD NEVER AFTERWARDS TELL, BUT HE GROWS WEARY... WEARY....

WITH A CACKLING LAUGH "TIME" HURLS HIS SKINNY ADVERSARY AMONG THE WORLD'S DISCARDED TOYS.

AS VAL STUMBLES OUT OF THAT FANTASTIC CAVERN HE HEARS A THIN, CRACKED VOICE GLOATING, "ALL CONTEND WITH 'TIME' AND ALL ARE VANQUISHED."

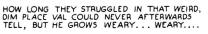
SAVE THIS STAMP
DOLOROUS GARDE
MORGAN LE FEY

AT THE CAVE'S MOUTH THE WITCH-WOMAN CALMLY WAITS THE RETURN OF ALL THAT REMAINS OF A PROUD PRINCE.

"YOU MUST BE TIRED, GRANDFATHER, SIT DOWN AND REFRESH YOURSELF."

116   430-39

VAL DRAINS THE CUP.

NEXT WEEK: THE WANDERER

HAL FOSTER
SAVE THIS STAMP
CAERLEON
SUMMER PALACE OF KING ARTHUR

colorful exploits in which he had once engaged. Val continued to travel and fight, but he also lived day-to-day; he also lost some bloody fights. Domestic affairs became as much a part of the strip as cast-of-thousands battles. Under Foster's magnificent tutelage, however, *Prince Valiant* was not thereby weakened or dulled but rather deepened and made more mature. Val's personality was displaying different sides, and there was a reason: "He does what we should do," Foster once reflected. "Yes, he is brave and strong—he has every virtue that I missed. All I have to do is think of my failings and correct them all in Prince Valiant.... He became more and more of an actual character to me; I began to visualize him. I could almost feel him standing at my shoulder when I wrote a story that was out of line; why, he would just shake his head there!"

Discussions of a comic strip reflecting an artist's conception of the fifth century as opposed to the strict archaeological record highlight just how unique *Prince Valiant* was. And Foster had a unique format—a full newspaper page from the start (and this in the Depression days when newspapers were shrinking, not expanding, Sunday comics) with the best color separation available at the time. Foster learned to exploit the "spectacle" aspect of his full pages by frequently designing huge panels filled with detail. He proved himself a master at drawing gloomy interiors with dozens of props, huge battle scenes crawling with figures, and vast exterior panoramas.

Foster set three goals for himself in *Prince Valiant,* which he met almost from his first page. He aimed for a feeling of reality, which meant knowing his subject thoroughly and how to document or distort elements for narrative demands. He wanted a strong dose of fantasy, and although the initial preoccupation waned, Merlin, various sorcerers, giants, and dragons remained in the wings for cameo appearances. He also sought a visceral spirit of adventure. The sword fights—especially after Val received the Enchanted Singing Sword, consecrated to Justice—were heady, and so were the colorful jousting tournaments. But, as noted, Foster eventually found, and promoted, heroism in everyday life.

The work of illustrator Howard Pyle was Foster's inspiration as he created *Prince Valiant,* and as a matter of fact many panels are visual references to illustrations of the King Arthur and Robin Hood stories by Pyle. Like Pyle, Foster discovered that nobility is not found just within the nobility; that the everyday can be as important, as interesting—and as noble—as participation in epic battles for romantic causes.

Foster's saga provided a resonant chord for twentieth-century readers, probably due in equal parts to his literate, understated text and his impressive artwork. Yet, in looking at *Prince Valiant,* we are struck by the fact that it is not—in strict and classical terms—a comic strip. *Val* appeared in the comic sections, and it utilized successions of panels to tell its story, yet it never had any dialogue balloons. It was presented, at least at first, as an old-fashioned picture-story, with clipped captions and the drawings in a subservient role, no matter how magnificent they appeared. There was no logical flow from image to image; there was rather a disproportionate (for comic strips) reliance on "bridges" and explanations in the hand-lettered captions.

As the theme and premise in *Prince Valiant* matured, Foster became a comic-strip cartoonist rather than an illustrator working among strips. He developed an imaginative use of panel progression, mixing close-ups and long

Our Story: FROM A WINDOW HIGH IN THE GALLERY PRINCE VALIANT AND ARN LOOK DOWN AT THE PAGAN WARBAND AS THEY SURGE FORWARD. THEY ARE STRANGELY QUIET AS IF OVERAWED BY THE STILL, SILENT GRANDEUR OF THE RUINED ABBEY.

THEN A CLOUD OF SMOKE BELLOWS UP FROM THE WOODEN SCREEN, WHICH OPENS, SEALING OFF THE ALTAR. FOR A MOMENT THE WHOLE END OF THE BUILDING IS OBSCURED, AND THIS IS ENOUGH IN ITSELF TO BRING FEAR TO THE PRIMITIVE MINDS OF THE BARBARIANS.

A GASP OF HORROR RUNS THROUGH THE PAGAN THRONG AS A SHADOWY FORM APPEARS DIMLY IN THE SWIRLING CLOUD. THEN THE SMOKE THINS, REVEALING A MONSTER SO HUGE AND MENACING THAT PANIC AKIN TO MADNESS GRIPS THE WATCHERS AND, SCREAMING, THEY TRAMPLE EACH OTHER IN A WILD SCRAMBLE TO ESCAPE.

NEXT WEEK—**The Dancers**

3-25-61

Prince Valiant

IN THE DAYS OF KING ARTHUR

BY HAROLD R. FOSTER

Synopsis: DAWN COMES AND, ONE BY ONE, PRINCE VALIANT AND HIS FRIENDS UNTANGLE THEMSELVES FROM THE HUDDLE THEY HAD FORMED TO KEEP WARM....... ALL EXCEPT YOUNG ARF. HE SEEMS STUPEFIED WITH COLD AND STUMBLES AS HE WALKS.

THE AVALANCHE OF SOFT SNOW THAT HAD BLOCKED THE PASS IS NOW FROZEN HARD, AND THEY MAKE THEIR WAY CAREFULLY BUT SAFELY ACROSS.

VAL WATCHES HIS BOY SQUIRE ANXIOUSLY, HIS LIPS MOVING IN A SILENT PRAYER, FOR WELL HE KNOWS THE AGONY THAT IS IN STORE FOR THE LAD.

NOW THE WAY SLANTS DOWNWARD. FRANCE IS BEHIND THEM, ITALY AHEAD. FOR A TIME MIST OBSCURES THE WAY. THEN THE WIND DRAWS IT ASIDE LIKE A CURTAIN AND THEY LOOK DOWN ON A BILLOWING SEA OF CLOUDS THROUGH WHICH GLITTERING PEAKS GO MARCHING ACROSS THE SKY.

THE WAY LEADS DOWN INTO THE CLOUDS, A WET AND TWILIGHT WORLD OF SWIRLING MISTS.

741 4-22-51

THEY CAN GO NO FURTHER. IN A SHELTERED SPOT MEN AND ANIMALS HUDDLE TOGETHER FOR WARMTH, WAITING FOR THE CLOUDS TO LIFT. SNOW FALLS... AND NIGHT.

HAL FOSTER

MORNING COMES AT LAST, BRIGHT AND CLEAR, AND VAL LOOKS ANXIOUSLY AT ARF. THE LAD'S FACE IS WHITE WITH PAIN. HIS FROZEN FEET ARE THAWING OUT!

NEXT WEEK—Arf's Danger.

Synopsis: PRINCE VALIANT TAKES DRINK FOR DRINK WITH HIS GRIM HOSTS, FOR HE MUST APPEAR AS CRUDE AND BRUTAL AS THEY. THEN COMES THE TOAST TO KING ARTHUR AND VAL LEAPS TO HIS FEET, TANKARD RAISED HIGH. TOO LATE HE REALIZES HE HAS BETRAYED HIMSELF. HIS TERRIBLE COMPANIONS RISE IN OMINOUS SILENCE.

NOW THE PRESENCE OF DANGER CLEARS VAL'S NUMBED BRAIN. HE LAUGHS: "SO YOU WISH TO DRINK TO ARTHUR? THEN, COME, JOIN HIS OTHER MONGREL FOLLOWERS!"

HE STANDS, SWAYING, PRETENDING NOW TO BE VERY DRUNK. "SHAME ON YOU, DRINKING THE HEALTH OF OLD KING ARTHUR WHOM YOUR NOBLE FATHER HATES!"

"BUT I WILL FOLLOW THE GREAT KING TOURIEN AND HELP HIM RULE THE WORLD! ALREADY I HAVE PLANS!"

THEN HE FUMBLES FOR HIS BENCH, SITS DOWN HEAVILY AND FALLS ASLEEP ACROSS THE LITTERED BOARD.

THERE IS A LONG SILENCE AND VAL VENTURES A PEEK. THE THREE LIE SPRAWLED IN DRUNKEN BUT PEACEFUL SLUMBER, SO HE KNOWS THEIR SUSPICIONS ARE ALLAYED.

THE SMOKY TORCHES BURN OUT AND ONE BY ONE THE CANDLES SPUTTER AND DIE. ONLY THE HEAVY TREAD OF THE SENTRIES BREAKS THE STILLNESS. IN THIS DREAD FORTRESS DWELLS A SMALL, MAD KING WITH MAD AMBITIONS. HIS MURDEROUS CAREER MUST BE ENDED, BUT HOW? A THOUSAND KNIGHTS COULD NOT TAKE THIS IMPREGNABLE CASTLE!

HAL FOSTER

NEXT WEEK — Plans.

For all the elements of history's great sweep, *Prince Valiant* was still an epic tale of personalities in situations. Foster created believable characters with consistent traits. In the end there was empathy between readers and Val as much for homely virtues as for heroic ones.

shots. He dropped backgrounds when, graphically, heavy detail would have subtly but definitely overwhelmed the eye. He used negative white space. And although his captions were usually at the bottom of every panel, he nonetheless integrated his text, either to lead the reader's eye according to his purpose or to prevent intrusion on the visual elements. These techniques of textual placement and visual variation were never quite grasped by the two other major cartoonists who also eschewed balloons. Alex Raymond, in *Flash Gordon*, always seemed uncomfortable with captions, balloons, and dialogue, and he was forever awkwardly experimenting; and Burne Hogarth, who succeeded Foster on *Tarzan*, consciously chose to reject Foster's oases of quiet moments. Hogarth's work was always alive

with movement, motion, and kinetic hyperactivity, even in backgrounds and props. It fit Hogarth's goal of pictorializing the mythic elements (which to Foster seemed silly preoccupations in the first place) but provided none of the release or contrast that Foster achieved in his more stately tales.

The question pales to irrelevance as to whether *Prince Valiant* was more than a comic strip or less than a comic strip. It became a very special comic strip wherein the absence of dialogue balloons became not a defect of form but simply a stylism. Hal Foster adopted the other conventions of comic-strip storytelling, from graphic composition and narrative flow to cliff-hangers and limited use of visual symbols (motion lines but never sound effects).

Hal Foster contributed mightily to the growth and diversity of the American comic strip. As the first true illustrator to devote himself to a major comic-strip success, he opened an enormous category of strips—the realistically drawn adventure—which continues today, and by implication he invited a corps of talented creators to join him. Also, by his achievements with *Prince Valiant,* he earned the role and the title of the comics' supreme classicist. Through his example the American comic strip was proving adaptable to new creative challenges and willing to explore new terrain.

In 1971 Foster (after his 1,789th page) relinquished the artwork to John Cullen Murphy, and he died in 1979. He was typically modest about his own place in comics, and human, history: "To understand is to appreciate, and to appreciate is to enjoy. Success is not wealth and the accompanying approbation of people for whose opinion one does not give a tinker's dam, but the ability to enjoy every minute of every day.

"The piling-up of possessions is regarded with such approval that many incompetents strive to do so all their lives. Monkeys and blue-jays also collect bright objects. So few people take time off to enjoy what they already have that trout streams and hedgerows are left peacefully for such leisurely incompetents such as I.

"To contribute something lasting to the sum of human knowledge or enjoyment is, to me, the real success."

Considering comic-strip history in musical terms, it could seem appropriate to chronicle Roy Crane's career and artistic evolution like the movements of a Baroque *concerto grosso: Wash Tubbs* (exuberant); *Captain Easy* (determined); and *Buz Sawyer* (full of virtuosity). Likewise Alex Raymond's development can be likened to the four movements in a Classical symphony. He drew four major comic strips, each with its own distinguishing theme (both narrative and stylistic), and like the movements in a Classical symphony they

sometimes attained grandiose heights of structure and accomplishment, yet they displayed little of the improvisational touch. There were no cadenzas, as it were, in *Secret Agent X-9, Flash Gordon, Jungle Jim,* and *Rip Kirby.* Except in *Kirby,* Alex Raymond was not personally devoted to mature narrative technique, and he often sacrificed the flow of the drawings-in-succession to the seductiveness of individual images. At times, his panels seemed more like snapshots rather than reticulated pieces of a cohesive whole, and he usually eschewed balloons for awkwardly placed quotations. Nevertheless, Alex Raymond is truly one of America's great comic-strip artists. His influence among colleagues was great, and his work is genuinely memorable.

Alexander Gillespie Raymond was born on October 2, 1909, in New Rochelle, New York, which, during his childhood, was an artists' colony of the first rank and home to such leading illustrators as the Leyendecker brothers (J.C. and Frank) and Norman Rockwell. Several prominent cartoonists also lived in the New York suburb, among them Fontaine Fox (*Toonerville Trolley*)

Alex Raymond signed many signatures and copied many styles during his apprentice period in the early 1930s. His work here on Lyman Young's *Tim Tyler's Luck* (November 21, 1931) was as realistic as he was asked to draw, or perhaps could do at the time.

and Russ Westover (*Tillie the Toiler*). A boy possessing artistic talent might almost have acquired dedication and ambition by osmosis. Raymond had talent; after schooling at the local Iona Prep, he took art instruction at New York's Grand Central School of Art.

To support his training, the young Raymond worked in a Wall Street brokerage house, where he witnessed the horror and despair of Black Tuesday and became convinced that even a career in cartooning was stabler than one in the "real" world. Back in New Rochelle, he signed on as an assistant to Russ Westover, a cartoonist known within the profession for using ghost artists—he was not an accomplished draftsman—and paying them poorly, if at all. Within a year Raymond was working in the bullpen at the King Features Syndicate.

By late 1930 Raymond found himself handling the bulk of the work on *Tim Tyler's Luck* for Lyman Young, another cartoonist whose hand never seemed to touch his own strip through the years. And in 1932 Raymond assumed most of the chores—drawing all the artwork except the major characters—on *Blondie*, a strip by Chic Young, Lyman's brother. (Ironically, Alex Raymond's brother, Jim, became the full-time ghost artist on *Blondie* a few years later and remained with the strip until his death in 1982.) Alex Raymond contributed to *Blondie* from the time it featured a millionaire playboy and his flapper girlfriend, through Dagwood's hunger strike staged to gain his family's assent to marry Blondie, to the wedding sequence and the Bumsteads' new life and new roles as the comics' most sympathetic and representative family. From a minor humor strip, *Blondie* eventually became the most popular strip of its generation.

In the meantime Raymond was adapting his style, meeting deadlines, and refining his skills. His compositions and figures grew more sophisticated almost by the week, even in the humorous strips, but it became evident that his skills were more suited to "straight" art. When, in late 1933, King Features conducted an extensive talent search to launch a new strip, Raymond provided their answer literally in their own backyard.

King president Joe Connolly was obsessed with the success of *Dick Tracy* at a rival syndicate; its creator, Chester Gould, had long been on the King payroll and slipped away after creating a host of failures. And, quite simply, *Tracy* was electrifying—overflowing with violence, danger, suspense, romance—a comic-strip mirror of lurid tabloid headlines. Connolly decided to challenge *Tracy's* success by launching not one but four similar strips. *Radio Patrol* was picked up nationally from a Boston paper; Lyman Anderson was hired to draw a strip version of Edgar Wallace's *Inspector Wade;* former sports cartoonist Will Gould

now you can

SEE

the thrill-a-minute excitement of AMERICA'S GREATEST DETECTIVE STORY WRITER

in smashing, vivid, action PICTURES!

SECRET AGENT X-9

daily detective strip by today's most popular, fastest-selling author of detective novels ..

DASHIELL HAMMETT

Only Dashiell Hammett could have created the swift, breathless suspense and excitement of this great new daily strip. Here is all of the stark, stirring drama, grim humor and baffling mystery that made Hammett's detective novels the favorites of all America—plus the added thrill of SEEING the story in PICTURES that bring you the action with vivid, gripping realism. There has never been a sleuth like Secret Agent X-9. He fights gun-fire with gun-fire — matches racketeers' cunning with his finely trained wits—faces any danger or runs any risk to bring the underworld into the hands of the law! Be sure to watch for Secret Agent X-9.

drawing by the sensational new illustrator ALEXANDER RAYMOND

begins Monday, Feb. 12, in

The Scranton Times.

(no relation to Chester) created a stark, impressive reflection of Warner Brothers gangster films in *Red Barry;* and King commissioned the master of the pulp detective genre, Dashiell Hammett, to create a comic strip. *Secret Agent X-9* was that strip, and the young, virtually unknown Alex Raymond was chosen to draw it.

The conceptualization of *X-9* was Hammett at his best, even if the prose was not (Jim Raymond remembered years later that Hammett had a chronic inability to structure dialogue balloons to fit characters' positionings), and Raymond's art—yet another style flowing from his versatile brush—was done in the contemporary drybrush look that dominated in the pulp magazines. Raymond was still feeling his way, as manifested in occasional stiff poses and awkward compositions, but even that look fit the mannered style of the script and premise. The character of X-9 was a combination of Hammett's Continental Op and Sam Spade and was mysteriously nameless like the Op.

Raymond delighted in drawing X-9 squinting through his cigarette smoke, snapping the brim of his fedora, and wisecracking with dames. Considering that only a year earlier the cartoonist had been spending his days drawing stock-company doctors and oafish swains in *Blondie,* his realistic artwork is even more impressive.

While planning *Secret Agent X-9,* Raymond was also preparing two more

comic strips. Like *X-9,* they were created as if by prescription, in answer to other successes in the field. *Flash Gordon* was to be King's answer to *Buck Rogers,* and *Jungle Jim* a slick, sophisticated *Tarzan.* They both made their debuts in January 1934 as Sunday pages, while *X-9* ran daily.

Buck Rogers, for all its success, seemed to be an easy target. It was one of the worst-drawn features in comics history—matched only by its outlandish premises and bizarre characterizations—yet it possessed a singular, attractive élan. Raymond and ghost writer Don Moore were probably told to avoid the silly gadgets and props that glutted *Buck Rogers.* In so doing, they created a different type of science-fiction strip, one that relied more on fiction than science, and on personalities more than situations. In fact, *Flash Gordon* was destined to become one of the worst-written strips in comics history, featuring unlikely premises, one-dimensional characters, and stilted dialogue. Its basis was a reworking of Philip Wylie and Edwin Balmer's recent *When Worlds Collide* (interestingly, Wylie's *Gladiator* was the precursor of another comics classic, *Superman*); the origin page opens with a newspaper headline announcing "World Comes To End"

X-9 did not just feature the stock gunfights and car chases of the detective genre. Supporting Hammett's strong suit, Raymond was actually best at the visual characterization that upheld pulp-flavored patter.

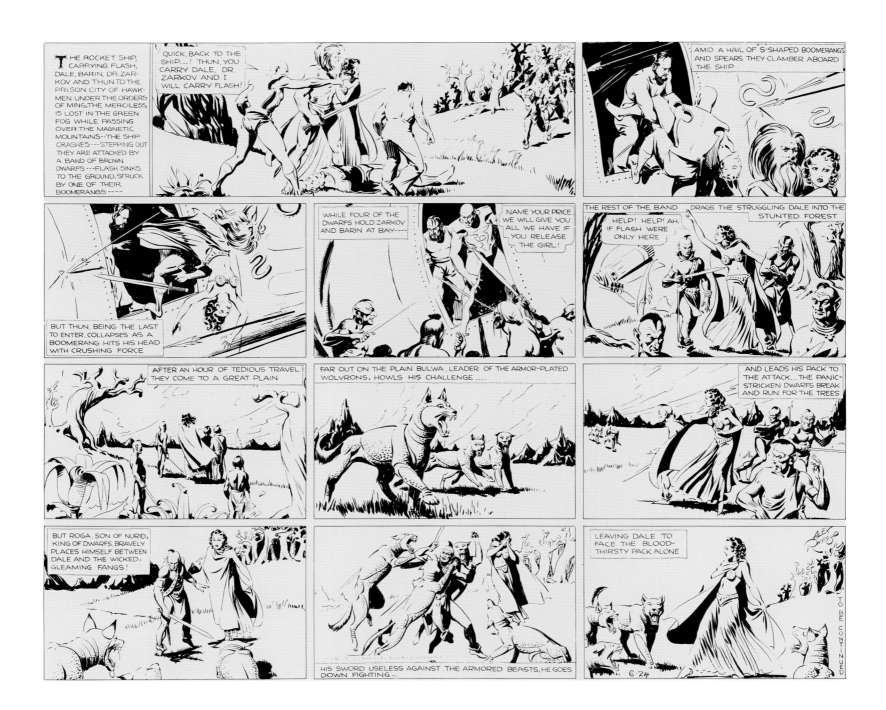

From the beginning *Flash Gordon* contained the science-fiction elements of rocket ships and armor-plated monsters, but it also pictured capes and drawn swords. There were captions galore, making the three balloons almost superfluous. Raymond was still feeling his way; this is the twenty-fifth *Flash* page, June 24, 1934.

as Flash Gordon ("world-renowned polo player") and comely Dale Arden are spirited away a moment before destruction on a spaceship of the seemingly crazed Dr. Zarkov.

Thereafter most of the action in *Flash Gordon* occurs on the mysterious planet Mongo, and the nemesis is that incarnation of evil, the Emperor Ming the Merciless. Writer Moore evidently ransacked every dime novel and pulp story he could find for clichés, and even the strip's central relationship, between Flash and Dale, was almost caricatural. She was a heroine of the sort with whom Buster Keaton cast himself—a helpless, purposeless, vacuous decoration. But for Flash she was motivation enough to risk entire planets and expend armies. As the strip aged, however, jealousy emerged as the characters' chief motivation, rather than standard devices like revenge, ideals, material salvation, and so forth. *Flash Gordon* became mythic at best, soap opera at worst, instead of true science fiction. Also, in a manner peculiar to the 1930s, futuristic elements were combined with the trappings of ages-old adventure stories: ray guns alternated with swords, and the well-dressed cast member combined high-tech breastplates with medieval

SWIMMING TO SHORE, FLASH DRAGS THE REVIVING ZARKOV TO THE BEACH···· DALE RUSHES TO MEET THEM··········

When Raymond's art improved, he combined lush brush-strokes with formal composition and romantic imagery. *(Facing page)*

In this outstanding *Flash* from 1936, Raymond balanced captions and balloons and let the visuals crisply tell a moment-to-moment story. The device of the mad Zarkov's eyes meeting the readers', in panel 2, is stunningly effective. At this period Raymond's art was at its most sensual and attractive level.

capes. And there seemed to be as many mounted steeds as there were rocket ships in Flash Gordon's universe.

None of this mattered, as it turned out, because Alex Raymond was illuminating the abysmal scripts. Never has art so transcended story in comics history, and never has there been an artist like Raymond. During the first several months of *Gordon,* he simply transferred the drybrush look he developed for *X-9* to this ersatz otherworldly epic. His work matured to a powerful, lush style of intense portrayals of personality, majestic poses, dramatic compositions, and a totally unique method of realization—romanticism in the comics. Raymond had discovered the elegant but moody illustrators John LaGatta and Matt Clark in the slick magazines, and he adapted their approach to the comics page. Characters were strongly delineated, and every element in a frame conspired to create an overall mood or flavor. Inspired by the frequent underwater settings of his script, Raymond took to rendering backgrounds with swirling, almost pulsating brush-strokes that unified his pages in a way that individual panels could not. *Flash Gordon* took on a throbbing, obsessive, sensual mantle that exploded like a bombshell in the comics pages of the 1930s. There was nothing like it—its imagery so compelling that premise, plot, and dialogue became almost superfluous details.

Four pages from the Witch Queen sequence of *Flash Gordon* in 1935 show that Raymond was experimenting with the "drybrush" illustrator's technique, which can be seen in the rendering of shading and figures. During this period the Hearst papers converted to a tabloid format for their Sunday comics; otherwise *Flash Gordon* was less expansive than in these pages, sharing a full sheet with *Jungle Jim*. Never were comic strips more exotic or sexy than in this period of Raymond's *Flash Gordon*; certainly they seem tamer more than half a century later.

In the midst of this artistic revolution—as other cartoonists rushed to imitate Raymond's romantic style—he created yet another strip, a companion piece to the color *Flash Gordon* page: *Jungle Jim.* Again another feature was the inspiration, and *Jim* was to be an upper-class *Tarzan,* with Greystoke, as it were, never going savage. Jim Bradley was the great white hunter, accompanied by his Hindu servant, Kolu, and his sexy sidekick, Lil, in adventures against poachers and pirates from Africa to the Orient.

In *Flash Gordon* Raymond used balloons fitfully, as they suited him, and usually they did not; the action, such as it was, was propelled via captions, as was the dialogue. In *Jungle Jim* Raymond retreated further from the accepted strip convention of utilizing and placing dialogue balloons in a unique and strategic manner. Unconsciously, no doubt, Raymond harked back to the picture-stories of the early 1800s, and *Jungle Jim* was more like heavily illustrated fiction than true comic strip. Without closely following every word of the text, the reader could not tell from the panel drawings whether the action was spaced minutes or weeks apart or whether embracing characters were saying hello or good-bye.

In the late 1930s Raymond hired an illustrator as his assistant—Austin Briggs, who, after ghosting and eventually handling all the chores on *Flash Gordon* (including a daily strip that was launched in 1940), became one of the most influential illustrators of the next generation and a founder of the Famous Artists School. It seemed inevitable that Alex Raymond would shift entirely to illustration.

By the early 1940s, both *Flash Gordon* and *Jungle Jim* had evolved to near-prototypes of bad comics storytelling, the deficiency being not so much in the words as in the techniques of structure and cohesion. The strips and pages of Raymond's work had no internal unity, no graphically logical progression from panel to panel. Nevertheless the artwork—with its romantic, elegant, and powerful images—carried the day.

Having worked very little on *Flash* during the war years, Raymond abandoned the feature completely when he joined the Marine Corps in 1944. Commissioned a captain, he served in the Pacific as a public-information officer and combat artist. He also illustrated stories for the Hearst magazines and experienced a rather remarkable catharsis. After more than ten years as a successful strip artist, flattered by public acclaim and the admiration of his fellow cartoonists, and after following his star through experimentations and evolutions of style, Alex Raymond rediscovered the comic strip. Illustration became a false god, and he found value in the conventions of the strip form that he had been ignoring or abusing through the years.

"I decided honestly that comic-art work is an art form in itself," he said. "It reflects the life and times more accurately and actually is more artistic than magazine illustration."

But his vehicle was not to be *Flash Gordon* or any other strip created (or created for him) in imitation of another. Raymond set about to create a new strip, focusing on a new type of hero and an unconventional premise. Everything was new for the cartoonist; for the first time in his career he used the pen as his main tool instead of the brush, and he secured ownership of his new creation, a rare allowance by syndicate moguls at the time.

Rip Kirby made its debut in 1946. Rip was a detective, but he relied more

A week of *Rip Kirby* strips from 1947. By this time Raymond was using captions sparingly and with total effectiveness; balloons carried the plot line forward, as well as the dialogue; the establishing shots and camera angles were interesting and fresh. Always a masterful cartoonist, Alex Raymond was now a master comic-strip creator.

on brains than brawn. He wore glasses, smoked a pipe, and read books on psychology. Like his creator, he was an ex-Marine, so could be relied upon to provide the requisite chases and fights, and he had a romantic interest in the person of blonde girl friend Honey Dorian. But mostly the cerebral Rip and his valet Desmond pursued hunches and donned disguises as they cracked cases.

This final movement in Raymond's symphonylike contribution to comics history was certainly his most mature. In an approach unlike any in his earlier strips, Raymond moved the point-of-view camera around with as much verve as did Milton Caniff; long shots, close-ups, severe down shots—all combined to make *Rip Kirby*'s unfolding stories as arresting as Raymond's individual images. He developed a method, now standard, of providing an establishing shot of a landscape or cityscape with accompanying balloon or caption. It is a facile device for setting a scene and serving readers who might have missed a portion of the continuity.

If Alex Raymond borrowed techniques from any of his fellow artists, it was no longer the illustration community; his action and fights seemed inspired by the hyperactive pen of Roy Crane, and his bizarre gallery of villains—not the least of whom was the beautiful, seductive, but deadly Pagan Lee—were worthy of Caniff's brands of extreme characterization. Raymond had always been influenced by Hal Foster, but in *Kirby* he broke with Foster's, as well as his own, reliance on captions instead of balloons. *Rip Kirby* displayed a sophisticated use and placement of character dialogue. Interestingly, Raymond took to the mode naturally, without even the occasional fallback to captions that one might have expected from an artist once so dependent upon them. Furthermore, Raymond's dialogue was sparse and snappy.

Also snappy was Raymond's lifestyle at this time. As handsome and dapper as any of his leading men, Raymond was a sports car enthusiast and had a license to race them, which he frequently did on weekends in Connecticut. One of his

JUNGLE JIM BY ALEX RAYMOND

Flash Gordon

Tune in on Your Radio for More Thrilling Adventures of **JUNGLE JIM**

A vignette from *Rip Kirby*. Raymond never forgot the dramatic value of eye contact with readers.

B y the 1940s Alex Raymond's brushwork was slicker than before, but his storytelling powers had diminished. He admired illustrators more than cartoonists, so his purpose was to illustrate the captions. In comic-strip terms it seems a waste to devote one-fourth of the *Flash Gordon* page to showing Dale merely pointing the way, and the action in the last panel is not shown but described. The artwork is left only to illustrate the fact that Flash is no longer a lone rear guard. *Jungle Jim*, the top strip, was always a succession of snapshots. *(Facing page)*

friends was Stan Drake, a cartoonist whose career resembles Raymond's in uncanny ways; he has been as versatile, drawing "straight" in *Heart of Juliet Jones* and comic in the current *Blondie*, which he inherited from Raymond's brother, Jim. They also shared an interest in fast cars.

On a rainy September afternoon in 1956, Raymond visited Drake's Westport studio while his Mercedes 300 SL Gullwing was in the shop having platinum plugs installed. Raymond expressed interest in driving Drake's new Corvette, and the pair hit the wet, winding roads around Green's Farms. Forty-five miles an hour hardly seems an excessive speed, except on the glorified paths of rural Connecticut. Raymond, behind the wheel, hit a turn and dip on Clapboard Hill Road, and the sleek Corvette arced sixty feet in the air—Drake remembers Raymond's exclamation and the strange sight of a pencil floating off the dashboard—before crashing into a tree. Raymond was killed instantly; Drake was thrown thirty feet and seriously injured.

Raymond was only ten days ahead of publication with *Rip Kirby* at the time (cartoonists are expected to work six weeks in advance), so King Features had to scramble for a new artist while still shocked by the tragedy. A young illustrator, John Prentice, was asked to draw a sample strip; he drew two, showed one, and was hired. Prentice has drawn *Rip Kirby* very capably in the Raymond style ever since.

The hurried transition was possible partly due to Prentice's talent and skills, but also partly to the fact that Alex Raymond had influenced, at the time of his death, a whole generation of artists such as Prentice. There were, and are, many cartoonists whose work reflects the anatomy, poses, compositions, shading, and pen techniques of Raymond, especially from his heady, romantic period with *Flash Gordon*.

Flash under Raymond ultimately stands as a paradox. Coulton Waugh (in *The Comics*, 1947) called it a "pulp product," and so it was. Only an Alex Raymond could have produced the romantic, evocative artwork that transcended faulty technique and inferior scripts. A restless genius, he never rested on his considerable artistic laurels, but was always evolving, experimenting, and absorbing. Unfortunately for the cartooning profession, for every John Prentice who proved able to inherit Raymond's vision as well as his comic strip, there have been dozens of artists content to exalt technique and imagery over style and substance.

Alex Raymond, who was one of the comics' great teachers by example, was also a student of the comic strip until the day he died. It is remarkable that someone of such achievement could be termed a late bloomer, but Raymond's understanding of comics as an art form was still evolving at the end, and such a dedication, as much as all of his considerable work, made him one of America's great comic-strip artists.

12

There have been two births of the comic strip. The first occurred around 1895, when the "founding fathers" defined the medium and established conventions like panel progression and balloon dialogue. For a generation the thematic preoccupation was largely humor and the graphic expression was exclusively comic. The second birth of the comic strip came in the 1930s and featured—for the first time—adventure, suspense, realism, violent continuities, and an illustrative style of drawing. Milton Caniff was at the center of this second wave, which was actually a revolution in the art form.

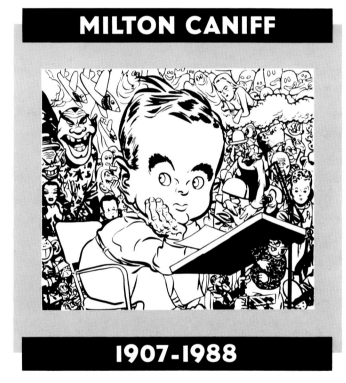

MILTON CANIFF

1907-1988

many another attribute, a singular vision—that he, as a cartoonist, was more than a mere entertainer, even more than an illustrator, as some of his notable contemporaries were striving to become. He saw himself as someone akin to a novelist or a film-maker. In his modest fashion he claimed to be only a "glorified newsboy," selling papers by producing cliff-hangers, but when he sat at the drawing board he also confessed to feeling like an "armchair Marco Polo." Indeed he explored worlds, but he also created them—and conquered them.

Entering the comic-strip field at a time when realistic continuities were a recent innovation, he almost instinctively took to the new mode of expression. He knew how to craft a compelling story within the confines of little panels and balloons, and he mastered a stunning brand of visual storytelling, creating vital characters that spoke with authentic voices. Art, characters, and dialogue—these are the basic components of the cartoonist's art, after all, and Milton

Caniff was widely acknowledged as an expert in all aspects of the comics field.

Milton Arthur Paul Caniff was born in Hillsboro, Ohio, on February 28, 1907. He was raised in Dayton, Ohio, where the Wright brothers had developed the airplane a scant four years before his birth, and while in high school he evinced an interest in cartooning. He contributed to the Dayton *Journal* and did spare-time work at the nearby Miami *Daily News,* owned by onetime presidential candidate James M. Cox of Dayton. While in high school, the young Caniff created a strip for the school's paper, and at graduation time he collected the series, called *Chic and Noodles,* in book form.

Caniff attended Ohio State University, where he majored in fine arts and where he developed an interest that rivaled cartooning—acting. While filling yearbook pages with illustrations and decorations, he was also starring in campus theatricals. Eventually he was dissuaded from a life before the footlights by Billy Ireland, the Ohio editorial cartoonist whose style was an inspiration to a generation of Midwesterners: "Stick to your inkpots, kid; actors don't eat regular."

A part-time job on the Columbus *Dispatch* during college became a full-time position in the art department after graduation in 1930, but he was fired shortly thereafter. The ravages of the Depression were hitting newspapers, and "last in, first out" was the dictum during economy moves. Caniff opened an art studio with fellow Ohio cartoonist Noel Sickles, who had worked on the *Ohio State Journal,* and he also served in various capacities with a theatrical company.

Only three months after losing his job at the *Dispatch,* Caniff received an offer from the Associated Press of New York. It seems that the AP's midwestern bureau chief had been sending clippings of recommendable talent to headquarters, and Caniff's spot art and cartoons had impressed the editors.

Arriving in New York City on borrowed money in 1932, Caniff soon began to enhance his reputation as well as the polished aspect of his artwork, which moved away from cartooney figures toward the illustrative look of magazine art. He was assigned a dizzying array of tasks at the AP: news and spot art; portrait and feature graphics; a panel with a blowhard Major Hoople-type character, *Mr. Gilfeather* (inherited from a youngster named Al Capp); its eventual reincarnation as *The Gay Thirties* (a human-interest feature of the type popularized by Clare Briggs, H.T. Webster, and J.R. Williams); and a children's poem-and-cartoon panel called *Puffy the Pig.*

Then, in 1933, Caniff was offered the opportunity to draw an adventure comic strip. He seized the chance, not only because he had been wanting to draw a strip for years (with many rejections to show for his efforts) but also because he could escape art-room drudgery like photo retouching. The strip was to appeal to children while also containing action, adventure, and romance. In *Dickie Dare* Caniff displayed a flair for adventure and humor—much as, for the previous ten years, other pioneers of the second wave like Roy Crane and Harold Gray had been tempering their adventure stories.

Dickie was an average American boy, graced with a livelier imagination than most. Initially the strip concerned itself with Dickie's daydream encounters with romantic heroes of fiction, legend, and history. Like a Little Nemo in Hollywood, Dickie rode with Robin Hood, sailed the seas with pirates, and even spent a week in Bethlehem at the Savior's birth.

Among Milton Caniff's early work for the Associated Press in New York was the children's feature *Puffy the Pig.*

The Gay Thirties was a human-interest panel in the style of genre cartoonists TAD, Clare Briggs, H. T. Webster, and J. R. Williams, except that Caniff frequently added familial homilies.

Caniff in 1934 attempted to mix humor and adventure, the comic with the realistic. In the space of two years, with the help of Noel Sickles, he would master the combination and learn to draw figures in action.

Caniff's artwork steadily improved, and after a few months he was producing a charming kid's strip. But changes were in the wind. Caniff was maturing as a cartoonist at a time when continuity strips were growing in sophistication. *Dickie Dare* began in the tender tradition of *Little Orphan Annie* and *Bobby Thatcher*—children's strips with adventurous, sometimes violent, elements, but still kid's strips. *Tarzan* and *Buck Rogers* seemed to belong to another genre. But a remarkable burst of creativity in 1933 and 1934 resulted in a proliferation of new and exciting adult-oriented continuity strips: *Secret Agent X-9, Flash Gordon, Red Barry, Brick Bradford.* Even *Tim Tyler's Luck,* begun as a rather routine young-boy's strip, took on real-life undertones in exotic settings.

Caniff acted on two pieces of advice he had once received about his new craft. "One was that drawing a newspaper feature is not a matter of fashioning paper dolls for the kiddies. If the feature doesn't sell papers, it is useless. The second thing came from a remark by the late Heinie Reiker, managing editor of the *Dispatch*. He said, 'Always draw your stuff for the guy who pays for the paper. Kids will never see it if the old man doesn't buy the paper and bring it home.' "

So in May of 1934, *Dickie Dare* underwent an abrupt thematic adjustment. At the conclusion of an airy daydream adventure in the public library, Dickie walks home at dusk, suddenly downcast and jealous that his escapades are all imaginary. But as fast as Caniff could make it happen, Dickie meets Dynamite Dan Flynn, a handsome friend of the family, who persuades Mr. and Mrs. Dare to let their son accompany him on a cruise to faraway lands.

Instantly *Dickie Dare* became a new strip with a new premise—and a new maturity. Dickie's world became very real as he dealt with gun smugglers and bad guys who lied, cheated, kidnapped, and murdered right before the eyes of Dickie and the readers. Caniff's drawing style at this time was still largely cartooney but showed a decided effort toward the "straight"; it was not yet realistic, but it contained little exaggeration or comic distortion.

There seems to have been one more inspiration for Caniff's, and Dickie's, transformation at this time. Feelers had reached the cartoonist from Captain Joseph Patterson of the New York *Daily News.* The paper and its syndicate were looking for a new adventure strip, something not only for the kids, but for the adults—the readers and buyers—too. While working on *Dickie Dare,* Caniff began fashioning and negotiating for the strip that was to be called *Terry and the Pirates.* Legend has it that Patterson chose the name Terry from a long list compiled by Caniff, and added "the Pirates" only as a euphonious appellation, not as a thematic prescription. Few pirates of the classical sort would ever appear in *Terry.*

Caniff's first *Terry* strips appeared in October of 1934, and at first the transition was rocky. As his last *Dickie*s appeared, his initial *Terry*s made their debut; he had been paid in advance by the AP and had to wait for royalties from

The syndicate's promotional strip introducing *Terry* to readers, 1935.

the News Syndicate. The young cartoonist had two strips running simultaneously but was starving nonetheless.

The more interesting transition occurred on the drawing table. "The child is father to the man," and the last *Dickie Dare* episodes bore a distinct resemblance to the first year of *Terry and the Pirates*. Obviously Caniff used the earlier strip as a sounding board; it contained elements of structure and character that appealed to him, and he adapted and fine-tuned them. Dickie was a dark-haired boy; Terry, also evidently about ten, was blond. Dan Flynn, the adult protector, was Irish, handsome, dashing, a bit shy about women; his mirror image (except for blond hair turned black) was Pat Ryan in *Terry*. The love interest in *Dickie* was Kim Sheridan, rich and spoiled, and in *Terry* her counterpart was Normandie Drake; both were involved in tentative romances with the boys' protectors.

The very first *Terry* episode found Terry and Pat (and a Chinese comic-relief character named Connie) in the Far East, and the appearance, at least via Caniff's artwork, portends epics of a prepubescent Douglas Fairbanks cast. Yet with an astonishing, sophisticated transformation rivaled only by that of Alex Raymond at the time, Caniff within a year had created a masterpiece of realism and emotion.

The foremost factor in this evolution was the addition of a studio mate—Caniff's old Ohio chum, Noel Sickles. The AP had hired Sickles to draw another adventure strip, *Scorchy Smith,* an aviation epic created by John Terry, brother of animation pioneer Paul Terry. Sickles had quickly adapted to realistic artwork and dramatic storytelling. Having been inspired by a set of illustrations Harold Von Schmidt had drawn for Willa Cather's *Death Comes for the Archbishop* several years earlier—employing lush black brushwork, defining objects by shadows as much as by outlines—Sickles introduced ultrarealism and impressionistic linework to the comics. He constantly experimented—with tones and shading media, for instance—and was to continue his techniques and experiments through the years. Eventually Sickles illustrated many important works, including Hemingway's *Old Man and the Sea,* and is regarded as one of the century's great illustrators.

Sickles's effect on his friend Caniff was electrifying. The figures and backgrounds in *Terry* grew more realistic, and finally the relationship between the two cartoonists grew not only symbiotic but collaborative. For several years Caniff did most of the writing on both their strips and Sickles did most of the artwork. Sickles continued to lend a hand on *Terry* well into 1941 (several years after he abandoned *Scorchy*) and evidently encountered no objections to his delineating Pat Ryan and Scorchy Smith identically.

Both strips are from one studio. Noel Sickles's brushwork, impressionistic shading, and constantly moving "camera" are evident in his *Scorchy Smith*, above. At the same time these techniques entered the world of *Terry and the Pirates*—Scorchy Smith and Pat Ryan of *Terry* even looked identical! Caniff was concentrating on the writing while Sickles took the lead on the artwork. In short order Caniff absorbed all from his studio mate, then made quantum leaps beyond as a comic-strip creator.

Another influence on both artists was the motion picture. The pair would play hooky from deadlines and slip away from their Tudor City apartment on Manhattan's East Side to haunt the movie palaces. What started as fun ended up affecting their work: Caniff's techniques primarily in dialogue and characterization and Sickles's techniques in composition and transition. Their particular fascination, viewed many times during one of its revivals, was D.W. Griffith's immortal *Birth of a Nation*. (Ironically, a generation later, European filmmakers like Resnais and Fellini acknowledged Caniff's influence on *their* work!)

The continuities in *Terry and the Pirates* grew markedly more mature in late 1935, more mature than they had been and more mature than those in other strips, then and ever after. They were sometimes more violent, sometimes more exotic, but always more complex, and therein lay the maturity. Pat Ryan, for instance, had a tentative romance with Normandie Drake; it was ruptured not only by a meddling aunt but by a fitful type of quarrel so common with impetuous lovers. Normandie, almost out of spite, married a society fop. Here was an adventure strip that dealt for a while not with guns and fistfights but with authentic emotions and resonant situations. Caniff was able to project empathy—for the first time in the comic-strip medium—and readers responded.

The role of comic-strip characters, their function and genuine importance, took on new dimensions under Caniff. More than any other humor strip, more than any other adventure strip (especially visual showcases like *Flash Gordon*), *Terry and the Pirates* featured characters with strong and multifaceted personalities. *Little Orphan Annie* was the only other comic strip with finely etched characters, but Harold Gray designed them purposely along different lines; his were symbols rather than portraits.

Many Sunday-page cartoonists leave open spaces for color to do its work, but Caniff always remembered that solid blacks make colors all the more effective, besides setting important moods. *(Above)*

During the first few years of *Terry*, Pat Ryan carried the romantic burdens, such as they were. The sexuality in the work of Raymond and Caniff has never been approached in newspaper comics since. These consecutive dailies are from 1936.

In the beginning *Terry and the Pirates*—like *Dickie Dare* at its close—strove to combine several elements for several audiences, as this Sunday page from 1935 demonstrates. *(Facing page)*

Caniff loved last-panel interruptions. His composition here is brilliant: all the elements—the turned heads, the perspective of the ceiling beams, the blackness of the door-opening, and the off-center, sexy Dragon Lady—direct the reader's eye masterfully.

Caniff occasionally fashioned his players after friends, acquaintances, and even movie stars (he said they not only provided inspiration but gave him a shorthand reference to stereotyped traits for his readers). His most compelling exercise in personality delineation is a high point in comics history.

In 1940, with war raging in China, Terry, Pat, and some friends found themselves stranded on the desolate plains, only to stumble across a helpless band of Chinese war orphans shepherded by, of all people, a proper American heiress. The icy blonde, Raven Sherman, commandeered the assistance and protection of the nonplussed Ryan, and several adventures ensued for the unlikely band.

For a year Raven was a major player or a background figure, but she was a presence, and a realistic one. Little by little, her hardness softened, especially when she met and fell in love with Dude Hennick, a rough-and-tumble roustabout. This unlikely courtship was all the more interesting to readers who had grown and changed with Raven. Then something happened that occasionally occurs in real life but very seldom in the comics: Raven was killed.

In a memorable daily strip—one long, bleak panel—Terry and a grief-stricken Dude buried Raven in a makeshift grave on the Chinese plain. Readers were stunned, many nearly as shocked as the characters in the story. Caniff received thousands of letters and telegrams and even floral memorials. Every year until his death he received communications on the anniversary of Raven's death. All this over a two-dimensional jumble of pictures and words in a few

Two strips show more awesome techniques by Milton Caniff. The first, from 1936, has a strong flavor of violence and action, yet not one punch is thrown; Pat is actually re-strained. But the dialogue and particularly the dizzying change in point of view result in a kinetic strip. The second strip features a silhouetted junk in a long shot, a close-up, and a medium shot—all while very little actual action takes place.

Raven Sherman (with Pat Ryan) during her transition from iceberg to warm friend.

inches of daily newspapers. Under Caniff's approach, the comics became something new on the American cultural landscape.

Caniff's main vehicle for projecting personality was not facial expression or body language, masterful as was his handling of these elements. It was dialogue. He was the first cartoonist since the birth of comics (with the possible, and again idiosyncratic, exception of Harold Gray) to provide his characters with individual voices—speech patterns, accents, quirks, mannerisms. They could be revelatory or superficial, but they had the ring of authenticity. Caniff may well have been inspired by movie dialogue, but he proved that his ears were as talented as his hands while producing *Terry*.

Among a long stream of characters and episodes, a shining moment of dialogue from 1943 endures. America had entered the war, and Terry was a young man in the armed services. Colonel Flip Corkin had replaced Pat Ryan as mentor (he was based on a friend from Ohio State days, Colonel Phil Cochran), and in a Sunday page Corkin paused to deliver a fatherly lecture to Terry on the war—the average guy's role in it and the communal values behind every action. It was a page of "talking heads," with a wordy monologue and absolutely no action. Nevertheless the page was a masterpiece of prose, gripping and sincere, a Gettysburg Address of World War II. It was as compelling, and as effective, as President Roosevelt's Four Freedoms speech or Ernie Pyle's dispatches or Frank Capra's *Why We Fight* films; it was inserted in full in the *Congressional Record,* the only comic strip ever so recognized.

LOVE NOT, YE HOPELESS SONS OF CLAY'

AS IT MUST TO EVERY ONE

Two daily strips from October of 1941. Millions of Americans grieved with Terry and Dude.

TERRY AND THE PIRATES
by MILTON CANIFF

LET'S TAKE A WALK, TERRY...

YES, SIR, COLONEL CORKIN!

I'M GOING TO MAKE A SPEECH — AND IT'LL BE THE LAST ONE OF ITS KIND IN CAPTIVITY — SO DON'T GET A SHORT CIRCUIT BETWEEN THE EARS...

NO, SIR

WELL, YOU MADE IT...YOU'RE A FLIGHT OFFICER IN THE AIR FORCES OF THE ARMY OF THE UNITED STATES...THOSE WINGS ARE LIKE A NEON LIGHT ON YOUR CHEST...I'M NOT GOING TO WAVE THE FLAG AT YOU — BUT SOME THINGS YOU MUST NEVER FORGET...

...EVERY COUNTRY HAS HAD A HAND IN THE DEVELOPMENT OF THE AIRPLANE — BUT, AFTER ALL, THE WRIGHT BROTHERS WERE A COUPLE OF DAYTON, OHIO, BOYS — AND KITTY HAWK IS STRICTLY IN NORTH CAROLINA... THE HALLMARK OF THE UNITED STATES IS ON EVERY AIRCRAFT..

...SO YOU FIND YOURSELF IN A POSITION TO DEFEND THE COUNTRY THAT GAVE YOU THE WEAPON WITH WHICH TO DO IT... BUT IT WASN'T JUST YOU WHO EARNED THOSE WINGS... A GHOSTLY ECHELON OF GOOD GUYS FLEW THEIR HEARTS OUT IN OLD KITES TO GIVE YOU THE KNOW-HOW...

...AND SOME SMART SLIDE RULE JOKERS SWEAT IT OUT OVER DRAWING BOARDS TO GIVE YOU A MACHINE THAT WILL KEEP YOU UP THERE SHOOTING ... I RECOMMENDED YOU FOR FIGHTER AIRCRAFT AND I WANT YOU TO BE COCKY AND SMART AND PROUD OF BEING A BUZZ-BOY...

...BUT DON'T FORGET THAT EVERY BULLET YOU SHOOT, EVERY GALLON OF GAS AND OIL YOU BURN WAS BROUGHT HERE BY TRANSPORT PILOTS WHO FLEW IT IN OVER THE WORST TERRAIN IN THE WORLD! YOU MAY GET THE GLORY — BUT THEY PUT THE LIFT IN YOUR BALLOON!...

...AND DON'T LET ME EVER CATCH YOU BEING HIGH-BICYCLE WITH THE ENLISTED MEN IN YOUR GROUND CREW! WITHOUT THEM, YOU'D NEVER GET TEN FEET OFF THE GROUND! EVERY GREASE MONKEY IN THAT GANG IS RIGHT BESIDE YOU IN THE COCKPIT — AND THEIR HANDS ARE ON THAT STICK, JUST THE SAME AS YOURS...

...YOU'LL GET ANGRY AS THE DEVIL AT THE ARMY AND ITS SO-CALLED RED TAPE...BUT BE PATIENT WITH IT... SOMEHOW, THE OLD EAGLE HAS MANAGED TO END UP IN POSSESSION OF THE BALL IN EVERY WAR SINCE 1776 — SO JUST HUMOR IT ALONG...

14th AIR FORCE U.S.A.F.

OKAY, SPORT, END OF SPEECH...WHEN YOU GET UP IN THAT "WILD BLUE YONDER" THE SONG TALKS ABOUT — REMEMBER, THERE ARE A LOT OF GOOD GUYS MISSING FROM MESS TABLES IN THE SOUTH PACIFIC, ALASKA, AFRICA, BRITAIN, ASIA AND BACK HOME WHO ARE SORTA COUNTING ON YOU TO TAKE IT FROM HERE! GOOD NIGHT, KID!

This way TO TOKIO!
Next stop U.S.A.

"Pirates" like the Dragon Lady eventually grew more high-tech in their villainy, while Pat Ryan mellowed and Terry matured (Hotshot Charlie was a replacement for the stereotypical Connie). The unseen, but commented-upon, reaction of the Dragon Lady in the last panel is masterful.

In possibly the most famous Sunday-page comic strip ever published, certainly the most powerful and effective, Caniff used a lot of words—but what words!—and superbly varied angles and colors. *(Facing page)*

What also made that particular Sunday page so brilliant was the artwork. Instead of showing a succession of faces, Caniff moved his point of view radically and dramatically. Here is the remaining substantial contribution of Caniff the cartoonist. No doubt again inspired by the cinema, Caniff shifted from close-ups to long shots to silhouettes to down shots in order to heighten or complement the action inherent in a story. Thus the plot line, the characters' personalities, the particular dialogue, and the artwork worked in concert to make a comic strip. Most cartoonists previously were content to concentrate on one or two aspects alone.

The techniques of the Sickles–Caniff style certainly attracted the readers' attention, but set the cartooning profession on its collective ear. Their brushwork and chiaroscuro were actually used as time-saving devices. When they depicted shadows and wrinkles and textures, they used an impressionistic approach that, when reduced on the newspaper page, created the effect of photographic realism. A generation of cartoonists began laboring ceaselessly to achieve the "Caniff look" in their own work.

Between 1936 and 1941 *Terry and the Pirates* virtually sang; there was nary a character nor an episode that failed to arrest attention or that does not hold up critically years later. Among the more memorable characters through the years were many women—and Caniff was famed for covert and overt sexuality in his material—including the sultry Burma, April Kane, Taffy Tucker, Hu Shee,

Rouge, and Nasthalia (Nasty) Smythe-Heatherstone. And for all the gritty realism in *Terry*, in its early years it was still a sort of fantasy strip filled with exotic locales, bizarre villains (like Captain Judas and the Charles Laughton-inspired Sandhurst), and sexy women.

America's entry into World War II changed all that. It would have seemed that a real war—involving genuine pirates, as it were—would provide the strip with an element it had lacked, ever so slightly, before; that a documentary component would round out Caniff's realistic tales. The opposite was the case. The magic element in *Terry*—in all of Caniff's work—was the release valve represented by romantic, otherworldly, even picaresque (to recall one of Caniff's cherished self-characterizations) aspects. The effect was particularly evident in the figure that was perhaps Caniff's strongest character, certainly a sharper personality than Terry himself: the Dragon Lady.

The original Dragon Lady was an inspired creation. To have the embodiment of evil, a sinister half-Oriental eminence with venomous proclivities, appear as an agonizingly tempting beauty was masterful. And true to life—if all evil were ugly, would not sinning be easier to resist? But in the war years, Caniff had to make a choice—would she side with the enemy (with whom she had previously collaborated when they were China's, not America's, foes) or stick with the Chinese? She joined the good guys, remaining as ambiguous as possible for story situations, but her persona was violated. And the same thing happened, basically, to *Terry* as a strip. It might not have seemed so apparent, except that Caniff, for the rest of his career, seemed more wedded to promoting military themes, loyalties, and causes, than reviving those picaresque situations.

Ironically, his last burst of exotic, if not otherworldly, attention occurred in the thickest of wartime settings. Caniff did not serve in uniform, so he tirelessly served the war effort through drawings and special efforts; he designed a run of

Terry specifically for camp newspapers—racier by a wide shot than the traditional version in home-front papers. The News Syndicate objected, however, so Caniff simply created a new strip and a new star: *Male Call Starring Miss Lace.*

If Thomas Nast had been, in President Lincoln's words, "the North's most effective recruiting sergeant" through his cartoons, then Milton Caniff was surely America's most effective morale officer in World War II. The strip abounded with inside jokes about the military and with cheesecake galore. After running in hundreds of camp newspapers, it was collected twice in book format.

In 1945 it was announced that Caniff would switch syndicates and create a new comic strip. The move was bold—retiring from a classic success voluntarily— but Caniff was looking for new worlds to conquer. Specifically, he was looking also for greater creative control and a larger degree of ownership rights. He switched to the *Chicago Sun-Times,* flagship paper of liberal newspaper mogul Marshall Field (with distribution help from King Features Syndicate) and created *Steve Canyon.*

Canyon starred a former Air Transport pilot who set himself up in business as a soldier-of-fortune-of-the-air in the days after the war; the strip commenced on January 19, 1947 (while *Terry* continued until 1973, drawn by George Wunder). The premise of *Canyon* fulfilled, in a high-tech manner, Caniff's vicarious wanderlust and picaresque leanings. Early stories were exciting, and the cartoonist once again provided a memorable cast, most of them women like the sinister Copper Calhoun, Poteet Canyon, Herself Muldoon, Miss Missou, Princess Sunflower, Madame Lynx, and Doe Redwood.

Then another war came along—Korea—and yet another in Vietnam, with the endless twilight of the Cold War as a constant backdrop from the fifties through the seventies. Canyon re-enlisted and was often pictured in uniform; for a time he worked with the CIA. To many readers it seemed, at best, that Canyon was a seven-day-a-week recruiting poster and, at worst, that his creator had lost the magic formula for mixing plot, character, dialogue, and art as he had so supremely in *Terry and the Pirates.*

Many stories seemed strident rather than subtle. Caniff began fashioning characters, it seemed, after every acquaintance, so that readers were left wondering if each name were a pun; where once real characters had trod, there now were obvious caricatures of real chums. His dialogue tended to evolve to the stagey, and more and more humor entered *Canyon,* both in plot lines and exchanges. Finally, Caniff's art took on a static appearance—at least compared to the sweeping vistas and emotional close-ups he juxtaposed so masterfully in *Terry.* One reason might have been that his last assistant (he employed several through

During the war Caniff drew a special *Terry* strip that never appeared in "civilian" newspapers. He renamed it *Male Call*, replaced Burma with a gal named Miss Lace, and a classic was born.

Terry And The Pirates

Wow Chow

the years) was the first who penciled instead of inked, so that Caniff surrendered the vital function of arranging compositions and points of view. During a period when adventure strips declined in the 1970s and 1980s, Caniff turned to lighter stories, many featuring Canyon's niece, Poteet, and her unorthodox friend, Bitsy Beekman. He also married Canyon to Summer Olsen, in a move that characterized the abandonment of any more picaresque pretensions.

Any remnants of exotic adventures in the last years of Caniff's work on *Steve Canyon*—the cartoonist died on April 3, 1988—were in prolonged dream sequences where Steve played roles in history or engaged in fanciful adventures. Caniff's career had come full circle, as the closing *Steve Canyon* episodes resembled *Dickie Dare* stories—but it did not seem fitting.

During its first few years *Steve Canyon* recaptured the verve and excitement of *Terry*. Caniff evidently relished the art chores too; among the methods he experimented with at the time (this dramatic page is from 1951) were direct inking without a pencil sketch and drawing images larger than the framed panels. White opaquing ink and the engraver's tool adjusted for the artwork outside the borders.

The drama in *Steve Canyon* was set around the world—and in Steve's head. The strip became personal and even domestic, and eventually Steve married.

In truth, the forty-one years of *Steve Canyon* could not hold a candle to the twelve years of *Terry and the Pirates*. The creative tragedy is mitigated by the fact that neither could the output of virtually any other cartoonist. In his best period, Caniff achieved many tangible successes, but his major triumph was the capturing of elements that elude many cartoonists, as well as creators in other popular arts: mood, evocation, and atmosphere.

In comic-strip history, in the second wave of which Milton Caniff was so prominent a player, there have been great names. Alex Raymond, the romanticist, is honored. Harold Foster, the classicist, is respected. Harold Gray, the expressionist, is studied; Chester Gould, another expressionist, is analyzed. But Milton Caniff, the realist, was all those things and has been copied widely, while none of the others has been to any great degree. There remains today, almost sixty years after he burst upon the scene, a discernible Caniff school; there are still new cartoonists who adopt his brushwork, his angles, his pacing, even his wrinkles.

To categorize the great American comic-strip artists in another manner, cartoonists like McCay, Raymond, and Foster tended to emphasize the visual over the narrative. Segar, Capp, and Kelly leaned the other way, a no less honorable or justifiable approach. Harold Gray and Milton Caniff not only juxtaposed but fused the two traditions, elevating the comic strip to a unique form of expression, finally and firmly.

Those exotic locales and memorable characters in *Terry and the Pirates* were indeed otherworldly. They are immortal.

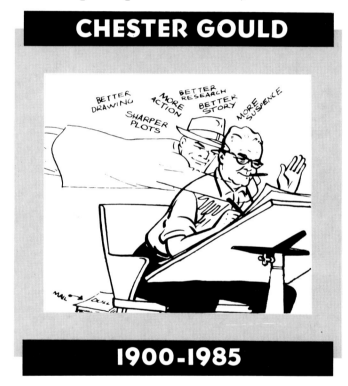

13

With Chester Gould we come to probably the worst artist in this book. Why, then, is he considered one of the best cartoonists—or comic-strip artists—in the history of the art form? Quite simply, Gould reminds us that comic-strip creators are not just portraitists—they are storytellers as well. They tell special kinds of stories, utilizing the dynamics of time and space, constantly showing parallel actions and differing points of view.

Gould was a comic-strip expressionist, like Harold Gray—making his pen lines reflect his world view, employing personification, relating morality plays instead of episodes in a serial—but to really understand Gould's contributions it is more revealing to contrast him with a cartoonist like Alex Raymond, not a soulmate like Gray. Raymond, the creator of such notable strips as *Flash Gordon* and *Jungle Jim,* was arguably the comics' best artist, but he was an inferior storyteller for the first dozen years of his career. It was the compelling brilliance of his images and his eventual mastery of strip conventions that put Raymond in the front rank of America's great comic-strip artists. Chester Gould, on the other hand, had chronic problems with anatomy and perspective—arms jutted from elsewhere than shoulders, foreground figures were smaller than background figures—but they were of no great significance in the overall structure of Gould's comic-strip work.

He may have had problems with drawing, but Gould was a master of narration, and drawing is but one part of the comics' unique vocabulary. The graphic component of the comics seems most important because it is most apparent to the reader, but the essence of the comic strip is narration—literary and visual. Gould knew how to blend the ingredients, and his comic-strip expression was unique, personal, and powerful. His artwork became not bad but personal and idiosyncratic.

If Gould's artistic approach is a lesson in comic-strip creation, then his career is a Horatio Alger story of pure determination. Neither his indulgent contemporaries nor history, with the benefit of hindsight, could have pegged Gould for immortality on the basis of the awful succession of cartoons and strips he doggedly produced for the ten years preceding his .357-magnum opus, *Dick Tracy.*

Chester Gould was born in Pawnee, Oklahoma Territory, on November 20, 1900. His father worked on a local newspaper, so young Chester grew up reading out-of-town papers and syndicate proof sheets and followed all the popular strips of the day, his favorites being *Mutt and Jeff,* the *Katzenjammer Kids, Mama's Angel Child, Hairbreadth Harry,* and *Slim Jim,* which was about a rural police trio forever in pursuit of a skinny hobo. Gould followed the usual path of young cartooning aspirants: he painted show cards, caricatured local celebrities, entered cartooning contests in children's magazines, and subscribed to correspondence schools.

He took the W.L. Evans cartooning course by mail and showed himself to be as much a self-promoter as an accomplished cartoonist by writing a testimonial letter for the school, which was published in national magazine ads in 1919. The reproduced letter read "Chester Gould, Cartoonist, *Tulsa Democrat"* and praised the Evans course for its content and methods. In reality Gould worked for the *Democrat* less than four weeks, contributing several cartoons during a local political campaign.

In 1921 Gould left Oklahoma for Chicago. He held odd jobs, many of them in the world of newspaper art; he filled in briefly doing sports cartoons for the Chicago *Journal* and worked a year for a mat-art service, drawing spot pieces labeled "year-end sale" and such. Every week he made the rounds of the Windy City's six newspapers, never with any luck or job offers. But Gould was determined. The cartooning business was glamorous, and this was also the decade of *The Front Page* in Chicago journalism.

Finally Gould was hired by the *Chicago Tribune,* but worked in the copy and art department—where once again he was drawing nothing more demanding than gimcracks for advertisements—then he went over to Hearst's *Chicago American.* On the *American* he was assigned several strips and even made some noise up and down the Hearst chain, where his work was occasionally picked up. He drew a strip called *Radio Cats,* about a feline family hooked on the wireless craze then captivating America, and was also assigned *Fillum Fables.*

Ed Wheelan was one of the few cartoonists who ever deserted William Randolph Hearst; mostly the traffic went in the opposite direction. Wheelan had created the popular *Midget Movies,* which simultaneously parodied movie serials and provided a group of ensemble players in a vehicle for continued stories. When Wheelan left to draw a new version (*Minute Movies*) for the George Matthew Adams Service, the Hearst organization plugged the hole with Gould's *Fillum Fables.*

Gould's imitation was dishwater strong and soon forgotten; the cartoonist's heart was never in the effort anyway. Another strip for the Hearst stable that was meant to fill the void fared somewhat better: E.C. Segar's *Thimble Theatre.*

Chester Gould, wanting to draw his own comic strip and be his own boss, made a few moves in that direction in the late 1920s. He created a new feature for the *American* called *Why It's a Windy City,* but the cartoon interviews with celebrities did not catch on. He took part-time courses at Northwestern University, finally earning a degree in commerce. He took a job on the Chicago *Daily News,* where he drew *The Girl Friends,* a frivolous, pretty-girl strip that, when the Depression set in, seemed out of place.

After securing a position with the mighty Hearst organization to no effect, Gould methodically set his sights again on the *Chicago Tribune.* Cousin to the *Trib*'s owner was "Captain" Joseph Patterson, who was publisher of the New York *Daily News.* Gould heard that the *News* was looking for a political cartoonist and began drawing a daily political cartoon and shipping it express by train, delivered to Patterson's desk, every day. It cost Gould fifty dollars a month, besides the effort (and ink), and resulted in no job; C.D. Batchelor became the *News* political cartoonist. But Gould caught Patterson's attention. The Captain was a good friend to have, for not only did he publish the *News,* but he ran the Chicago Tribune–N.Y. News Syndicate, which rivaled Hearst's King Features with popular features like *Little Orphan Annie, The Gumps, Harold Teen, Moon Mullins, Winnie Winkle,* and *Smitty.*

It was 1931. Gangsters seemed to be overrunning Chicago; their activities were certainly overrunning the headlines. After countless comic-strip submissions in a variety of humorous categories, Chester Gould responded to both the headlines and the recent trend in strips toward adventure. He worked up five dailies of a strip he called *Plainclothes Tracy* (Tracy being a vague pun on a detective's activities) and drew them as realistically as he could. The hero was inspired by Sherlock Holmes—and his square-jawed profile was reminiscent of the most famous of Holmes's impersonators, the stage actor William Gillette. Into the short sequence Gould crammed violence, guns, tough-talking dames, and lots of action.

Patterson must have realized that finally something new had come across his desk—not just a new something from that persistent loser, Gould, but something new in comic strips. Continuities were not new in 1931, but adventure strips were. Yet most of them were exotic: *Buck Rogers* took place centuries in the future; *Tarzan* was swinging through picturesque jungles; *Tailspin Tommy*

"Plainclothes Tracy" was the first strip of the week of samples that Chester Gould submitted to Captain Joseph Patterson.

portrayed the glamorous world of aviators like Lucky Lindy. Even *Little Orphan Annie,* which could be considered realistic, was more melodramatic than adventurous. And virtually no strip was violent. The front pages chronicled violence—why not the comic pages? What if a Sherlock Holmes met up with an Al Capone?

On Patterson's next trip to Chicago he summoned Gould to discuss the strip. He doubled the pun and gave the detective the first name of Dick (underworld slang for detective). He suggested an origin story that would establish the strip's violent tone and provide a premise and motivation; Gould would be hard-pressed to offend the conservative Patterson when dealing with crime, retribution, and violence. In the opening story, as suggested by Patterson, Tracy is an average Joe—not yet a cop—who one night calls on his sweetheart, Tess Trueheart. She lives with her parents above the family delicatessen. After Tracy arrives, thieves break in for the day's receipts, kill Mr. Trueheart, and, implicitly, rape Tess. Over the body of Tess's father the young Tracy vows eternal vengeance on criminals.

It is possible that Captain Patterson harbored some doubts about *Tracy's* reception, because the strip commenced not in the syndicate's flagship papers in Chicago or New York, but in the small *Detroit Mirror.* Public interest and acceptance were swift, however, and *Dick Tracy* soon became a national sensation.

Tracy's cast began, and was to remain, small. There was Tracy himself; a few police companions; the orphaned Dick Tracy Junior, as he was known, created for the younger readers ("Junior" became a police sketch artist and eventually was adopted by Tracy); and a dizzying, ever-changing cast of villains.

In truth there were two Tracy strips through the years, so markedly did Gould change his structure. Through the 1930s *Dick Tracy* was a crime-solving strip, dwelling on the commission of crimes, the villains, and their schemes. Like Sherlock Holmes, Tracy followed clues and solved mysteries, with readers present every step of the way. Villains were cruel, often sadistic, but sometimes showed a human side, and in the early stories Gould frequently depicted innocent folk caught in the crossfire—and by circumstance.

Around 1940 *Tracy* evolved into a new structure. In spite of the fact that Gould relied on props ranging from state-of-the-art to make-believe police paraphernalia, *Tracy* became less documentary and more symbolic. The number of bit players was distilled further; although battles were fought for the protection of innocents, their presence was less evident, and anyone appearing in *Dick Tracy,* it seemed, was either good or bad—there was no middle ground.

SILHOUETTE

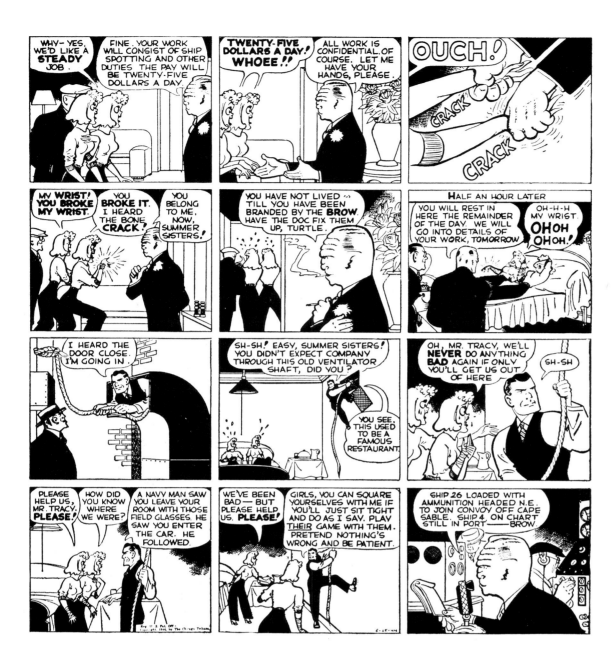

The villains became more bizarre, although this was only the most obvious change. No longer did Gould pattern his bad guys after motion-picture heavies or selected gangsters in the headlines. The new rogues' gallery in *Dick Tracy* contained virtual abstractions who became trademarks of the strip and are still living today in America's cultural consciousness, generations after their comic-strip demise.

The major alteration in Gould's technique and structure, however, was in the type of story. Virtually every sequence after 1940 was not a mystery; the commission of a crime was not always focused upon. Usually readers knew who the villain was and had no clues to track. *Dick Tracy* became instead the eternal chase.

Gould achieved several things simultaneously. With Tracy as the hunter and a changing cast of villains as the hunted, there was little opportunity for nuances about relativism, points of law, or psychological motivation—which was fine, according to Gould's (and Patterson's) theory of social philosophy. Gould's world became black and white, just as Harold Gray's was, and so the eternal chase in *Tracy* acquired overtones of retribution rather than justice. Further, Gould

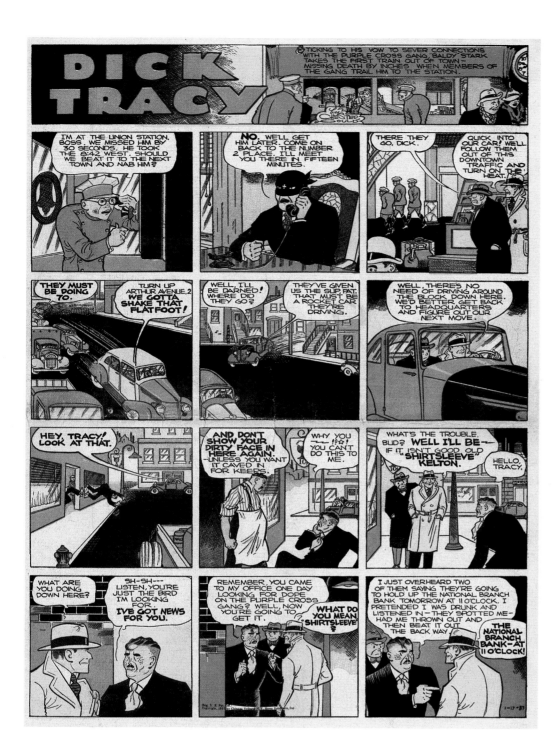

established a style of pacing in his stories that was more breathless than that of other strips; he constantly shifted the reader's point of view from Tracy to the villain to Tracy, splicing a terse narration throughout the panels and employing all manner of cliff-hanging devices. For weeks a villain would elude Tracy's best efforts by means as logical as careful planning or as unlikely as unexpected coincidences, and the result was at once as compelling as crime movies and pulp novels (both of which Gould preceded and no doubt inspired) and as believable as front-page news stories.

The chase became a motif, and the characters—Tracy's ubiquitous profile and the bizarre villains' visages—became virtual icons. There is no evidence that Gould was conversant with the historical tradition of morality plays, but *Dick Tracy* was certainly in that tradition. The strip can be seen as much an editorial as an entertainment feature in the newspapers, but was a remarkable and sophisticated saga, with fierce integrity and consistency on several levels.

232

Like Gray, Gould was not an inept realist, and neither was his rogues' gallery populated with virtual stereotypes because he lacked a deeper imagination. His villains, like those in *Little Orphan Annie,* are the personification and manifestation of evil. If crime is ugly, Gould reasoned, criminals should be presented as ugly. If the city, infested with miscreants, provides scant haven for decent folk, it should be depicted as icily neutral, which is how *Tracy's* settings invariably looked. The action in *Dick Tracy* is almost abstract; Gould seemed to draw backdrops instead of backgrounds.

Chester Gould was a Platonist in an increasingly Aristotelian world, a moralist fighting the tide of situational ethics. The main difference between *Annie* and *Tracy* was that Annie's world was more ordered—frequently threatened, but ruled by an omniscient authority. In *Tracy* there was an implied value system (implied with the force of a sledge hammer!), but ultimate victory for those values was forever just beyond reach. Annie could be serene, while Tracy was

constantly on the prowl; Annie was hunted by evil, while Tracy hunted the evildoers.

Gould had a fascination with objects. After he achieved success with *Tracy*, he hired one of America's pioneer police sketch artists, A.A. Valanis, to consult on investigative procedure and equipment. One of his assistants, Rick Fletcher, prided himself on being "the best gun artist in the comics." And Gould filled his strip with polygraph machines, oscilloscopes, microscopes—and his famous panoply of gadgets like the two-way wrist radio and the magnetic, antigravitational "space coupe." Ironically, it is usually some very mundane prop that does the villain in. After a dozen slithery escapes, the Nazi spy Brow is impaled by a flagpole; B-B Eyes is immobilized by a used tire; Flattop becomes wedged between pilings and drowns; Mumbles accidentally punctures his life raft. Gould was not implying irony in creating simple solutions after mechanically complicated pursuits; rather, he was implying that—in his Providential value system—the universe itself, via small objects even, conspires toward the good.

On such assumptions Gould built a style. But fully half of his style was the artwork, and we can return to a discussion of Gould's singular graphic contributions. Apart from addled anatomy and perspective (or, one is tempted to think, partly because of it), *Dick Tracy* showcased a visual style that was not pretty but was attractive. Gould spotted his blacks masterfully, leading the reader's eye through the panels, providing balance or asymmetry as the sequence demanded. Critic Donald Phelps has observed that "Gould's blackness is not always darkness, not the dimming or withdrawal of light but the supplanting of light by a vigorous, surface-rending presence that commands the design in its perverse, roughshod energy."

Gould used his "camera" in an odd manner. He would shift between close-ups, middle ground, and long shots readily enough, but he almost invariably showed his characters either full face or in profile. The practice may have been due to his own limitations, but it gave the strip a friezelike flavor in its most classical interpretation, and a mug-shot flavor in its tabloid interpretation. However—and here Gould proved himself as innovative with his point of view as Milton Caniff in *Terry and the Pirates*—his "camera" often focused on a prop exclusively, or on a character's furtive actions or on a pointed firearm. A common Gould panel would be a dialogue balloon and the character from the waist down, counting loot or fondling a gun.

Artistic inconsistencies were molded by Gould into the functional equivalents of his famed labels and arrows ("Two-way wrist radio"; "That prison uniform label") that were silver platters for readers. An exaggerated forearm with a gun or a severely distorted setting attracted readers' attention and allowed Gould to "command the design," to set the agenda for the few seconds readers spend with a comic strip.

It was in the 1940s that Gould created a spate of memorable villains—the Mole, Littleface, B-B Eyes, Flattop, The Brow, Shakey, Mumbles, Breathless Mahoney—and some unforgettable types who started as, or turned out to be, good guys—Vitamin Flintheart, Gravel Gertie, B.O. Plenty. At that time *Dick Tracy* became a cottage industry as well as a comic strip, with reprint comics, Big Little Books, movie serials, and all sorts of toys serving a waiting public; eventually there would be a television program and an animated series as well.

Throughout the fifties and sixties the essence of *Tracy* hardened but grew lighter at the same time. Gould grew more preachy, especially during the permissive sixties. The label "Law and Order First" floated willy-nilly through the panels as conspicuously and as often as "Two-way wrist radio." Episodic interludes pictorialized the offenses of court rulings that allowed criminals to go free while Tracy raced to document some meaningless shred of evidence at a judge's demand. During that same period, however, Gould indulged in fantasy; it was the early days of America's space program, and he had his characters travel to the moon and meet a new species of being. Junior Tracy even married the Moon Maid. (It is unclear whether Gould was merely evolving his style or reacting to the public's changing preference for humor strips at the time.) One incident was revealing: Gould once drew Tracy in an impossible situation and had the detective look out of the panel and instruct Gould to extricate him. Gould then drew his own hand with an eraser eliminating the crisis. The sequence was never printed; the avuncular Captain Patterson advised Gould never to violate the "reality" of his comic strip's world.

One bow to changing times was a diminution of bullets through the head, at one time a Gould stock-in-trade. They whizzed, with blood and brains exiting and "splat" sound effects dutifully lettered astride the ear, through villains' and Tracy's head with seeming abandon—and inspired references in *Li'l Abner's* long-running strip-within-a-strip spoof of *Tracy*, Fearless Fosdick.

On Christmas Day 1977, Chester Gould retired from the chase. The chase continues, for *Dick Tracy* was passed to a new team (the fine crime-novelist Max Allan Collins and, today, the Pulitzer Prize-winning cartoonist Dick Locher), but Gould did what few busy cartoonists have managed to do in their last years. He pushed the chair away from the drawing board and enjoyed the fruits of his labor. *Dick Tracy* was always one of the most popular strips once Gould hit his individualized stride, and his peers honored him in rare fashion by twice awarding him the National Cartoonists Society's Reuben award.

Gould died at his home in Woodstock, Illinois, on May 11, 1985, much honored and assured of his place in history. His achievements were undreamed of by anyone but—undoubtedly—himself. After so many years and so many attempts, Chester Gould succeeded. He learned to draw comic strips—and to craft them in brilliant fashion. And contrary to his own epigram, crime, in his case, *did* pay.

14

"I am sure that [Al Capp] is the best satirist since Laurence Sterne," wrote John Steinbeck. "He has taken our customs, our dreams, our habits of thought, our social structure, our economics, examined them gently like amusing bugs. Then he has pulled a nose a little longer, made outstanding ears a little more outstanding, described it in dreadful folk poetry and returned it to us in a hilarious picture of our ridiculous selves."

In a real sense Al Capp is the other side of the coin represented by Harold Gray of *Little Orphan Annie*. Both cartoonists made their strips intensely personal statements of their own beliefs and prejudices, their world views. Capp took the posture a step further by consciously making his strip, *L'il Abner*, an extension of his own personality as well—and it was a personality as vivid and controversial as any in the cartooning world. Between the 1940s and 1970s Al Capp was arguably the most famous, and certainly the most visible, strip artist in America. When *L'il Abner* made its debut in 1934, the vast majority of comic strips were designed chiefly to amuse or thrill their readers. Capp turned that world upside down by routinely injecting politics and social commentary into *L'il Abner*, wearing his grouses with modern life on his ink-stained sleeve. *Abner* became a soapbox for Capp's satirical forays, many of which escaped the formal bounds of the strip's premise and setting. The strip was the first to regularly introduce characters and story lines having nothing to do with the nominal stars of the strip. The technique—as invigorating as it was unorthodox—was later adopted by cartoonists like

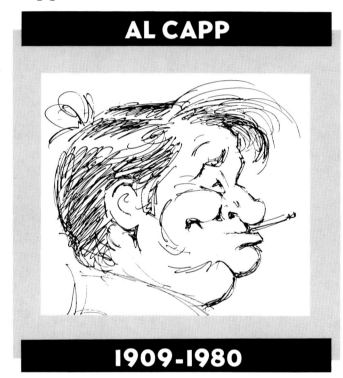

AL CAPP

1909-1980

Walt Kelly and Garry Trudeau, whose strips (*Pogo* and *Doonesbury*) also inherited Capp's penchant for political commentary.

Just as he invested new functions other than simple entertainment in his comic strip, Capp helped draw new attention and respect to his chosen profession. Through *L'il Abner* the newspaper comic section achieved unprecedented importance, attracting new readers who were more intellectual and attuned to the news. Cartoon historian Coulton Waugh reported that many poll respondents who claimed they ordinarily ignored comic strips admitted that *L'il Abner* was their sole exception.

Al Capp was born Alfred Gerald Caplin in New Haven, Connecticut, on September 28, 1909; forty years later his pen name became his legal name. Two events in his youth affected his later career and, undoubtedly, his outlook on life: at the age of nine he lost a leg, and at fifteen he hitchhiked through the South and first encountered hillbillies in the Ozarks.

The young Capp lost his leg when he was run over by an ice truck. It is difficult to assess the effect this accident and the subsequent handicap had on Capp's outlook. In later years he referred to the incident with the ice wagon matter-of-factly. He even joked about his wooden leg, relating the time he carelessly retired for the night in a hotel, and the next morning a room-service waiter, noticing the leg on the floor, inquired whether the gentleman under the bed desired any breakfast. In spite of his phlegmatic attitude toward disability, Capp maintained that cruelty and a desire to feel superior were the ingredients that underlay all comedy. Indeed, the body of Capp's work in *L'il Abner* reflected this point of view, far more sardonic than lighthearted in spirit.

Al Capp temporarily left home in the mid-1920s to visit his uncle, a rabbi in Memphis, Tennessee. Although this was the period of the South's most celebrated displays of insularity, Capp left few records of incidents that involved prejudice or even inconvenience during his trip—but he did absorb copious impressions of memorable backwoods folks and colorful settings, which he would use to build his career a decade later.

Al Capp's father was an amateur cartoonist who regularly amused his children with drawings. This early pastime obviously had a strong influence on both Al and his brother Elliot (who went on to script more than a dozen notable comic strips, including *Abbie an' Slats, The Heart of Juliet Jones, Dr. Kildare,* and *Dark Shadows*). Young Al decided on a career in art and attended a succession of art schools—including the Pennsylvania Academy of the Fine Arts and Boston's Museum School—always keeping one step ahead of tuition bills. Finally Harry Resnick, Capp's uncle, arranged a job interview for his nephew at the Associated Press in New York.

In the early 1930s the AP offered newspapers a complete package of news by wire, features, photos, maps, decorations, and comics. Capp was hired in 1931 to take over the single-panel feature *Col. Gilfeather,* a weak imitation of cartooning's classic Major Hoople, the overstuffed, prevaricating blowhard. Capp inherited *Gilfeather* from Dick Dorgan, the younger and deservedly forgotten brother of cartooning legend TAD Dorgan (*Indoor Sports, Judge Rummy's Court*) but quit after three fitful months. In turn, young Milton Caniff became Capp's successor.

Confident that he could now create his own comic strip, Capp left the AP

MISTER GILFEATHER   by A. G. Caplin

HOWDY DO!

— MR. GILFEATHER — MEET 'SOAPY' WATERS, — HE'S THE NEW DISHWASHER HERE AT THE MANSION HOUSE — THE PLACE IS SO CROWDED WITH THE SUMMER FOLKS, THEY AIN'T NO PLACE TO PUT HIM EXCEPT IN WITH YOU! — — WE LIKE TO GIVE THE BREAKS TO THEM AS PAYS REGULAR!

AS WELCOME AS A HORNET

Al Capp (then still A. G. Caplin) drew an early and earnest effort, *Mister Gilfeather*, for the Associated Press in 1931.

shortly after quitting *Col. Gilfeather*. Legend has it that while Capp was walking along Central Park one afternoon with a bundle of comic-strip samples under his arm, a limousine pulled up to the sidewalk. The chauffeur announced that he and his employer in the back seat had a bet about the bundle under Capp's arm. Did the package contain comic strips, as his employer claimed, or did it contain some other sort of oblong object? The chauffeur lost.

As it happened, the winner of the bet was cartoonist Ham Fisher, creator of the popular boxing strip *Joe Palooka*. At the time, *Palooka* was a humorous continuity about an oafish fighter and his scheming manager; it had not yet gained the widespread reputation of later years, when it was eventually transformed into a maudlin melodrama. Fisher's reputation for hiring others to do his work was already well established, and soon Capp was a full-time ghost artist, producing story and art on *Palooka* over Fisher's signature.

In spite of the low pay traditionally afforded Fisher's assistants, as well as the requisite anonymity, Capp's stint on *Palooka* was wonderful on-the-job training in the craft of comic-strip creation. Capp dealt with deadlines and reproduction problems, syndicate relations, plotting, pacing, and character development. Among the characters he introduced was a dumb hillbilly, Big Leviticus, a creation forged from memories of his trip through the Ozarks. The hillbilly proved popular and, in fact, shared the spotlight with Palooka himself through several story lines.

Bolstered by a year of experience, Capp once again set out to draw his own comic strip, and quit *Palooka*. When he eventually sold a new comic strip based on a family of dumb hillbillies—even with no boxers anywhere in sight—Ham Fisher became enraged, inaugurating a feud that continued until Fisher's death in 1956. The feud went public, and each year Fisher reprinted pages of the Big Leviticus sequence to remind readers that his was the comics' *first* hillbilly, a dig at Capp's *L'il Abner*. Capp, for his part, regularly caricatured Fisher in his own strip and even wrote articles about his trying days under Fisher (including "I Remember Monster," for the *Atlantic Monthly*). The fight culminated with Fisher attempting to get Al Capp expelled from the National Cartoonists Society by presenting enlarged *L'il Abner* panels that revealed pornographic details. After it was discovered that Fisher had doctored the examples (and if there was ever a strip that was racy without tampering, it was *L'il Abner!*), Fisher himself was expelled from the NCS, a fact that may have contributed to his eventual suicide.

Controversies notwithstanding—and perhaps, in a small part, because of them—*L'il Abner* was an instant success after making its debut on August 13, 1934. Capp later boasted that when his Uncle Harry showed his samples to King Features Syndicate, largest of the comic distributors, he was promptly offered $250 a week, the equivalent of four or five times that amount today. There is another side to this story, however. The president of King Features, Joseph Connolly, was reported to have commented about the *L'il Abner* samples: "Great strip, great art; yes, sir. A couple of things, though—that Abner's an idiot. Make him a nice kid, with some saddlestripe shoes on him. And Daisy Mae's pretty, but how about some pretty clothes? As a matter of fact, why don't you forget that mountain bit and move them all to New Jersey?"

Capp was distressed by these suggestions, yet attracted to the large guarantee

Al Capp (signing Al G. Cap) introduces the denizens of Dogpatch to America. In the beginning of *Li'l Abner*—this is the first week of strips, from 1934—there was much that was traditional, taken from dialect literature and the movies, in the hillbillies.

One of the first *Li'l Abner* Sunday pages. America was receptive to things of the hills; country-music radio programs were broadcast nationwide, and singers of hillbilly music like Jimmie Rodgers were enjoying major commercial success. The "top strip"(as companion strips were called on color pages, even when they ran below the main features) was *Washable Jones*, a short-lived but inspired fantasy strip.

Connolly offered. In the end his own determination won out. After all, the very reason he left Fisher was to create a comic strip completely on his own, so Capp ultimately accepted an offer from United Feature Syndicate—then one of the smallest distributors—for only $50 a week, without any editorial interference. Later, when *L'il Abner* was a national success, Capp constantly bristled at syndicate interference.

When the syndicate interfered, it was usually to pass on readers' complaints about raciness, political commentary, or contemptuous satire (on targets like Frank Sinatra, Liberace, and *Gone with the Wind*), which sometimes necessitated apologies. Actually, these factors were precisely what helped make *L'il Abner* unique among strips. On the other hand, Capp also observed, "The syndicate had control. I could be fired at any time—they owned it [L'il Abner]. I couldn't take that after a while and said, 'I'm quitting. You can keep the strip.' I meant it. They all got upset, of course, and after a lot of running around they offered me a deal of a brand-new contract, with new terms, and at the end of ten years the strip would become mine. . . . There was an unwritten law that a successful strip had a life-span of ten years . . . and it was figured that a strip had had it after a dozen years. Of course after ten years I was going hotter than ever."

L'il Abner had a defined cast of characters, a strong premise, and a clearly delineated flavor and posture. The central figures were the Yokums—Pappy, Mammy, and Abner; the beautiful hillbilly girl who pined for Abner, Daisy Mae; and their mountain friends and relatives. The premise was the rather audacious assumption that Abner was so dumb, and his family and friends so gullible, that anything could befall them—and did. Other strips presented dense characters as heroes—Happy Hooligan comes to mind—but they were usually redeemed by occasional victories and token dignities at the hands of their creators. Not so for Abner and his friends. Capp, virtually alone among strip creators, consistently displayed no respect for his lead characters; all were so dumb, shiftless, or conniving (or all three) that they could not recognize a triumph even when one hit them over the head. Abner was frequently cheated, beaten, starved, and disgraced, although he continued to remain either cheerful or altogether befuddled through it all. Even when Daisy Mae was chasing him, Abner was too dense to evince a romantic response.

Similarly, Capp's craft was an audacious exercise of verbal and visual techniques. After Abner was launched, Capp was aghast to realize that his strip was one among dozens of others—easily lost amid strips that ran, in those days, over three or four pages of American newspapers. Capp was determined to have Abner immediately stand out in that crowd. To accomplish this, he began to use visual devices—previously available to but underutilized by strip cartoonists—that produced the effect of neon signs festooned upon his daily feature: heavy black panel borders, electric balloon flashes, bold and arresting lettering, black shading, and a colorful vocabulary of aural onomatopoeia, rivaled in the comics only by Roy Crane's sound effects. Occasionally Capp would even draw an elongated vertical panel, obliging the reader to revolve the newspaper in order to follow the action. Earlier cartoonists had achieved impact through decoration, such as George McManus in Bringing Up Father and certainly Winsor McCay in Little Nemo; George Herriman did so via surreal elements in Krazy Kat. But Capp's graphic technique was concerned only with impact, not decoration. His artistic touches were akin to the circus barker's invitations: the best was inside. Abner was essentially a narrative strip.

By carrying the basic traits of his characters' personalities to the nth degree, Capp not only manufactured clean slates on which to design outrageous types, but he harked back to a literary tradition as old as John Bunyan's. Herein is Capp's similarity to Harold Gray, whose Little Orphan Annie, as serious as Abner was humorous, also used extremes to portray vice and virtue. If Abner was supposed to be innocent, he was vacuous to the point of imbecility. To represent the business community, Capp drew General Bullmoose, the most venal and corrupt capitalist this side of radical union tracts. Sexy women? Capp created

Abner got into his predicaments in the strangest ways . . . and Al Capp usually saw to it that they were demeaning, outrageous, and hilarious ways.

The 1937 Li'l Abner (page 244) demonstrates Capp's masterful use of composition—spotting blacks, framing characters in a big, bright moon, and capturing readers' attention with silhouettes and bold lettering. Daisy Mae was perpetually frustrated, never respected, and always thwarted by Capp if not Abner. On page 245, in a 1941 page, Capp showed that he accorded the same feelings toward his leading man.

LI'L ABNER
by AL CAPP

THE ARTISTIC OFFICES OF THE GREAT **ROOT TOOT ZOOT SUIT** MANUFACTURING COMPANY

WASHINGTON CROSSING THE DELAWARE

THE ONLY WAY TO MAKE THIS NATION **ZOOT SUIT CONSCIOUS** IS TO CREATE A GREAT NATIONAL HERO WHO PERFORMS INCREDIBLE DEEDS OF VALOR—ALWAYS DRESSED IN A ZOOT SUIT!!—

SO, NATURALLY, EVERY RED-BLOODED YOUNG MAN IN AMERICA WILL WANT TO EMULATE THIS HERO. WE'LL SELL **MILLIONS** OF ZOOT SUITS!!

BUT—WHERE CAN WE FIND SOMEONE **STUPID** ENOUGH TO CONTINUALLY RISK HIS LIFE TO ADVERTISE OUR PRODUCT?

HM!—IT'D HAVE TO BE SOMEONE WITH A **VERY LOW** I.Q.!!

RIGHT!! FIND ME THE MAN WITH THE LOWEST I.Q. IN AMERICA!!

YES, SIR!

ONE MONTH LATER—

E-EGAD! WHAT'S **THAT**?

I FOUND HIM, DANGLING FROM A TREE IN YELLOWSTONE NATIONAL PARK, BOSS! HE HAS THE LOWEST I.Q. IN **AMERICA**!!

MAYBE IN THE **WORLD**!

MY MAN—ER—YOU **ARE** A MAN, AREN'T YOU?—YOU CERTAINLY AREN'T **IMBECILE** ENOUGH TO ACCEPT A JOB THAT MEANS RISKING DEATH, EVERY DAY?

WHO **SAYS** I'M NOT?—

SPLENDID!—**THAT'S** THE STUFF! SIGN YOUR NAME HERE—WITH THIS PEN.

I AIN'T **GOT** NO NAME. THEY CALLS ME "**HEY, YOU!**"——AN'WHAT DOES "SIGN" MEAN?—AN' WHAT'S THIS—SOMETHIN' T'EAT?

NO, **NO!**—JUST PLACE IT IN YOUR HAND—LIKE THIS—AND MAKE A MARK—**ANY** KIND OF A MARK——

WITH WHICH END?

HOLD EVERYTHING!!

BOSS!!—I'VE JUST FOUND SOMEONE WITH AN EVEN LOWER I.Q. THAN **HIS**!!

IT CERTAINLY CAN'T BE **HUMAN**!!

OH, **AH** IS AS HOOMIN AS TH' NEX' FELLA. AH WERE TOLE THAR WERE SOME QUESTION AS TO WHETHER AH GOT TH' INTELLY-GUNCE T'**HANDLE** THIS JOB!—WAL, JEST LISSEN T'**THIS**! TWO AN' TWO IS THREE; THREE AN' THREE IS FO'; FO' AN' FO' IS-IS—*GULP!* IT'S S-SOMETHIN'!!—OH—MAH **BRAIN**—IT'S **STRAINED**!!

SEE!

YOU'RE FIRED—MORON!!

MORON?—**MY**—THASS PURTY!—"**MISTAH MORON**"—THASS WHUT AH'LL USE FO' A NAME. ALLUS WANTED ONE. MIGHT COME IN HANDY, SOMETIME——

TO BE CONTINUED—

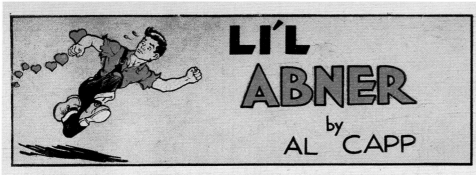

244

many of them—Dogpatch had its own Appasionata von Climax. (Capp was always mystified that he never received a complaint about her name.)

The narrative structure in *L'il Abner* was a clear reflection of, actually an enlargement on, these personality types. Whatever could go wrong did, and usually to the most outrageous—or, occasionally, tragic—ends. The lovable Shmoo was a creature that fulfilled everyone's whims, from the desire for romantic companionship to the desire for a plate of ham and eggs. The Kigmy was another lovable creature, who happened to have a target painted on its posterior. Its name was a pun for the Kigmy's sole function in life: to be kicked by frustrated and hostile humans. The Bald Iggle was a cuddly creature with dreamy eyes; gazing into those eyes impelled one to tell the truth, the whole truth, and nothing but the truth.

In Capp's cosmology these charming creatures were not boons to *L'il Abner's* world—they were menaces. Society could not tolerate the amity and harmony they brought. The Shmoos were beaten back into the Valley of the Shmoon, and the Bald Iggle was slaughtered in the strip by government agents at the behest of businessmen, the military, salesmen, and spouses, who all preferred a world ruled not by the truth but by prevarication.

Many great cartoonists had made their reputations by cleverly ridiculing society and illuminating the foibles of human nature. Opper had begun the tradition, and Rube Goldberg, Milt Gross, TAD, Clare Briggs, and H. T. Webster continued it, but none was as sardonic as Capp. Couched in outlandish fun, his statements were harsh. Capp was calling society absurd, not silly; human nature not simply misguided, but irredeemably and irreducibly corrupt. Unlike any other strip, and indeed unlike many other pieces of literature, *L'il Abner* was more than a satire of the human condition. It was a commentary upon human nature itself.

Dogpatch had a cast of thousands, and the extreme character types among its population were (as Capp would have stated it) merely exaggerated reflections of—shudder!—ourselves. Among the memorable players were Hairless Joe and his friend Lonesome Polecat the Indian; they lived together in a cave and concocted Kickapoo Joy Juice. The term was to become a byword and eventually a licensed soft drink. Sadie Hawkins was an early citizen of Dogpatch whose hunt for a husband inspired an annual Leap Year-with-a-vengeance in the hills and, during the 1940s and 1950s, tag days known as Sadie Hawkins Days on college campuses across the United States. Fearless Fosdick was a commentary on the lowly lives of policemen in general and a parody of *Dick Tracy* in particular. Although Fosdick was Abner's "ideel," the hapless cop's misadventures often took over the strip for weeks on end. Fosdick would trample old ladies and shoot innocent citizens full of holes in the process of apprehending a poor soul who walked on the grass when expressly forbidden to do so. As readers became devotees of the character, Fosdick outgrew his function as mere parody. Chester Gould, creator of *Tracy*, once praised Capp as the only cartoonist doing full-time press-agent work for another cartoonist's strip.

Despite the memorable characters and astonishing plots, Capp was sharply challenged in 1952 when one of his own syndicate staffers attributed the success of the strip to other reasons. As Capp recalled years later, "One guy . . . had not the faintest respect for me. As a matter of fact, it was one day he said rather

Two episodes from the first great Shmoo story (they proved too popular to disappear permanently) are from 1948. Any resemblance to anything, living or dead. . . .

The Kigmies were creatures that allowed Capp to make a comment on prejudice against classes and racial groups.

contemptuously, 'Hey, don't think of yourself as another Dickens. You're a guy who knows a trick: Abner doesn't marry Daisy Mae. Be grateful you thought of it, because that's what makes the strip go—nothing else.' Well, I was horrified. So I got them married. And it went, and we got a lot of publicity besides."

The offhand challenge to Capp resulted in one of the most famous marriages of the century (*Time* and *Life* both accorded it major coverage). The marriage eventually shifted the focus of the strip, although Abner and Daisy Mae's honeymoon sequence was a rather tortured affair, at least for Daisy Mae Yokum, whose

One of the most potent comments on human nature to appear in *Li'l Abner* was the "Bald Iggle" sequence of 1955. Here are the first episode and the last three of the classic story.

Two Sunday pages from the middle period of *Li'l Abner*. The cartoonist depicted in the top page is one of Capp's periodic caricatures of his old boss Ham Fisher. *(Facing page)*

Fearless Fosdick was a strip within a strip—Abner's favorite comic, it sometimes ran for weeks as a separate feature instead of *Li'l Abner*.

LI'L ABNER

BY AL CAPP

Due to a delicate brain transfusion, Li'l Abner now has the great Rumbrandt's genius. He has been hired by Happy Vermin, the world's smartest cartoonist.

("All Ah does is drawr th' pitchers!"—An' he signs 'em!! An' merely fo' that, he pays me a dollah a day!! He's all heart!!")

Excuse me. I must speak to an old friend.

Honest, boss—nobody's seen me in this closet, all day, drawing your comic strip!! Nobody even knows I'm alive!!—I've given up all my friends and pretended I'm dead—like you asked me to!!

You're fired!!—I told you, 20 years ago, this job was temporary!! I've found someone who'll work cheaper!!—

This is your studio.

It looks a li'l like a closet to me.

Naturally!! I have a big reputation!! No one must know that a stupid lout like you is doing all my work for me!!

—And don't forget—if you have to stop to rest for a minute—turn off the light!! No sense running up unnecessary expenses.

Yassuh. Yo' is all heart—

Vermin!!—your comic strip is slipping badly!!

But, how about that original idea I thought of last year? I married my hero to my heroine!!—that's always put new life in other strips!!

It made yours even (yawn!!) duller!!—unless you get some new characters, you'll have to go back to your old racket!!

I can't do that. I sold my mother the shoe-shine box!!

He's all heart.

?!—What are these sketches!! Have you been taking time off?

Oh, no, suh!!—Ah drawed yore strips wif mah hands!! One pen in each!! Them was done wif mah toes, whar ah has quite a bit o' talent also.

Hillbillies?—H-m-m—Yokum!!—I'm proud of having created these characters!!—they'll make millions for me!! And, if they do—I'll get you a new light bulb!!

Oh, sob!!—Yo' is too good fo' yore own good—yo' is all heart.

husband was too dense to consummate the union and carried around a strangely shaped cured ham for much of the trip.

The 1952 marriage probably was the high-water mark in Capp's creative output, although *L'il Abner*'s popularity continued well beyond that year. In the 1950s a Dogpatch theme park was opened in the Ozarks, several best-selling book collections were published, and a Broadway play was a smash hit and later made into a movie.

Through the 1960s *L'il Abner* experienced profound changes. There was less *cherchez les femmes* in the strip (perhaps due to Abner's domesticity) and more politics (certainly due to Capp's own politics, which were changing). Capp had been regarded as a darling of the liberal establishment because of his frequent jabs at conservatives and Republicans, but during the protest era of the 1960s his stance altered. Actually, Capp claimed that only his targets, not his politics, changed. Maintaining that he had always spoken for the people who were "shamed, disgraced, and ignored by other people," during the sixties he spoke up for the "poor son-of-a-bitch who *worked,* who was being denounced by liberals."

In his strip Capp attacked hippies and bureaucrats, introducing Joanie Phonie, a protest singer modeled after Joan Baez, and SWINE—Students Wildly Indignant about Nearly Everything—an SDS-type group. In addition to producing jibes in print, Capp went on the road with his politics, touring the college lecture circuit—where he relished hecklers—and frequently appearing on television talk shows.

Capp could even evoke a sardonic chuckle from his new role and the problems it caused with his traditional readership. "I talked about it, and I continued to talk, because one of the things I found was that when I was all for the liberal

Abner's devotion to Fearless Fosdick was such that he followed his "ideel" to the marriage altar, such as it was. Fosdick's wedding, as Abner respectfully read in the comic books, turned out to be a dream, but Abner's did not. Two weeks later Daisy Mae—now Mrs. Yokum—was carrying a giant ham on her honeymoon while the marriage remained unconsummated. The ham (which gets shot through the door) was the object of unconfirmed sightings, not only by Capp's nemesis Ham Fisher. What the ham resembled was clear; whether Capp meant a reference to Ham himself is open to speculation.

Does Not Pay," which featured garishly exploitative covers that usually included a legendary lamster such as John Dillinger or Baby Face Nelson being caught in a hail of machine-gun fire, as he shouted something to the effect, "You'll never take me, you dirty G-Men." Meanwhile, looking on over in a corner, was the inevitable Veronica Lake/Lizabeth Scott-like blond bombshell, spilling out of her satin evening gown.

On a considerably more respectable level, however, there were the comic strips that appeared in the daily papers that Dad brought home each evening. Deemed suitable for reading on the living room rug right out there in the open, these were considered so inoffensive that even politicians could read them over the radio.

Although we certainly didn't know it at the time, it now turns out that the comic strip was also one of the truly unique American art forms. Come to think of it, something else we didn't know was that the guy who drew "Little Orphan Annie" was influenced by Bunyan, Dickens, Hugo, Goethe, Woolf, Dreiser, Pirandello and Joyce. Or that the creator of those creepy "Dick Tracy" villains was "a Platonist in an increasingly Aristotelian world."

Such observations are proffered in "America's Great Comic-Strip Artists" (Abbeville Press, 295 pages, $55), a hefty new coffee-table book that is weighing in for the holiday season.

"In less than a century, the comic strip—with its own language, structure and integrities—produced a great many artists who worked masterfully within a complex set of rules," writes Richard Marschall, author of the book, which is highly readable despite its sometimes-overreaching propensity for literary contrasts and comparisons. "Accorded little recognition in its birthplace, the comic strip is widely celebrated around the world, where American cartoonists of the past are culturally lionized and their works anthologized."

Marschall—who is editor-in-chief of Nemo, the only magazine devoted to the history and criticism of comics—selects what he considers to be the 16 finest: R.F. Outcault (the "Yellow Kid," "Buster Brown"), Rudolph Dirks (the "Katzenjammer Kids"), Frederick Burr Opper ("Happy Hooligan," "Alphonse and Gaston"), Winsor McCay ("Little Nemo in Slumberland"), George Herriman ("Krazy Kat"), E.C. Segar ("Thimble Theatre," with Popeye), Cliff Sterrett ("Polly and Her Pals"), Roy Crane ("Wash Tubbs," "Captain Easy," "Buz Sawyer"), Harold Gray ("Little Orphan Annie"), Hal Foster ("Prince Valiant"), Alex Raymond ("Flash Gordon," "Rip Kirby"), Milton Caniff ("Terry and the Pirates," "Steve Canyon"), Chester Gould ("Dick Tracy"), Al Capp ("L'il Abner"), Walt Kelly ("Pogo") and Charles M. Schulz ("Peanuts").

In a recent phone conversation from his home in Ardsley, Pa., the 40-year-old Marschall said he got turned on to comics—particularly "Happy Hooligan"—as a youngster, when he discovered some of his father's books on the history of the form.

"The choices for my own book were arbitrary. There were three more who could have made it: Frank King ("Gasoline Alley"), Billy DeBeck ("Barney Google") and George McManus ("Bringing up Father"). I was looking for cartoonists who really turned some corners in that lifeline of comics' history, who did something new, who brought distinct personalities to their characters."

"There have been two births of the comic strip," writes Marschall, who also teaches the history of illustration at the School of Visual Arts in New York and at the Philadelphia College of Art. "The first occurred around 1895, when the 'founding fathers' defined the medium and established conventions like panel progression and balloon dialogue. For a generation, the thematic preoccupation was largely humor and the graphic expression was exclusively comic. The second birth of the comic strip came in the 1930s and featured—for the first time—adventure, suspense, realism, violent continuities, and an illustrative style of drawing."

Marschall traces the evolution of comic strips through the work of the Chosen Sixteen, such as the experimentation in form and theme before 1910, and the standardization of themes (suburban life, working women) during the '20s.

As for specifics, a sampling:

● Herriman was "the most celebrated comic-strip artist of all time, and by common agreement the greatest," while his "Krazy Kat" was "the surreal masterpiece generally acknowledged to be the greatest comic strip of all time.... Very few readers understood it at the time, or even to this day." Analyzed exhaustively, "it has been portrayed as a variation on the eternal triangle of tragic romances; as a grand statement on freedom versus authority; as an allegory on innocence meeting reality; and, of course, as a comic cacophony of obsessions."

SWIMMING TO SHORE, FLASH DRAGS THE REVIVING ZARKOV TO THE BEACH..... DALE RUSHES TO MEET THEM ......

Alex Raymond's "Flash Gordon" used romantic, evocative artwork.

George Herriman's

"Terry and the Pirat[es]"

● Segar's "Thim... "compensated for i... destrian artwork w... memorable charact... the wildest scenari... tory."

● "Terry and the... than any other ... characters with "s... tifacted personaliti... was "the first carto... his characters with ... es—speech patt... quirks, mannerisms...

● Kelly "clearly ... virtuosity than an... greats.... 'Pogo' c... at by children for i... tion, and marveled

Comics

The funnies ... seriously

A celebration of the comic strip: America's little orphan art form

By Clifford Terry

Years ago, in what some of our children not-so-wryly refer to as the Dark Ages, a kind of pre-Elvis adolescent rebellion took shape in the form of that cross-generational bane of American parents: the dreaded comic book. There wasn't anything much more satisfyingly sneaky than reading these contraband items under the covers by the faint beam of the flashlight.

A particular favorite in my bed-

Harold Gray's Daddy Warbucks and Orphan Annie. The strip start-

From left: Chester Gould's Dick Tracy, Charles Schulz's Charlie Brown and Frederick Burr Opper's Happy Hooligan.

attitudes—and I believed in them—the conservatives showed me only icy contempt. I never got a letter from them. They just hated me. When I began attacking liberals, the conservatives maintained their icy silence, but the liberals began denouncing me by the thousands of letters every week!"

Increasingly dominated by Capp's strident commentary, *L'il Abner* became less subtle and clever. Capp inaugurated a newspaper column and was planning to host a television talk show when political complaints and a scandal involving him and a college coed derailed that particular digression. Talk of Capp's candidacy to run against Senator Ted Kennedy also ceased. Critics who had recently called him the great comic historian of his time now denounced him as a bitter fascist. He maintained that the sources of his inspiration were changing, a thought that bolstered him in believing his work was as fresh in the 1960s and 1970s as it had been during the 1930s and 1940s.

Actually, his themes had changed, but his artistic inspirations remained constant; even as a youth, he had admired and imitated the parallel-line shadings of British cartoonist Phil May. He also admired the surrealism of Cliff Sterrett's *Polly and Her Pals:* "To think that a whole generation grew up worshipping Picasso when the guy who did it far better was Sterrett!" As an aspiring cartoonist, he had cut his teeth on Opper's *Happy Hooligan* and *Alphonse and Gaston.* Capp's literary inspirations included Charles Dickens, Robert Benchley, and Booth Tarkington, as well as S. J. Perelman, of whom he said, "I loved him because I understood everything he said!" He also admired "the great army of American humorists—totally unknown but named Nat and Sol—all of whom were writing for radio. They were good, but nobody knew who they were. *Today* nobody knows who they were, but they were the great American humorists."

Toward the end of his career (*L'il Abner* ceased publication on November 13, 1977), Capp's thematic inspirations had certainly changed. No longer was human nature the subject of his dissection; he now dissected each morning's screaming headlines. Partly to blame was the tendency toward general overpoliticization that was so prevalent during the 1960s and that decade's aftermath. Now Capp was forced to deal with his new targets on their own turf: everywhere. In the past, politics represented only a small percentage of what he attacked; when politics pervaded the entire culture, *L'il Abner* followed suit.

There were second thoughts along the way. After his retirement Capp admitted that the strip may have suffered at the end but stated that he thought his critiques were needed in the marketplace of ideas. Through it all Capp preserved his self-assured role as a commentator, a position as well defined and fiercely asserted as it was during the first years of *L'il Abner.* He saw the cartoonist primarily as commentator: "Comic art not only should say something about the status quo—it must. The message is in the art that is brought to any medium. A work of art is a work of art regardless of form, size, or material. People have been brainwashed: If it's a comic strip, in a daily newspaper, and done with pen and ink, it's supposed to be a contemptible trifle. That's self-swindling snobbishness."

For a brief moment Capp hopped onto the contemporary bandwagon when he created Pop Art silkscreen prints of his Dogpatch denizens, but he doggedly continued to defend comic art as a separate and respectable art form, not a weak sister of some distantly related form. "Modern art," he said in reaction to critics'

LI'L ABNER by AL CAPP

This Neighborhood Restricted —

dismissal of the comics, "is the revelation of disordered minds. It is created by the untalented, sold by the unscrupulous, and bought by the uninformed. Genuine art today is found . . . in comic strips. And comic strips are the best art being produced in America today. I judge them by the same standards I apply to Daumier and Michelangelo. And by those standards comic strip art is damn good."

Al Capp's virtuosity was astonishing. He logically belongs within the group of American humorists populated by the great local colorists and dialecticians. No matter that he was a Jew from the Northeast or that Dogpatch hardly resembled the real Ozarks or anywhere else, for that matter. Capp's milieu and methods put him squarely and prominently in the bloodline of Sut Lovingood, Artemus Ward, Petroleum V. Nasby, Mark Twain, Kin Hubbard, Ring Lardner, and, following Capp himself, the comics' own Walt Kelly, whose *Pogo* further continued the precious tradition. Capp represents a type of literary humor as purely American as the comic strip itself.

For all the apparent insouciance that Al Capp brought to *Li'l Abner*, his classic strip was actually built on a very structured view of life and the human condition. With his deceptive blunderbuss, Capp seemed as freewheeling as his characters when aiming at targets through his Dogpatch chronicles. But he was, in fact, an impeccably appointed sharpshooter. In making his readers laugh— and in making them think—Al Capp first determined to make them take notice. No strip cartoonist more deftly juggled creativity and publicity. His greater feat was creating characters who were blatantly absurd yet became virtual folk heroes, or at least enduring symbols. Although Capp may have debunked traditions, he inaugurated several of his own, most notably Sadie Hawkins Day. In spite of his evident contempt for his characters, history will accord respect aplenty for them, for him, for the strip, and for the unique manner in which he drew comic strips while making profound observations.

Al Capp was not a master satirist who happened to draw funny pictures. He was, proudly and fiercely, a cartoonist who happened to do what he did better than virtually anyone else in the select circle of comic-strip masters—and with a real sense of himself and his times.

15

Few cartoonists have exhibited talents in several areas in one career or through one feature. Fantasy was the specialty of Winsor McCay; George Herriman made it his bailiwick too, while staking ground in the realm of literary and intellectual expression. Cliff Sterrett also appealed to intellectuals, as Charles Schulz would later do in *Peanuts*. Farce and parody were the domains of E.C. Segar, and the graphic sense he lacked was displayed with seeming instinctiveness by Frederick Opper. Dialogue—incisive, distinctive—that revealed not only the personalities of characters but also the world view of the cartoonist was the special gift of Al Capp.

WALT KELLY

1913-1973

In the company of great cartoonists such as these, one stands out as a monumental talent in that humorous tradition. Walt Kelly was master of all that could be surveyed, the many tools and techniques available to comic-strip artists. *Pogo,* the only newspaper strip he ever drew, generously included ele-ments of fantasy, literary and intellectual touches, farce and parody, graphic brilliance, and wonderful dialogue, but it also contained philosophy, politics, whimsy, poetry, metaphysics, social commentary, and good old-fashioned slapstick.

Kelly did not set out to assemble recipe ingredients from the masters of comic art who had preceded him; neither did he structure *Pogo* to showcase his varied proclivities on the quota system. Rather, he was gifted enough to be able to drink from all creative springs, where earlier artists had drunk from at most one or two. Whether his broader landscape earns him a higher place than his predecessors is open to question, but ultimately the question

is pointless; genius is too slippery to measure, and perhaps Walt Kelly's crowning laurel is that he clearly displayed more virtuosity than any of his fellow greats.

Kelly was also creative with biographical facts. He penned his autobiography many times in articles, books, press releases, and interviews, but a reasonably reliable story of his early life can be discerned, and it is a story that is remarkable for its unremarkable aspects. Although evincing an interest in drawing and exercising an appetite for the funnies, Kelly evidently did not follow the pattern of other great comic-strip artists by drawing cartoons early, often, and obsessively.

Walter Crawford Kelly, Jr., was born on August 25, 1913, in Philadelphia. When he was two, his family moved to Bridgeport, Connecticut, where his father was to work in munitions factories. Kelly sometimes credited his father with "putting a pencil in his hands" in inspirational fashion and sometimes with having no effect at all on his artistic bent, but he did recall his father (who had dropped out of school at age nine) expounding a theory that the "true means of communication" was the picture, not the word. His father argued, wrote Kelly, that "We are . . . bad at talking, bad at remembering language, and bad at spelling; but we are just great at remembering pictures. 'Language,' he said to my mother one evening at supper, 'is the worst means of communication known to man.' "

Nevertheless young Walt did not abandon speech or the written word. He did remember years later that he and his friends were enamored of *Mutt and Jeff* reprint books, "all of us determining to become cartoonists and rich." Curiously, it was the inspiration of Bud Fisher, *Mutt and Jeff* 's creator, that similarly seized young Al Capp—also a Bridgeport resident in his youth—and the similarity centered on the publicity about Fisher's wealth and his showgirl affairs as much as, if not more than, his cartooning talents.

Another parallel with Capp is that Walt Kelly suffered a debilitation in his teens, although it was not as severe as Capp's amputation; the young Kelly sustained two years of a paralysis that affected his left side. This may have turned his interest toward drawing; certainly it obliged more sedentary activities than those followed by fellow teenagers. It seemed not to affect Kelly's outlook on life or humor—except perhaps to turn his views, respectively, more tolerant and beneficent. Kelly would later comment on his friend Capp's observation that cruelty was the basis of all humor by noting that the dictum revealed more about Capp than it did about humor.

While in high school, Kelly started to submit work to the local big-city daily, the *Bridgeport Post*. As a writer he was, at first, the correspondent for Warren G. Harding High School, and as a budding cartoonist, he drew work for the weekly junior page. Kelly graduated from high school in 1930, right into the dingy but heady city rooms of the old *Post* building on Lafayette Street. According to a cartoonist's rite of passage that sadly no longer applies, Kelly worked at almost every job in the art and editorial departments, learning his trade and somehow, by osmosis, receiving a transfusion of printer's ink for the blood in his veins. Kelly was probably the last major comic-strip artist who considered the title *newspaperman* as noble as *cartoonist,* and he remained to his end a colorful specimen of the stereotypical cigar-chomping, saloon-haunting, deadline-crunching worker. Often he drew on a propped-up drawing board—not a fancy mechanical table—with a fedora on his head or, comically, the liberated brim of an old fedora as an eyeshade.

A panel from an early *Pogo* Sunday page, when fantasy was a stronger element than in later years.

As his cartooning improved, Kelly handled more interesting assignments than decorations and silver-print portraits. Once he illustrated a protracted comic-strip life of the Bridgeport legend P.T. Barnum, and eventually he drew editorial cartoons. Kelly scored some hits with his paper's endorsement of a Socialist candidate for mayor. The rest of the country looked askance at the candidacy, but in Bridgeport—somehow appropriately, in view of the way Kelly's singular sense of humor developed—it was an unusual campaign for unusual reasons. The candidate, with the unlikely name of Jasper McLevy, was not really controversial in town; the other major paper, the *Herald*, also supported him. And as a Socialist, McLevy was a Rugged Individualist. He was loath to spend public money, and many times during the years he was in office (Kelly's cartoons helped elect him to the first of many terms), McLevy defended his refusal to buy snow-removal equipment by stating, "God put the snow there, and God will take it away."

Perhaps the mayor's theory of public service attracted Kelly to municipal bureaucracy, for he left the *Post* after several years to take a job as an investigator for the Bridgeport Welfare Department. He also worked at various other jobs and even attended art school in New York—one month at the Phoenix. He decorated shop windows in New York, too, until he was swindled by neighboring shop-owners who contracted for one job, told him he had done the wrong window, and fired him for the mistake after he completed the second.

While in New York, Kelly also contributed some work to the very first of the modern-era comic books; he drew children's pages for National (later Superman/DC) in the days immediately preceding the superhero period. And he drew for *St. Nicholas* magazine, forming an unlikely artistic bridge with such figures as Howard Pyle and Frederic Remington, who drew illustrations during the magazine's heyday.

By 1936 Walt Kelly determined to investigate his own welfare. He moved cross-country to California, lured by "the WPA of the cartooning world," Walt Disney Productions, which at the time was hiring thousands of artists and providing classes in the various aspects of cartooning and animation. The studio was rapidly expanding from shorts to full-color feature animation, and the program, a practical move for the "Mouse Factory," trained an entire generation of drawing-board cartoonists and animators. Kelly was to work there until 1941; co-workers were Hank Ketcham, later to draw *Dennis the Menace;* Virgil Partch (VIP), a prolific magazine cartoonist; and Eric Gurney, who moved on to a career as one of America's great animal-cartoon book illustrators. While at the Disney Studios—he left during the bitter strike that disrupted the vaunted, paternalistic harmony there—Kelly worked on *Pinocchio, Fantasia, The Reluctant Dragon,* and *Dumbo.*

Kelly returned to New York. During his time with Disney, the comic-book business had mushroomed into an industry, and Kelly would spend the better part of the next decade in comic books, but not in the superhero realm. Buttressed, perhaps, by the story and art training he got at the Mouse Factory, he decided to specialize in funny animals.

Although his career was briefly interrupted during part of World War II by service in the army's foreign-language publications department, Kelly came to dominate the independent titles at Dell Comics from his drawing board at

Walt Kelly's initial conception of Pogo.

Western Printing, the company that packaged the funny-animal books. Appropriately, he drew covers for a number of Disney titles, whose interior stories were sometimes produced by Carl Barks, another anonymous Disney artist who eventually came to be revered as one of the great comic-book cartoonists. Mostly, however, Kelly worked on his own titles in *Fairy Tale Parade, Santa Claus Funnies,* and *Animal Comics.* He also contributed heavily to *Raggedy Ann and Andy, Our Gang,* and *Looney Tunes.* It was a story of his own, in *Animal Comics* no. 1 of 1942, however, that laid the foundation for Kelly's final career.

The story, called "Albert Takes the Cake," begins with the captions "Once there was a big old alligator named Albert who loved chocolate cake. . . . One bright morning Pogo the Possum discovered that it was his birthday. . . . And when Mrs. Jay heard the news, she told Bumbazine, the little boy who lived on the edge of the swamp."

Such unpretentious and potentially saccharin origins nevertheless bore the trademarks of Kelly's individuality. Bumbazine is a little black boy, not drawn stereotypically nor speaking in dialect; Kelly had him star in the comic-book story at a time in America when the Army was still segregated. Also, the story takes bizarre comic twists, as Albert plans to eat child and possum first and have the chocolate cake for dessert. His scheme goes awry, of course, and the story ends with Albert consigned to the bottom of the swamp—firmly anchored by the misbegotten cake in his stomach—as Pogo and Bumbazine celebrate with watermelon.

Soon, of course, the swamp was identified as Georgia's Okefenokee, a real place except as depicted by Kelly, who made it as fanciful as Herriman's Cokonino County (Kelly eventually visited Okefenokee for the first time in 1955). Soon, also, Bumbazine disappeared. Try as he might to remain the star of the running feature—and it seemed that such was Kelly's intention—Albert eventually yielded the spotlight to Pogo. And, like Little Nemo before him, Krazy Kat at the time (then living out the last of his nine lives), and Charlie Brown in the future, Pogo, star of his strip, is the quiet character—the eye of the hurricane—among a very colorful and sometimes raucous cast.

Kelly had found his niche with *Albert/Pogo,* although at the time funny-animal work was not the most glamorous in comic books. He later recalled: "It was impossible for me to draw a naked woman. It was blinding work. I would no sooner have her clothes off than I would remove my hat, out of respect. With my eyes unshaded I couldn't see what I was doing. Besides, the editor said that, as an adventure man, I had better stick to drawing mice. So I concentrated on puppies, kittens, mice, and elves . . . every once in a while glancing back at the men who were grimly penciling out the Pueriles of Pauline, taking clothes off and dagging people with butcher knives."

The kiddie appeal and childhood milieu in *Pogo* were, however, excuses, not reasons. More than a stage or platform, the *Pogo* stories were launching pads for the multifaceted tales Kelly was to tell. *Pogo* could be laughed at by children for its silliness or action and marveled at by adults for its satire or wisdom—simultaneously, not alternately. Kelly could and did—and loved to—swing with abandon from Perelmanesque wordplay, witty and literate, to broad slapstick to tender pathos. This virtuosity would intensify later in the *Pogo* newspaper strip, but there was one more detour along Kelly's path.

Pogo Possum and Albert the Alligator looked a lot different in the early 1940s when they appeared in *Animal Comics* stories. Bumbazine was the little black boy who nominally—and briefly—was the star of the strip.

Kelly loved to draw detailed panoramas of his Okefenokee Swamp.

This was the first *Pogo* daily strip in the *New York Star* (1949); later the same year, when Kelly's comic strip was picked up for distribution by the Post-Hall Syndicate, it was used again to introduce the diminutive possum.

The newspaper *PM* was an experimental, left-wing, advertising-free daily in New York during the 1940s. Among its bright spots was the literate, intellectual strip *Barnaby,* but the bright spots evidently were too few, especially as postwar euphoria waned. Kelly worked a bit for *PM* just before its demise, and when a few staffers regrouped to found a new daily—the *Star*—Kelly was asked to handle the art direction (along with a number of other duties, in a pace reminiscent of the activities on the *Bridgeport Post* fifteen years earlier). He accepted the challenge, and for the crowded eight months of the New York *Star*'s existence, Kelly did an amazing amount of work, including spot art, design work, ads, political cartoons—and a comic strip. The political cartoons garnered national attention, for during the presidential campaign he pictured Republican Thomas Dewey as a robotized adding machine in a series of brilliant salvos; he also depicted Progressive candidate Henry Wallace as a blindfolded shepherd surrounded by wolves in sheep's clothing.

Kelly's comic strip was new but the characters were not. Pogo, though still

resident in the Okefenokee swamp, had found a new home and a new format, six days a week as a newspaper strip. Free of the comic-book environment, Kelly somehow became both sillier and more serious at the same time. He talked politics and made sophisticated allusions, and his daffy scripts became masterpieces of absurdities. The cast by now had expanded to include Howland Owl, an ersatz inventor and authority; Churchy Le Femme the zany turtle; Beauregard Bugleboy the hound dog; and Porkypine the porcupine, the swamp's resident grouch, a cynical but tenderhearted curmudgeon.

Neither Pogo nor Kelly himself could sustain the *Star,* but when the paper folded, the possum's reputation was such that his continuity was assured. Kelly submitted *Pogo* to the major syndicates but was picked up by the newest outfit on the block, the fledgling Post-Hall Syndicate. They were right for each other; *Pogo* was one of a handful of features that turned the syndicate into a major operation, and the strip was promoted with care and ferocity. Kelly's creation became a national sensation.

Syndication began in 1949, and within five years *Pogo* was appearing in

DR. OWL ONCE DUG THE SWAMP FOR A SQUARE ROOT

During the dawn of the "new-clear" age, Walt Kelly provided an explosion of literate wordplay and nonsense in *Pogo*. This daily is from the first year of the strip.

more than five hundred papers. It became the most controversial comic strip of its day because of the political commentary Kelly readily injected. Pogo graced the cover of *Newsweek* twice. Kelly became a noted public speaker, especially on campuses, and was interviewed on television by Edward R. Murrow and Alistair Cooke. A mock presidential bid by Pogo in 1952 grew to major proportions; Carl Sandburg, of all people, proclaimed, "I Go Pogo!" and a rally at Harvard turned into a four-hour near-riot. Simon and Schuster commenced publication of what ultimately numbered nearly three-dozen reprint books, and Kelly recorded an album of *Songs of the Pogo*.

The cast in the swamp grew too. It might not have been the proverbial cast of thousands, but it certainly seemed so. Through the years Kelly created well

I n Walt Kelly's world, animals—like beneficent Easter bunnies in dove-shaped boats—provided humanity that humans could not.

Pogo did not always need Pogo to put its gags across. Sometimes he would simply have provided too much sanity.

over 150 distinct, titled characters, and every one had a defined personality. No two were alike, and all were compelling.

The characters' language became like that in no other comic strip. Kelly's brand of Southern dialect was actually a cascading pastiche of white and black Southern, full of literalisms, puns, and free-association nonsense. It went beyond the bastard dialect concocted by Al Capp and beyond the Yiddish-Spanish-whatever of George Herriman (only Krazy spoke such lingo anyway, making the resonance as much Herriman's as his creation's). In *Pogo* the characters had different voices, different cadences, different idiosyncrasies. Again, the virtuosity can be compared to Caniff's in the adventure strips, but, of course, it had more comic turns and an almost profligate élan.

Kelly's ear for language (thank God he did *not* adhere to his father's theories

and prejudices on the subject) manifested itself in richer ways than putting clever words in his characters' mouths. He had a love affair with words that no other strip artist had, and he frequently composed poetry, both in the strip and in *Pogo* anthologies. His clear inspiration was another master of nonsense, Lewis Carroll, in verses like:

FOR GENEVIEVE MACANNULLA

A SONG NOT FOR NOW
YOU NEED NOT PUT STAY..
A TUNE FOR THE WAS
CAN BE SUNG FOR TODAY...
THE NOTES FOR THE DOES·NOT
WILL SOUND AS THE DOES..
TODAY YOU CAN SING
FOR THE WILL·BE THAT WAS.

> *Pick a pock of peach pits,*
> *Pockets full of pie,*
> *Foreign twenty blackbirds*
> *Baked until they cry . . .*

and (sung by the freckled cow Horrors Greeley):

> *Give me a home*
> *'Tween Buffalo an' Rome,*
> *Where the beer in the cantelope lay . . .*

Kelly always claimed he was more of a parodist than a satirist, which is evident in these examples, and that of his most famous rhyming:

> *Deck us all with Boston Charlie,*
> *Walla Walla, Wash., and Kalamazoo!*
> *Nora's freezin' on the trolley,*
> *Swaller dollar cauliflower, alleygaroo!*

What thrust *Pogo* onto the front pages, past the comics pages, was the political material Kelly routinely injected. It could range from playful, as during the strip's first few months ("Dewey or don't he?"), to savage. During the heyday of Senator Joseph R. McCarthy, Kelly fashioned a mean-spirited lookalike, the bobcat Simple J. Malarkey, who terrorized the swamp's denizens, even its blacker souls. His stories and characterizations—as well as likenesses—were masterful and excited fervent controversy. No complaints seemed ever to come from McCarthy

himself, but his editorial supporters and even detractors found themselves dropping selected strips, canceling the feature entirely, consigning it to editorial pages, or conducting readers' polls behind which to hide.

One paper, the *Providence Journal* in Rhode Island, was opposed to McCarthy but banned *Pogo* because "politics had no place on the comics page." Kelly soon fashioned a brief episode with a character named Miss Sis Boombah, a Rhode Island Red (the first tempting allusion), who was identified as being from Providence and, clearly, a chicken (the second reference) as she tangled with Malarkey's associates. It was a perfect, and clever, example of Kelly's virtuosity, for any reader could follow the surface story line with enjoyment, while some could discern the political undertones, and a few were aware of the inside joke being told. The *Journal,* by the way, eventually "surrendered" to Kelly in a good-natured editorial and reinstated the possum.

A not-so-happy ending for free expression occurred in 1962, when Kelly depicted two intruders in the swamp. A boorish pig resembled Soviet leader Khrushchev, and a seedy goat was the spitting image of Cuban dictator Castro. A Japanese client paper dropped *Pogo* after "inquiries" were made by the Russian embassy, and that paper never relented. Kelly fumed. "I can understand their position," he wrote; "they're so close to Vladivostok."

Kelly's political commentary was seldom subtle—he did not intend it to be—but it *was* clever, until his final years, when it grew ubiquitous, humorless, and strident. In the last half-dozen years of *Pogo,* characters lampooning Bobby Kennedy, Eugene McCarthy, George Wallace, Richard Nixon, Lyndon Johnson, Spiro Agnew, J. Edgar Hoover, and others glutted the strip.

Surpassing Kelly's understanding of poetry, parody, and politics, however, was his overwhelming sense of structure. Not only was *Pogo* an extension of his talents and sensibility, but the strip form itself was conquered, bent, and molded by him in every way. Sometimes Kelly was giving another of his knowing winks to readers, but mostly he was exercising his craft. Characters, when tired, would lean against panel borders. Voluble characters would have to crane their necks to avoid wordy speech balloons. A swarm of gnats in one episode kept arranging themselves in patterns of words and balloons over characters' heads, which—of course—"made" the characters speak against their will.

Only in the comic strip can traditional, literary artifacts serve visual and cognitive functions; Kelly had certain characters reveal their personalities, styles, and tones simply through the lettering in the balloons over their heads. Hence the firebrand Deacon Mushrat spoke in Gothic lettering straight from a King James Bible; Sarcophagus MacAbre, the grim vulture dripping with black crepe, spoke via balloons that resembled black-bordered death announcements; and the flea-bitten circus barker P.T. Bridgeport—in a wonderfully harmonious bit of homage—spoke in loud, colorful, festooned circus-poster word balloons. And, in one marvelous strip, Porky walks out of a last-panel scene muttering, "The humor of this strip eludes me." Kelly violated the "fourth wall" deliciously.

Kelly had a sense of space, a sense of his role, and, having mastered so many of comics' possibilities, also a sense of the limitations of a newspaper strip, and he lived happily therein. Like his strip, Kelly himself was, besides funny, at times political, sociological, metaphysical, whimsical, poetic, slapstick, philosophical—but very seldom pretentious. Along the way there were honors enough,

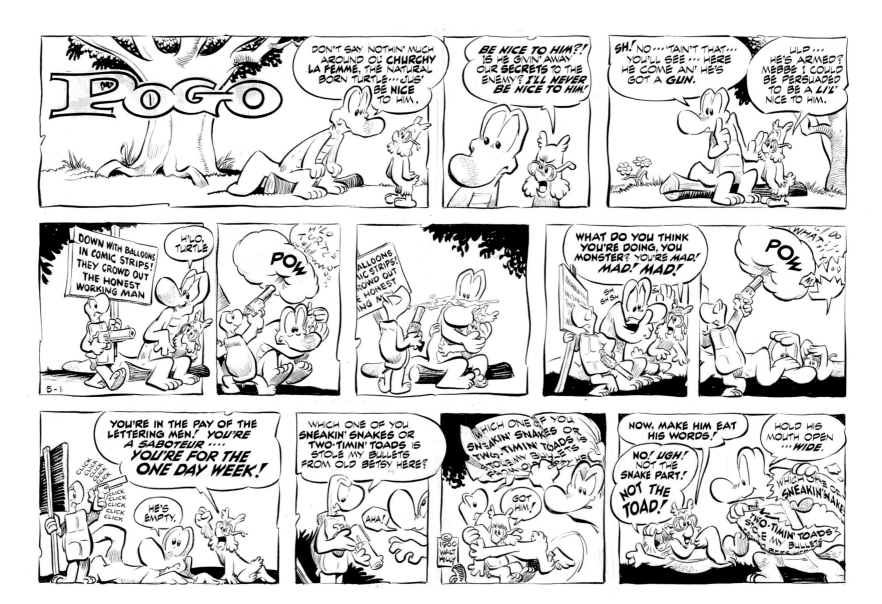

and Kelly's ego was as big as his strip's success, but he seemed to subscribe to the notion that the only thing worse than real modesty was false modesty. He did not have to pretend to things, because he was such a formidable presence and his accomplishments were so manifest.

Kelly won the Cartoonist of the Year award from the National Cartoonists Society when *Pogo* was but three tender years old, and in 1954 he was elected NCS president. During his term he testified forcefully before congressional hearings into the comic-book business—against contemporary trends and in favor of strict self-regulation, a fact that has dismayed some of his second-generation fans. Kelly was the first strip cartoonist to be invited to contribute originals to the Library of Congress. Besides his own anthologies, Kelly illustrated

The *Pogo* page above, reproduced from the original art, shows Kelly's working methods and sketching techniques. Blue pencil lines do not photograph in newspaper reproduction, so some cartoonists—especially former animators who were trained in freehand sketching—left the blue lines and avoided erasing. The Sunday strip, a brilliant page of in-jokes on the cartooning profession, demolishes the "fourth wall" between characters and readers by dissecting the form's conventions and clichés. The daily below is an inspired—though, happily, typical—piece of Okefenokee nonsense.

Pogo frequently tipped the straw hat to Bridgeport, Connecticut, winter home of the Barnum circus and boyhood home of cartoonist Kelly.

the works of others and wrote articles himself on a wide range of subjects. He designed a mobile, wrote educational materials for children, and campaigned for ecological reforms when Earth Day was yet a trial balloon in the movement. For a TV special featuring Pogo characters, he wrote the script, provided character voices, and renewed his animation skills.

Walt Kelly and *Pogo* seemed to splash onto the comic-strip scene, boldly going in new directions (usually simultaneously) and charting new paths. Although Kelly was doing what talented predecessors had done, it was the way he did it that made him such a monumental figure, and he seemed to explore all variations of expression, not just one or two. Ironically, his chosen stage and theme—

Absurd premises and preoccupations, changing backgrounds, brilliantly rendered expressions—Kelly brings all factors together in a wonderful romp from 1955.

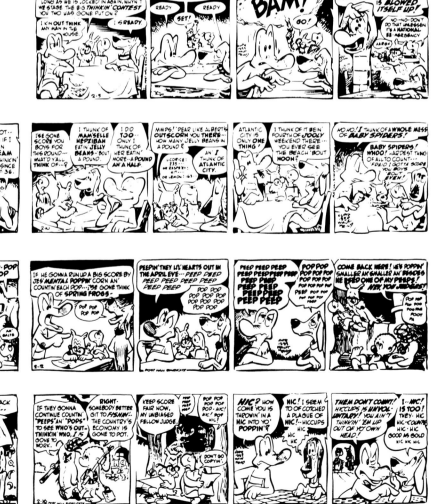

talking animals reflecting on the human condition—were not new forms but as old as literature and drama themselves.

It is tempting to call Walt Kelly a modern-day Aesop, but the comparison is ultimately more glib than honorific. Neither does it render full due to Kelly to explore his techniques of anthropomorphism or metempsychosis because doing so would tend to focus on the creatures instead of their souls, their physical manifestations rather than their intellectual preoccupations. After reading runs of Kelly's swamp saga, one can see that *Pogo* has genuine characteristics of the classic pastoral. As Edward Mendelson noted (in the *Yale Review,* Spring 1978): "Although the rustics of a classic pastoral are usually shepherds, Kelly's substitution of anglers is supported by a tradition that extends back through Sannazaro's

Every Christmas, in the *Pogo* strip and on his personal Christmas cards, Walt Kelly expressed these lyrical sentiments through the whole cast.

God rest ye merrie, Gentlemen~~~   ~Let nothing you dismay~~~

Eclogae piscatoriae to the twenty-first *Idyll* of Theocritus. In Kelly's pastoral, as in the classical and renaissance varieties, the rustics use their elaborately stylized language to speak about sophisticatedly urban issues. They write poems, suffer the pangs of unrequited love, and, for the most part, enjoy an innocence for which the reader feels nostalgia; while, at the same time, the pastoral artifice reminds him that such innocence has never existed outside of art."

It was a world that Walt Kelly created, and he just happened to use Okefenokee as a forwarding address and decorate his background props with Spanish moss. But readers were really visiting his mind. Pogo's swamp was as real as Hogan's Alley or the Katzenjammers' island or Slumberland or Popeye's Dice Island or Flash Gordon's underwater world of Mongo or Terry's Orient or Kokonino Kounty. Or as unreal—take your pick. And, like the other settings, it was wonderful in no small part because it was a place that could exist only in the comic strips— in no other medium, no other art form.

Walt Kelly died on October 18, 1973, from complications of diabetes; he had recently had a leg amputated. *Pogo* continued for about a year afterward, via scissors and glue pot and through the efforts of his son, Steve, and widow, Selby, and other associates. But without Kelly the task was quixotic. It would have been hard to imagine or invent a Walt Kelly, but it is impossible to replace him.

Through *Pogo,* when Kelly seemed to be pointing readers toward grand and distant statements, he was actually holding a mirror to our faces. As he said— revealing, in his predictably multifaceted manner, that even his prose could be poetic—"There is no need to sally forth, for it remains true that those things which make us human are, curiously enough, always close at hand. Resolve, then, that on this very ground, with small flags waving and tinny blasts on tiny trumpets, we may meet the enemy. . . and not only may he be ours, he may be us."

16

The humorous comic strip in America—the category that inaugurated the art form and dominated its themes for a full generation—has had three distinct periods. The first, coinciding with the birth of the comics, was the age of the one-premise gag strip. Casts were small, incidental characters few, and the strips were based on a small number of durable situations. The second era came when the scion of continuity was grafted onto the comic stock. In the 1920s and 1930s characters developed personalities slightly more faceted, mostly because they were found in continuing stories rather than unconnected situa-tions. The third era—which still dominates today—can rightly be called the Schulz era. In an exceedingly unassuming manner, reflecting its creator's own personality, the new comic strip *Peanuts* in the early 1950s established two structural modes that virtually every humor strip since has adopted. Charles Schulz began by establishing his prem-ise in a new way. He introduced a large cast of characters and imbued each with extremely strong personality traits. Then he manufactured a long list of settings, situations, and routines in which to place his characters. It is too simplistic to say that mixing characters and situations resulted in gags writing themselves—nor is such an analysis borne out by Schulz's method or intention—but it was the perfect prescription for the creation of an integrated comic universe.

CHARLES M. SCHULZ

1922–

Schulz's other device has subtly but assuredly influenced the succeeding generation of humor strips as well. He introduced a new type of gag construc-

tion, although he has never been recognized for it, evidently because his contributions have been enveloped by the universality of their usage. As continuities receded and gag-a-day strips reasserted themselves in the early 1950s, *Peanuts* pioneered certain conventions—the sarcastic punch line; the upturned-eyes response; eye-contact with the reader in final panels; the primal scream as reaction to a situation; an entire gag relaying one character's reflections rather than an interchange between two; the gag payoff in the penultimate panel; and a comment in the last balloon.

These conventions are not as elemental to the comic strip as an art form as, say, Rudolph Dirks's definitive use of successive panels and the vocabulary of visuals (motion lines, sweat beads), but they are certainly as pervasive. Such disparate features as *Doonesbury* and *Garfield* owe debts to *Peanuts* for their basic forms of premise, pacing, and character delineation. Even in the past dozen years—while *Peanuts* entered the echelons of venerable classics, approaching its fortieth anniversary—only *Calvin and Hobbes* among major strips has explored new forms of expression and gag delivery.

Charles Schulz remains a very quiet eye in the center of the invigorating hurricane for which he is responsible. He was born in Minneapolis, Minnesota, on November 26, 1922, and his fate was sealed from the beginning. In an unlikely, midwestern version of consecration out of mythology, when Schulz was just two days old an uncle nicknamed him Sparky, after the horse Spark Plug in the *Barney Google* comic strip. Sparky had just entered the strip and was becoming a national sensation, but why the uncle connected him with the Schulz family baby is unknown. Charles Monroe Schulz ultimately became a cartoonist, however, and still uses the sobriquet.

Schulz's father was a barber (as is the father of his lead character, Charlie Brown, one of many similarities), and Sparky grew up during the Depression. He retains strong impressions of his industrious father and his close-knit family. The boy was bright enough to leapfrog several grades in school, although this made him the smallest kid in the class and ultimately caused his grades to suffer. Episodes of rejection and alienation reinforced aspects of an already sensitive nature and were filed away for eventual reference. The young Schulz was a fan of many newspaper strips and showed an aptitude for drawing. At school he may have used it as a defense mechanism, since he fulfilled many requests for likenesses of Popeye for grateful classmates. But the inclination turned more substantial when Schulz's mother spotted a coupon ad for a cartoon correspondence course.

The strong fantasy element in *Peanuts*, often taken for granted by readers, is central to understanding the strip and its appeal.

276

" You're so intelligent, and I'm so tired of it all ! "

Since early in the century, mail-order cartooning had been popular, and one of the nation's most active mills was located in Minneapolis—the Federal School. During his senior year in high school Schulz decided to take the course instead of going on to college. Many of this century's professional cartoonists took correspondence courses, but Schulz is one of the few who completed every lesson to the end.

It took a world war to interrupt Schulz's progress—he was drafted in 1943—but it was not the prospect of battle that proved most traumatic. Just before he was shipped out of the Minneapolis/St. Paul area, his mother, who had been suffering a painful fight with cancer, prophetically offered a final good-bye to her son when he was home on a weekend furlough, and then she died the next day. The event shattered young Schulz and affects him to this day, only partially because she never lived to see the artistic success she had encouraged.

His mother's death and his army experiences in Europe (Shulz was mustered out a sergeant) brought him back to St. Paul accompanied by a newfound interest in Christianity; he was grateful, he said, that he had merely survived. He joined a local Church of God congregation and found solace in their warm and unintimidating fellowship. Through the years Schulz was to read through study Bibles several times, conduct classes in the Bible, and even occasionally preach on street corners. Eventually his faith became less structured than his denomination's, less public and more private.

After the war Schulz sought work in cartooning and soon found himself busy locally. He freelanced lettering and cartoons for a Catholic magazine and eventually secured a staff job with his correspondence school, renamed the Art Instruction Institute. He started specializing in kid cartoons and submitted work to the nation's major magazines. Remarkably, he was bought only by the biggest and one of the toughest markets to crack, the *Saturday Evening Post*. For the local St. Paul *Pioneer-Press* he inaugurated a weekly feature for the women's pages called *Li'l Folks*. The cartoons were signed "Sparky" and began highlighting two recognizable characters, a little boy with a round head and a distinctive spotted dog.

In 1950 Charles Schulz practiced the ritual undertaken by magazine cartoonists of the day: submitting to newspaper syndicates. *Li'l Folks* was rebuffed by several organizations, but United Feature Syndicate of New York was interested. Although he ultimately received a contract, there were several surprises: it was suggested that the single-panel format be changed to a daily strip and the title changed to *Peanuts*. On each count Schulz deferred to big-city syndicate moguls, but he resented the imposed title—and still does. To him it lacks dignity, is a non sequitur, and leads readers to assume one of the characters is named Peanuts. The title was chosen by executives from a list of ten suggested by production manager Bill Anderson, who had not even seen the samples. His inspiration was the kid's audience, called the "peanut gallery," for television's *Howdy Doody* show.

Peanuts it was, and when it made its debut on October 2, 1950, Shermy and Patty issued history's first recorded put-down of Charlie Brown before the readers of only seven newspapers. The early list of characters was rounded out by Snoopy, and at the beginning Schulz himself had not yet decided upon a lead. The large cast of strong personalities that populates *Peanuts* today was not present in the strip's early years. Characters were added slowly but with regularity;

the strip's famous tone—children speaking as adults—was not present from the start; there was a definite evolution toward Schulz's singular modes. All of which confirms the cartoonist's genius; his contributions have been arrived at instinctively rather than clinically.

Although a cult following soon developed, the growth in *Peanut*'s acceptance was gradual. After a year it was carried in thirty-five papers; forty-one a year later; and fifty-seven the next. In 1952 a Sunday page was added (in ten newspapers), and only in 1956 did *Peanuts* start appearing in more than one hundred newspapers. By then the avalanche had begun. Schulz's formulas were in place— Charlie Brown had become America's most notable neurotic; Schulz's gag pacing was mature; the economical punch lines were clever and eminently quotable; and the cast was rounding out. Snoopy was developing a personality that began to exhibit markedly human traits. Lucy the brassy fussbudget appeared, with her unflappable brother, Linus (he was phlegmatic in large part because of his security blanket, a prop and a term that Schulz contributed to the American language). Schroeder played the grand works of Beethoven on a toy piano.

Finally—the catalyst that brought *Peanuts* to more readers than newspapers did at the time—the Rinehart publishing company began issuing *Peanuts* reprint anthologies. In 1955 Charles Schulz was the recipient of the Reuben award, cartooning's Oscar, from his peers in the National Cartoonists Society, and in 1964 he became the first cartoonist to win the honor twice—but by that time his success and impact were becoming the stuff of legends.

The Great American Strip often takes place during the Great American Pastime.

Schulz was adding memorable characters to the strip at a rapid pace. Charlie Brown acquired a sister, Sally; and Lucy acquired a second brother, Rerun. Peppermint Patty—no relation to the original Patty—evinced a strong personality and eventually starred with her friend Marcie in sequences apart from the regular cast. Franklin was a black boy whose casual appearances comfortably integrated the American comic strip; Jose Peterson was to be another, albeit somewhat eclectic, ethnic representative. Snoopy acquired not just a brother, Spike, but a new persona. He was to provide a special brand of fantasy to a strip previously only tinged with that element.

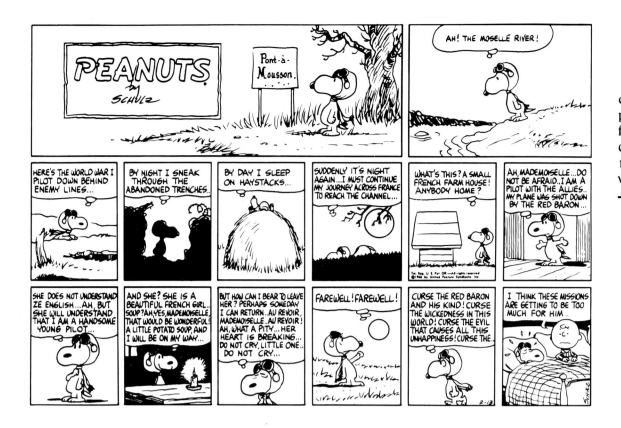

Coincident with Snoopy's fantasies—imagining himself to be the Red Baron, writing novels atop his doghouse (on a precariously perched typewriter), "conversing" with a bird named Woodstock—was an explosion in publishing spin-offs. The *Peanuts* books were predictable best-sellers, but a quantum leap occurred when *Happiness Is a Warm Puppy* appeared. It was a book of homilies accompanied by simple drawings, and it quietly rested atop best-seller lists for forty-five weeks. There were other such books in addition to the strip anthologies, and they inspired greeting cards, posters, and countless other forms of merchandise.

The ubiquitous presence of *Peanuts* cast members on the American cultural landscape, and their universal appeal, led in still other directions. In 1965 an animated cartoon for television, written by Schulz and produced with Bill Melendez and Lee Mendelson, not only was a major ratings success but captured two prestigious awards, the Peabody and an Emmy; *A Charlie Brown Christmas* is now a classic that is telecast every Christmas season. Dozens of other animated specials have followed. In 1967 an off-Broadway play, *You're a Good Man, Charlie*

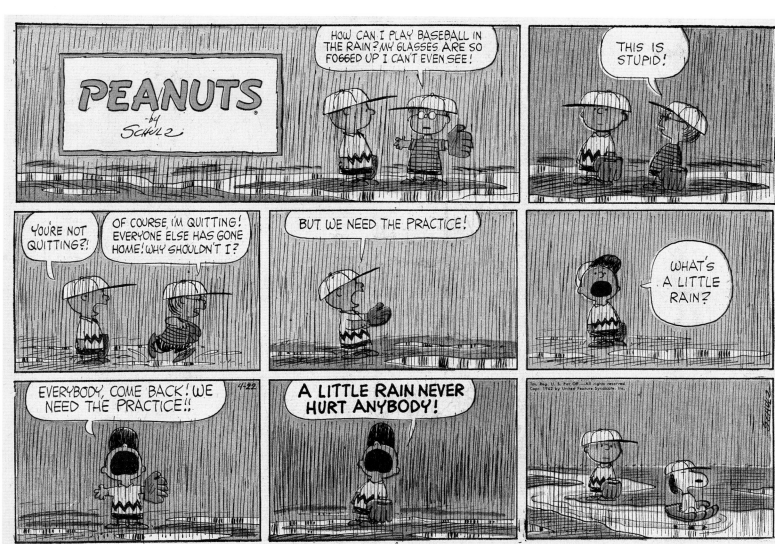

Brown, opened to rave reviews, a four-year run, and enough road and repertory performances to make it the most-produced musical in American theatrical history. In 1970 a theatrical cartoon, *A Boy Named Charlie Brown,* broke box-office records at Radio City Music Hall.

A host of other forums, formats, appearances, uses, and honors were tied in to the *Peanuts* cast—Schulz's story is as much a story of modern licensing as one of modern cartooning—but in 1969 a unique compliment was paid. The astronauts on Apollo 10 named their command module *Charlie Brown* and their lunar lander *Snoopy.* For millennia dogs had howled at the moon; Snoopy was a dog who visited it.

Currently *Peanuts* appears in more than two thousand newspapers, having become the most widely distributed comic strip in history. Its licensing activities are attributable to the strip's enduring appeal, even in these days when some strips use merchandising as a crutch or seem to be dictated by licensing considerations. Perhaps most remarkable about Charles Schulz in his later work is that he continues to experiment and innovate. Once again comparison with other strips is apt; other thirty-plus-year old strips have rested on laurels, simplified characters and situations, and grown routine. Schulz has kept fantasy alive with a thinking school building; has utilized the honored tradition of humorous continuities with summer-camp sequences; has engaged in melancholia with hospital episodes; and has altered his daily format to accommodate three-, two-, and even one-panel gags.

Peanuts is clearly a phenomenon, not just a comic strip. It was the first "intellectual" strip that also appealed to a broad readership and paved the way for *B.C., The Wizard of Id, Miss Peach, Doonesbury,* and *Calvin and Hobbes.* It has been different, but it has also been in the mainstream: the comic strip in America started with children as stars. In the beginning there were the Yellow Kid and the Katzenjammer Kids (Charlie Brown can even be seen in the lineage of large-headed bald boys stretching from the Yellow Kid through Henry). After the seminal kid strips, there were the gangs of comics history in the panels of John T. McCutcheon and Clare Briggs; in the Worry Wart drawings of J.R. Williams and in Mickey "Himself" McGuire of Fontaine Fox's Toonerville Folks; in the backlot groups in *Reg'lar Fellers* and *Just Kids* and the Rinkeydink gang in *Winnie Winkle.*

But in a real sense the kids in *Peanuts* are not kids. They do not converse like children, yet they *are* children—and by this device Schulz is not so much seeking a literary way to be profound but rather engaging in fantasy. He has fashioned a plastic environment in which no adults have ever appeared, where cast members are sometimes masters, sometimes subjects, of normal children's circumstances. When characters discuss metaphysics and theology, as they frequently do, readers are seldom reminded that the ontology of childhood is relatively foreign to *Peanuts*'s text, but they *are* amused (beyond the actual jokes) at the incongruity of half-pints talking about such subjects.

Skippy is a strip from comics history that bears a certain resemblance to what Schulz has accomplished, but its creator, Percy Crosby, alternated between street-gang toughness, poetic reflections, and political propaganda, ultimately reducing Skippy to a mouthpiece instead of a character. With Schulz and *Peanuts* it has been just the opposite. The sophisticated tone is integral, not optional.

Snoopy is transformed once again in a Schulz sketch paying homage to Lewis Carroll.

"Oh, you can't help that," said the cat: "we're all mad here. I'm mad. You're mad."
"How do you know I'm mad?" asked Alice.
"You must be," said the cat, "or you wouldn't have come here."

SCHULZ

Charlie Brown is not Charles Schulz's soapbox—or even his incarnation. True, he is the quiet center of humorous thematic swirls in the strip, and true, he resembles his creator in certain autobiographical ways. But almost all of the *Peanuts* crew displays traits that are part of Sparky Schulz's personality. Every comic strip is an extension of a cartoonist's talent and genius, but no strip has been more a reflection of self than *Peanuts*. Schulz has always been mystified when people refer to his philosophy in the strip, and well it is so, for *Peanuts* has been essentially an unself-conscious tour de force masquerading as a comic preoccupation with self-conscious doubts, identity crises, and anxiety attacks.

One of the elements of *Peanuts*'s notoriety and acceptance has been the consanguinity of such neurotic obsessions with crises in the American psyche. The 1950s ushered in the era of child psychology, but that was not Schulz's affinity. Rather, he struck chords with adult readers who openly or unconsciously shared the cast's problems with identity, respect, and self-worth. To other readers— and to the children among them—*Peanuts* was just plain funny. By these means Schulz became the modern counterpart to the humorists and cartoonists of the 1920s who created and chronicled the "little man" in the face of a confusing mechanized world. Charlie Brown is the little man of our day.

But it is ultimately fantasy, not commentary, that will assure *Peanuts* its immortality in comics history. Its sophisticated lexicon and conservative demeanor

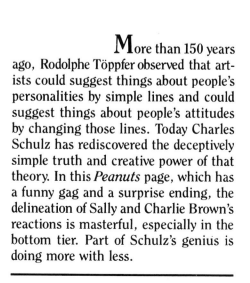
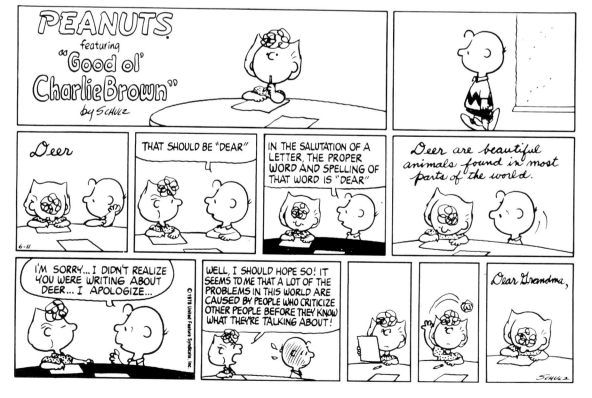

tend to obscure the fact that *Peanuts* is as much a fantasy strip as *Krazy Kat;* it is as internally consistent to its own rules and style as Herriman's masterpiece. Snoopy's humanity is accepted with equanimity. Schroeder's performances of Beethoven are devices beyond comic implausibility; via inspired structural playfulness, Schulz makes the musical notes hang physically in the air, for Lucy to observe and Woodstock to climb upon. Linus can, without fear of inconsistency, switch from learned discussions of saints and sages to an abiding faith in the Great Pumpkin, whose visitation he awaits every Halloween.

In criticizing and analyzing comic strips, many reductions are possible, and one of the most basic, most physical, is reducing to lines. The cartoonist draws with lines—straight lines that define the frame of action and, in succession, propel a narrative. Lines that point a piece of dialogue to a character's head. Lines that swirl and mix and combine to form figures. Lines that indicate motion and action. Somewhere between the two-dimensional hash of lines and the reader's brain there is shorthand employed and assumptions made. Truly the comic strip is a special, new, plastic, and expressive form of communication.

Significantly, Charles Schulz, the final cartoonist of this appreciation, uses lines as idiosyncratically as any cartoonist in strip history. In the current age of sterile drawing styles—as well as an astonishingly large number of amateurish comic strips in syndication—Schulz has rediscovered and celebrated the line. Snoopy's eyebrows bounce off his head; Woodstock "speaks" in chicken scratches; signs and symbols abound in speech balloons, enveloping sighs and exasperated *Aaaaaaughs*.

Schulz's line has, in recent years, become somewhat shaky, a source of some frustration to him. However, to those who study and love comic strips, it should be seen as a distinctive and comfortable thumbprint. In the 1840s Rodolphe Töppfer defined the role of lines in delineating personality (in his *Essay on Physiognomy*) and, by creating picture stories, became a godfather of the comic strip. The individuality of *Peanuts* has brought matters full circle.

Charles Schulz's comic strip may be a merchandising colossus, but it remains the product of one cartoonist—no assistant has ever touched the *Peanuts* strip—a cartoonist who reveres the American comic strip and revels in its creation. He has borne and transformed the heritage splendidly, and it remains to be seen whether his followers will be merely imitators or innovators in the fashion of the modern master who calls himself Sparky after a comic-strip racehorse.